The iMac For Dummies

W9-ASZ-883

What've You Got There?

To find out how much memory your iMac has and what system-software version, choose About This Computer from the menu (see Chapter 1). Write the answers down here.

Your iMac OS version: _____

Built-in memory: _____

Surviving the First Half Hour

You may need this information only at the very beginning of your iMac career — but you'll *really* need it.

Turning on the iMac

Press the On/Off button. It's the round button at the upper-right corner of your keyboard (see Chapter 1).

Turning off the iMac

1. If you've typed or drawn anything, make sure it's safely stored on your disk by choosing Save from the File menu.
2. Press the round On/Off button on your keyboard.
3. In the dialog box that appears, click Shut Down.

Troubleshooting Keystrokes

See Chapters 15 and 16 for details.

The iMac is frozen, but the cursor moves: Press ⌘-Option-Esc and then click the Force Quit button. Save your work in each program; then restart the iMac. (Works about half the time. Other times, read on.)

The iMac has crashed or locked up: Restart by inserting a straightened paper clip into the tiny, triangle-marked hole (behind the door on the right side). If that doesn't work, unplug and replug the power cord.

All icons appear blank: As the iMac starts up, hold down ⌘-Option. When asked to rebuild the desktop, click OK.

A weird problem keeps recurring: As the iMac starts up, press Shift until you see "Extensions Off." Only basic functions work now (no faxing, no Internet), but the iMac runs clean and pure. See Chapter 16 to finish the troubleshooting; this trick at least gets you into your iMac.

You're panicking: Call Apple's hotline: 800-500-7078.

Working with Icons

Finding a file

Each file you create is represented by an icon and is usually stored inside an electronic folder, which looks like a file folder on your screen. Everyone sometimes misplaces a file. Here's what to do.

1. Choose Find from the File menu (or the menu).
2. Type a few letters of the missing file's name.

   You don't have to type the whole name . . . only enough to distinguish it; type *Wonk* to find the file called *Willy Wonka Earnings*. Capitalization doesn't matter.
3. Press the Return key or click the Find button.

   The iMac roots through your files. When it shows you a list of all icons that match, click one (to see where it is) or double-click (to open it).

Renaming a file

1. Click an icon (once) and press Return.
2. Type a new name; then press Return.

A file's name can be up to 31 letters long. If you make a mistake, backspace by pressing the Delete key.

To insert a CD-ROM

1. Hold the CD by its edges (or the hole). Press the button on the iMac's CD-ROM panel to make the tray pop out an inch or so. Pull the tray out all the way.
2. Gently slap the CD-ROM into the tray, label side up.
3. Push the tray closed until it snaps shut.

Ejecting a CD or other disk

Drag the disk's icon onto the Trash can. Or click the disk icon (once) and choose Put Away from the File menu.

Copying a file onto a disk

You can't drag icons onto a CD. If you've bought a floppy drive, Zip drive, SuperDisk, or other disk drive for your iMac, however, just drag any file's icon (below, left) onto the disk's icon (below, right) and let go.

Alternatively, you can drag the file into the disk's *window*, instead of on top of the disk's icon.

The iMac For Dummies®

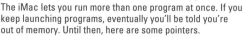

Cheat Sheet

What All These Little Controls Do

```
StyleWriter 1200                              2.1.1
Copies: 1      Pages: ◉ All ○ From:    To:         [ Print  ]
Print Quality: ○ Best ◉ Normal ○ Draft           [ Cancel ]
Paper Type:  [ Plain          ▼ ]                 [ Options ]
Image:       [ Grayscale    ▼ ]
Notification:[ None          ▼ ]
```

They call this box a *dialog box* because the iMac is asking questions it needs answered. Here are the elements of a typical dialog box.

Radio buttons

Print Quality: ○ Best   ◉ Normal   ○ Draft

Named after the pushbuttons on a car radio, where only one can be pushed in at a time. Likewise, only one iMac radio button can be selected at a time.

Check boxes

☒ **Clean ink cartridge before printing**

Used to indicate whether an option is on or off. Click once to place the X in the box; click again to remove the X (and turn off the option).

Text fields

○ **From:** [   ] **To:** [   ]

You're supposed to type into these blanks. To move from one blank to another, either click with the mouse or press the Tab key.

Pop-up menus

Paper Type: [Plain   ▼]

When you see this, you're seeing a *pop-up menu*. Point to the text, hold down the mouse button, and make a selection from the minimenu that drops down.

Buttons

[Cancel] [**Print**]

Every dialog box has a clearly marked button or two (usually OK and Cancel) that make the box go away — your escape route.

Click OK (or Print, or Proceed, or whatever the button says) to proceed with the command you originally chose from the menu. Click Cancel if you want to back out of the dialog box, as though you'd never issued the command.

See the thick black outline around the Print button above? You don't have to use the mouse to click that button; you can press either the Return or Enter key on your keyboard instead.

Working with Several Programs

The iMac lets you run more than one program at once. If you keep launching programs, eventually you'll be told you're out of memory. Until then, here are some pointers.

Determining what programs are running

Put the cursor on the icon in the upper-right of your screen; hold down the mouse button.

The *Application menu* drops down, listing all the programs you've launched. The frontmost one, the one you're working in now, is indicated by a check mark. (If you have iMac OS 8.5 or later, this frontmost program is also named in the menu bar, as you can see here.)

Quitting programs to free up memory

1. Use your Application menu, as illustrated above, to choose the program's name.
2. From the File menu, choose Quit.

Working with iMac Windows
Opening or closing a window

Every window was once an *icon* that you double-clicked to see what was inside.

1. Double-click any icon to open its window.
2. To get rid of a window, click the *close box* in the upper-left corner.

```
☐  Macintosh HD
10 items, 755.2 MB available
```

Bringing concealed icons into view

Sometimes a window is too small to show you everything within it. When that's the case, you'll see gray *scroll bars* along the bottom or right side.

1. Point to one of the small arrows on the scroll bar and press the mouse button continuously (below, left).

   Your view of the window slides in the direction of the arrow, showing you what's hidden beyond the edges (below, right).

2. To make the window as large as necessary to view all the icons (up to the size of your screen), click the *zoom box*.

```
☐  Macintosh HD
10 items, 754.6 MB available
```

...For Dummies: Bestselling Book Series for Beginners

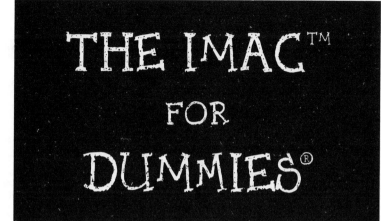

THE IMAC™ FOR DUMMIES®

by David Pogue

IDG
BOOKS
WORLDWIDE

IDG Books Worldwide, Inc.
An International Data Group Company

Foster City, CA ♦ Chicago, IL ♦ Indianapolis, IN ♦ New York, NY

The iMac™ For Dummies®

Published by
IDG Books Worldwide, Inc.
An International Data Group Company
919 E. Hillsdale Blvd.
Suite 400
Foster City, CA 94404
www.idgbooks.com (IDG Books Worldwide Web site)
www.dummies.com (Dummies Press Web site)

Library of Congress Catalog Card No.: 98-89716

ISBN: 0-7645-0495-9

Printed in the United States of America

10 9 8 7 6 5 4 3 2 1

1B/RX/RS/ZY/IN

Distributed in the United States by IDG Books Worldwide, Inc.

Distributed by Macmillan Canada for Canada; by Transworld Publishers Limited in the United Kingdom; by IDG Norge Books for Norway; by IDG Sweden Books for Sweden; by Woodslane Pty. Ltd. for Australia; by Woodslane (NZ) Ltd. for New Zealand; by Addison Wesley Longman Singapore Pte Ltd. for Singapore, Malaysia, Thailand, and Indonesia; by Norma Comunicaciones S.A. for Colombia; by Intersoft for South Africa; by International Thomson Publishing for Germany, Austria and Switzerland; by Distribuidora Cuspide for Argentina; by Livraria Cultura for Brazil; by Ediciencia S.A. for Ecuador; by Ediciones ZETA S.C.R. Ltda. for Peru; by WS Computer Publishing Corporation, Inc., for the Philippines; by Contemporanea de Ediciones for Venezuela; by Express Computer Distributors for the Caribbean and West Indies; by Micronesia Media Distributor, Inc. for Micronesia; by Grupo Editorial Norma S.A. for Guatemala; by Chips Computadoras S.A. de C.V. for Mexico; by Editorial Norma de Panama S.A. for Panama; by Wouters Import for Belgium; by American Bookshops for Finland. Authorized Sales Agent: Anthony Rudkin Associates for the Middle East and North Africa.

For general information on IDG Books Worldwide's books in the U.S., please call our Consumer Customer Service department at 800-762-2974. For reseller information, including discounts and premium sales, please call our Reseller Customer Service department at 800-434-3422.

For information on where to purchase IDG Books Worldwide's books outside the U.S., please contact our International Sales department at 317-596-5530 or fax 317-596-5692.

For information on foreign language translations, please contact our Foreign & Subsidiary Rights department at 650-655-3021 or fax 650-655-3281.

For sales inquiries and special prices for bulk quantities, please contact our Sales department at 650-655-3200 or write to the address above.

For information on using IDG Books Worldwide's books in the classroom or for ordering examination copies, please contact our Educational Sales department at 800-434-2086 or fax 317-596-5499.

For press review copies, author interviews, or other publicity information, please contact our Public Relations department at 650-655-3000 or fax 650-655-3299.

For authorization to photocopy items for corporate, personal, or educational use, please contact Copyright Clearance Center, 222 Rosewood Drive, Danvers, MA 01923, or fax 978-750-4470.

is a trademark under exclusive license to IDG Books Worldwide, Inc., from International Data Group, Inc.

About the Author

Ohio-bred **David Pogue** never touched a computer — nor wanted to — until Apple Computer suckered him into it by selling Macs half-price at Yale, from which he graduated *summa cum laude* in 1985. Since then, Pogue has merged his two loves — the musical theatre and Macs — in every way he could dream up: by spending ten years in New York as a Broadway theatre conductor; writing manuals for music programs like Finale; and becoming the Mac guru to every Broadway and Hollywood creative-type he could get his hands on — Mia Farrow, Carly Simon, Mike Nichols, Stephen Sondheim, Gary Oldman, Harry Connick, Jr., and others.

In his other life, Pogue writes the award-winning, back-page column, *The Desktop Critic,* for *Macworld* magazine. His résumé also boasts some *real* accomplishments, like winning the Ohio spelling bee in seventh grade, being the only nonlawyer in three generations, and getting a Viewer Mail letter read on David Letterman.

He lives in Connecticut with his wife Jennifer, son Kelly, and wonder-dog Bullwinkle, where he does magic tricks, plays the piano, and awaits the birth of daughter Tia. The family photos lurk on the World Wide Web at *www.davidpogue.com.*

Also by David Pogue:

Macs For Dummies
MORE Macs For Dummies
Macworld Mac Secrets (with Joseph Schorr)
Magic For Dummies
PalmPilot: The Ultimate Guide
Hard Drive (a novel)
The Microsloth Joke Book
The Great Macintosh Easter Egg Hunt
Tales from the Tech Line
The Weird Wide Web (with Erfert Fenton)
Classical Music For Dummies (with Scott Speck)
Opera For Dummies (with Scott Speck)

ABOUT IDG BOOKS WORLDWIDE

Welcome to the world of IDG Books Worldwide.

IDG Books Worldwide, Inc., is a subsidiary of International Data Group, the world's largest publisher of computer-related information and the leading global provider of information services on information technology. IDG was founded more than 30 years ago by Patrick J. McGovern and now employs more than 9,000 people worldwide. IDG publishes more than 290 computer publications in over 75 countries. More than 90 million people read one or more IDG publications each month.

Launched in 1990, IDG Books Worldwide is today the #1 publisher of best-selling computer books in the United States. We are proud to have received eight awards from the Computer Press Association in recognition of editorial excellence and three from Computer Currents' First Annual Readers' Choice Awards. Our best-selling ...*For Dummies*® series has more than 50 million copies in print with translations in 31 languages. IDG Books Worldwide, through a joint venture with IDG's Hi-Tech Beijing, became the first U.S. publisher to publish a computer book in the People's Republic of China. In record time, IDG Books Worldwide has become the first choice for millions of readers around the world who want to learn how to better manage their businesses.

Our mission is simple: Every one of our books is designed to bring extra value and skill-building instructions to the reader. Our books are written by experts who understand and care about our readers. The knowledge base of our editorial staff comes from years of experience in publishing, education, and journalism — experience we use to produce books to carry us into the new millennium. In short, we care about books, so we attract the best people. We devote special attention to details such as audience, interior design, use of icons, and illustrations. And because we use an efficient process of authoring, editing, and desktop publishing our books electronically, we can spend more time ensuring superior content and less time on the technicalities of making books.

You can count on our commitment to deliver high-quality books at competitive prices on topics you want to read about. At IDG Books Worldwide, we continue in the IDG tradition of delivering quality for more than 30 years. You'll find no better book on a subject than one from IDG Books Worldwide.

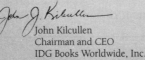

John Kilcullen
Chairman and CEO
IDG Books Worldwide, Inc.

Steven Berkowitz
President and Publisher
IDG Books Worldwide, Inc.

*Eighth Annual
Computer Press
Awards* ≥1992

*Ninth Annual
Computer Press
Awards* ≥1993

*Tenth Annual
Computer Press
Awards* ≥1994

*Eleventh Annual
Computer Press
Awards* ≥1995

Author's Acknowledgments

This book was made possible by the enthusiasm and support of IDG Books Worldwide's John Kilcullen; Project Editor Mary Goodwin; Acquisitions Manager Mike Kelly; and everyone else in the sprawling universe of IDG Books voicemail. Thanks, too, to Pam Dey, whose tireless research produced the Ultimate iMac Buyer's Guide of Appendix D, and to Apple's Rhona Hamilton and Sue Runfola.

Above all, thanks to Apple's cofounder Steve Jobs, whose vision and refusal to compromise produced the glorious, smash-hit, see-through machine called the iMac.

The David Pogue Pledge

As in all my Macintosh books, I make the following guarantee:

1. I will reply to every reader e-mail (except gratuitously nasty ones). My address is *david@pogueman.com*. (I'm not so great at responding to U.S. mail.)

2. I will not use trendoid terms in my writing: *the user* when I mean you; *price point* when I mean price; *performance* when I mean speed; *developer* when I mean a software company; *software package* when I mean a program; and so on.

3. I will never put an apostrophe in the possessive word *its*.

Publisher's Acknowledgments

We're proud of this book; please register your comments through our IDG Books Worldwide Online Registration Form located at http://my2cents.dummies.com.

Some of the people who helped bring this book to market include the following:

Acquisitions, Editorial, and Media Development

Project Editor: Mary Goodwin

Acquisitions Manager: Michael Kelly

Copy Editor: Bill Barton

Technical Editor: Tim Warner

Editorial Manager: Kelly Ewing

Editorial Assistant: Paul Kuzmic

Associate Permissions Editor: Carmen Krikorian

Production

Associate Project Coordinator: Tom Missler

Layout and Graphics: Lou Boudreau, Angela F. Hunckler, Jane E. Martin, Brent Savage, Jacqueline J. Schneider

Proofreaders: Christine Berman, Kelli Botta, Nancy Price, Kathleen Sparrow, Ethel M. Winslow, Janet M. Withers

Indexer: Anne Leach

General and Administrative

IDG Books Worldwide, Inc.: John Kilcullen, CEO; Steven Berkowitz, President and Publisher

IDG Books Technology Publishing: Brenda McLaughlin, Senior Vice President and Group Publisher

Dummies Technology Press and Dummies Editorial: Diane Graves Steele, Vice President and Associate Publisher; Mary Bednarek, Director of Acquisitions and Product Development; Kristin A. Cocks, Editorial Director

Dummies Trade Press: Kathleen A. Welton, Vice President and Publisher; Kevin Thornton, Acquisitions Manager

IDG Books Production for Dummies Press: Michael R. Britton, Vice President of Production and Creative Services; Cindy L. Phipps, Manager of Project Coordination, Production Proofreading, and Indexing; Kathie S. Schutte, Supervisor of Page Layout; Shelley Lea, Supervisor of Graphics and Design; Debbie J. Gates, Production Systems Specialist; Robert Springer, Supervisor of Proofreading; Debbie Stailey, Special Projects Coordinator; Tony Augsburger, Supervisor of Reprints and Bluelines

Dummies Packaging and Book Design: Patty Page, Manager, Promotions Marketing

♦

The publisher would like to give special thanks to Patrick J. McGovern, without whom this book would not have been possible.

Contents at a Glance

Cartoons at a Glance

By Rich Tennant

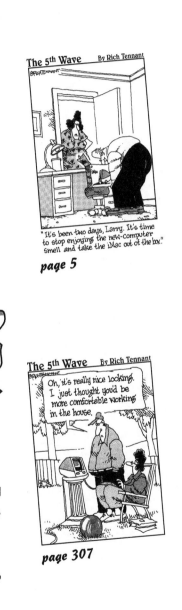

The 5th Wave By Rich Tennant

"It's been two days, Larry. It's time to stop enjoying the new-computer smell and take the iMac out of the box."

page 5

The 5th Wave By Rich Tennant

"Great! It comes with Quicken. Now maybe we can figure out where all the money around here is going."

page 101

The 5th Wave By Rich Tennant

"Come here, quick! I've got a new iMac trick!"

page 181

The 5th Wave By Rich Tennant

"Brad! That's not your modem we're hearing! It's Buddy!! He's out of his cage and in the iMac!!"

page 249

The 5th Wave By Rich Tennant

Oh, it's really nice looking. I just thought you'd be more comfortable working in the house.

page 307

The 5th Wave By Rich Tennant

INTERNET ACCESS .50¢ - Min.

page 209

The 5th Wave By Rich Tennant

Honey - is one of your AOL chat room friends an elephant herder from India?

page 287

Fax: 978-546-7747 • E-mail: the5wave@tiac.net

Table of Contents

· ·

Introduction

● ●

*I*f you bought an iMac, you're unbelievably smart (or lucky). You've neatly eliminated most of the hassle, frustration, and annoyance that normally comes with buying a computer. You've saved an incredible amount of money, while still getting a fast, state-of-the-art machine; and you've significantly enhanced your office décor. (Especially if your wallpaper is see-through blue-green.)

That's not just PR baloney, either; the iMac truly is a dramatically different machine. For example, on an iMac, cables emerge from the *side* of the computer, where you can get at them. Why did it take 20 years for the computer industry to realize that the *back* of a computer is the *least* convenient spot for connections?

The iMac also has everything you need built in: a modem (so you can use the Internet and e-mail), a CD-ROM (so you can easily install new programs), and a glorious color screen (so you don't have to set up your own). Selling a complete computer in one handy bundle isn't a new idea — but rarely has it all worked together so smoothly. And, of course, never before has all of this good stuff come in a futuristic-looking case that you can move from room to room without calling a bunch of friends over to help.

In short, the iMac is the gadget that comes closest to fulfilling the vision of Apple founder Steve Jobs: to make a personal computer that's simply another appliance. You don't have to buy memory upgrades for your TV, do you? You don't have to hire a consultant to install your toaster oven, right? So why should computers be any more complicated?

Who Needs an iMac Book?

If the iMac is so simple, then who needs a book about it?

Well, despite all the free goodies you get with the iMac, a *manual* isn't among them. You need somewhere to turn when things go wrong, when you'd like to know what the add-on software does, or when you want to stumble onto the Internet for the first time.

By the way, of *course* you're not a dummy. Two pieces of evidence tell me so: for one thing, you're learning the iMac, and for another, you're reading this book! But I've taught hundreds of people how to use their Macs, and an awful lot of them start out saying they *feel* like dummies when it comes to computers. Society surrounds us with fast-talking teenagers who grew up learning English from their Nintendo sets; no wonder the rest of us sometimes feel left out.

But you're no more a dummy for not knowing the iMac than you were before you knew how to drive. Learning a Macintosh is like learning to drive: After a lesson or two, you can go anywhere your heart desires.

So when we say *Dummies,* we're saying it with an affectionate wink. Still, if the cover bothers you even a little — I'll admit it, you wouldn't be the first — please rip it right off. The inner cover, we hope, will make you proud to have the book out on your desk.

How to Use This Book (Other Than as a Mouse Pad)

If you're starting from the very, *very* beginning, read this book from the end — start with Appendix A, where you can find an idiot-proof guide to setting up your computer.

Otherwise, start with the very basics in Chapter 1; turn to Chapter 15 in times of trouble; and consult the other chapters as the spirit moves you.

The book winds down with Appendix D, a sampler of cool add-on products that fit the iMac's special USB connectors; Appendix B has contact info for a number of important Mac companies and publications; and Appendix C, "The Techno-Babble Translation Guide." (You'd probably call it a glossary.)

Macintosh conventions

Macintosh conventions? Sure. They're called Macworld Expos, and there's one in Boston and one in San Francisco each year.

Conventions in this book

Oh, *that* kind of convention.

So that we'll be eligible for some of the more prestigious book-design awards, I've marked some topics with these icons:

Nerdy stuff that's okay to skip but will fascinate the kind of people who read Tom Clancy novels.

The Macintosh is the greatest computer on earth, but it's still a computer. Now and then it does unexplainable stuff, which I'll explain.

A shortcut so you can show off.

Denotes an actual You-Try-It Experience. Hold the book open with a nearby cinder block, put your hands on the computer, and do as I say.

A few new, cool things about Mac OS 8.5 and later. (See Chapter 1 to find out what Mac OS 8.5 is.)

Apple and obsolescence

One more thing before you delve in: Apple is the gigantic Silicon Valley computer company that started out as a couple of grungy teenagers in a garage. Each time Apple introduces a new Macintosh model, it's faster, more powerful, and less expensive than the model *you* already bought. People love Apple for coming up with such great products — but they also feel cheated at having paid so much for a suddenly outdated machine.

Feel whatever you want, of course. But if you're going to buy a computer, accept the fact that your investment is going to devalue faster than real estate in Chernobyl.

Here's a promise: No matter how carefully you shop or how good a deal you got on your iMac today, it will be replaced by a less expensive or souped-up version within a year. (It'll still *work* just fine, and be more or less up-to-date, for about five years.)

With that quick and inevitable computer death looming, how can people psych themselves into spending $1,300 for a computer? Simple: They believe that in those few short years, the computer will speed them up enough, and enhance their productivity enough, to cover the costs easily.

That's the theory, anyway.

Part I
For the Absolute iMac Virgin

The 5th Wave   By Rich Tennant

"It's been two days, Larry. It's time to stop enjoying the new-computer smell and take the iMac out of the box."

In this part . . .

There are three ways to learn how to use a new computer. You can consult the manual; unfortunately, your iMac didn't come with one. You can take a course (like you've got time for that?). Or you can read a book like this one. (Then again, no other book is quite like this one.)

In these opening chapters, you'll learn, as kindly and gently as possible, how to get up and running on your iMac — and nothing else.

Chapter 1

How to Turn On Your iMac (and What to Do Next)

· ·

In This Chapter
▶ How to turn the iMac on (and off)
▶ Confronting weird new words such as *mouse*, *menu*, and *system*
▶ Doing windows
▶ Mindlessly opening and closing folders

· ·

*I*f you haven't hooked up your iMac yet, go now to the mercifully brief Appendix A, which gently guides you through the ten-second experience of plugging everything in.

Box Open. Now What?

At this moment, then, you should have a ready-to-roll iMac on your desk, in all its transparent blue plastic glory, and a look of fevered anticipation on your face.

Switching on the iMac

In this very first lesson, you'll be asked to locate the On button. It's in the upper-right corner of your keyboard. It's round, and it bears the universal symbol for iMac On-Turning.

Try pressing this button now. If the iMac responds in some way — a sound plays, the screen lights up, missiles are launched from the Arizona desert — then your machine is working. Skip ahead to the following section, "The startup slide show."

If pressing that key didn't do anything, try pressing the identical-looking button on the face of the machine itself. If that works, your keyboard may not be plugged into the right side of the iMac. And if even the front-panel button doesn't work, your iMac isn't plugged into a working power outlet. I'll wait here while you get that problem sorted out.

The startup slide show

If your On-button experiment was successful, you hear a chord, and after a few seconds, an image appears on the screen. Now you get to witness the Macintosh Startup Slide Show, revered by millions. First, you see a quick glimpse of the smiling Macintosh. It looks like this:

(In the rare event that your smiling Macintosh looks like this —

— your iMac is upside-down.)

Next slide: You see the famous Mac OS logo, looking like Picasso's portrait of a schizophrenic:

During this time, the bottom of your screen fills with little inch-tall pictures. In Macintosh lingo, the term for "little inch-tall pictures" is *icons*. These particular icons represent the different features of your Mac, each turning itself on and preparing for action: One represents your CD-ROM drive, another's for dialing the Internet, and so on. Much, much, much more information about these startup-item doodads is in Chapter 8.

At last, the colored full-screen pattern, called the *desktop,* appears. Congratulations! You've arrived.

If you saw anything else during the startup process — such as a blinking question-mark icon, a strange error message, or thick black smoke — you've just met your first computer problem. Proceed directly to Chapter 15. This problem and many others are explained — and solved — for you there.

Your First Moments Alone Together

As any gadget lover can tell you, the most exciting period of appliance ownership comes at the very beginning. You're gonna love this stuff.

Moving the mouse

The *mouse* is the round, plastic, yo-yo-like thing on the desk beside your keyboard. Having trouble visualizing it as a rodent? Think of the cord as its tail and (if it helps you) draw little eyeballs on the sloping side facing you.

Now then, roll the mouse across the desk (or mouse pad), keeping the cord pointed away from you. See how the arrow pointer moves across the screen? For the rest of your life, you'll hear that pointer called the *cursor.* And for the rest of your life, you'll hear moving the mouse called *moving the mouse.*

Try lifting the mouse off the desk and waving it around in midair like a remote control. Nothing happens, right? The mouse controls the cursor only when it's on a flat surface. (The two-toned ball on the bottom of the mouse detects movement when you roll it around.) That's a useful feature — you can pick up the mouse when you run out of desk space, but the cursor will stay in place on the screen. Only when you set the mouse down and begin to roll it again will the cursor continue moving.

What's on the menu?

Let's try some real computing here. Move the cursor up to the light-gray strip at the top of the screen. It's called the *menu bar,* named after a delightful little pub in Silicon Valley. Touch the arrow on the word *Special.* (The *tip* of the iMac's arrow is the part you need to worry about. Same thing with real-life arrows, come to think of it.)

> **File   Edit   View   Special   Help**

Pointing to something on the screen in this way has a technical term: *pointing.* (Think you're going to be able to handle this?)

Now put your index finger on the button on the mouse and briefly, quickly, press the button down (and then release it). If all went well, you should see a list of commands drop down from the word *Special,* as shown here:

Congratulations — you've learned how to *click the mouse* (by pressing the button), and you've also learned to *pull down a menu* (the list of commands). Try clicking anywhere on the colored backdrop of your screen (or just waiting 15 seconds); the menu disappears.

The big turn-off

Before we get into 3-D color graphs, space-vehicle trajectories, and DNA analysis, I guess I should tell you how to turn the iMac *off.*

In a pinch, sure, you can just yank the power cord out of the wall. But regularly turning off the iMac by chopping off its power can eventually confuse the poor thing and lead to technical problems. Instead, you're supposed to turn off your iMac using one of these two delightful methods:

> ✔ **The keyboard way:** Press the power button (the same one you used to turn the iMac on) for a couple of seconds. This box appears:

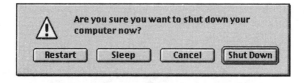

If you've had enough for one session, use the mouse to click the Shut Down button. (The computer turns itself off.) If you're ready to read on, though, confident that you now know how to turn this thing off, click the Cancel button instead.

✔ **The mouse way:** Click the word *Special* (hereafter known as the *Special menu*) again. When the list of commands appears, roll the mouse downward so that each successive command turns dark. When each menu command turns dark, it's said to be *highlighted*.

(The only commands that don't get highlighted are the ones that are dimmed, or *grayed out*. They're dimmed because they don't make any sense at the moment. For example, if no disc is in the CD-ROM drive, choosing Eject Disk wouldn't make any sense. So the Mac makes that command gray, which means it's unavailable to you.)

Roll the mouse all the way down to the words *Shut Down* so that they're highlighted.

If you do, in fact, want to turn the iMac off for now, release the mouse button. The Mac turns itself off completely. If you'd rather proceed with this chapter's teachings, don't let go of the button yet. Instead, slide the cursor off the menu in any direction and then click the mouse button. The menu snaps back up like a window shade and nothing else happens. (A menu command only gets activated when you release the mouse while the cursor's on a command.)

Hey, you've only read a few pages, and already you can turn your iMac on and off! See? This thing's no harder than a toaster.

If your thirst for knowledge is unquenched and you want to slog ahead with this lesson, read on.

Moving things around on the desktop

Take a look around the screen. You've already encountered *menus* (those words *File, Edit, View,* and so on at the top of the screen). Near the upper-right corner of the screen, you see an *icon*. (Remember? — a small symbolic picture.) Unless you've changed it, that icon is called *Macintosh HD.*

Icons represent everything in the Mac world. They all look different: One represents a letter you wrote, another represents the Trash can, another represents a CD you've inserted. Here are some examples of icons you'll probably be seeing before long:

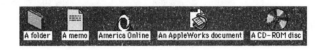

You can move an icon by dragging it. Try this:

1. **Point to the Trash icon.**
2. **Press and then hold down the mouse button continuously — and, while it's down, move the mouse to a new position.**

    This sophisticated technique is called, by the way, *dragging*. You're dragging the Trash icon now.

3. **Let go of the mouse button.**

Hey, this thing isn't so technical after all, right?

Other than the fact that there's a Trash can, nobody's really sure why they call this "home-base" screen the *desktop*. It has another name, too: the *Finder*. It's where you file all your work into little electronic on-screen file folders so that you can *find* them again later. If you have a recent version of the iMac's built-in software, in fact, the word *Finder* even appears at the top of the screen, as shown in the next illustration.

Used in a sentence, you might hear it like this: "Well, no wonder you don't see the Trash can. You're not in the Finder!"

Icons, windows, and Macintosh syntax

Point to the hard-disk icon (a rectangular box, probably called *Macintosh HD* — for *H*ard *D*isk) in the upper-right corner of the screen.

This particular icon represents the giant disk inside your iMac, known as the *hard drive* or *hard disk,* that serves as your filing cabinet. It's where the computer stores all your work, all your files, and all your software.

So how do you see what's in your hard drive? Where do you get to see its table of contents?

It turns out that you can *open* any icon into a window, where you'll see every item inside listed individually. The window has the same name as the icon you opened.

Before we proceed, though, it's time for a lesson in Macintosh syntax. Fear not; it's nothing like English syntax. In fact, everything that you do on the Macintosh has this format: *noun-verb.* Shakespeare it ain't, but it's sure easy to remember.

Let's try a noun-verb command, shall we?

1. Click the hard-disk icon in the upper-right corner of the screen.

The icon turns black, indicating that it's *selected.* Good job — you've just identified the *noun.*

2. Move to the File menu and choose Open.

You guessed it — Open is the *verb.* And, sure enough, your hard disk opens into a window, where you can see its contents.

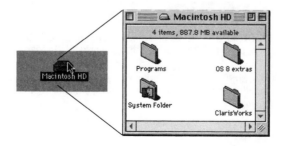

Did any of that make sense? In the world of Macintosh, you always specify *what* you want to change (using the mouse) and then you use a menu command to specify *how* you want it changed. You'll see this pattern over and over again: *Select* something on the screen and then *apply* a menu command to it.

The complete list of window doodads

Look over the contents of your hard-drive window, as shown in the following figure. (Everybody's got different stuff, so what you see on your screen won't exactly match the illustration.)

Better yet, look over the various controls and gadgets around the *edges* of this window. Using these controls and buttons, you can do all kinds of neat things to a window: stretch it, move it, or make it go away. (You'll find much more patient descriptions of these controls in Chapter 9.) These various gadgets are worth learning about — you're going to run into windows *everywhere* after you start working.

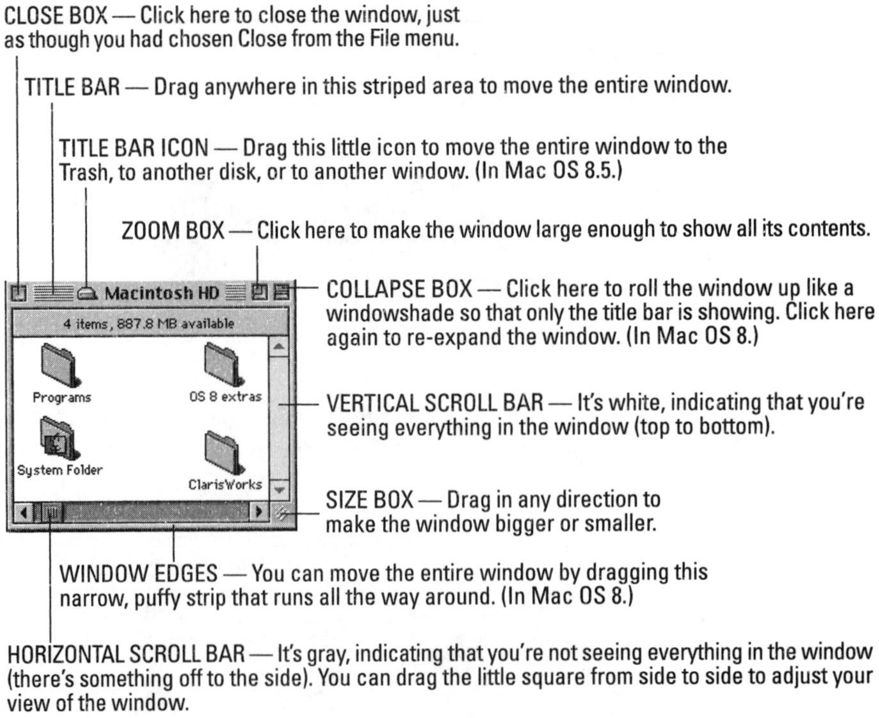

CLOSE BOX — Click here to close the window, just as though you had chosen Close from the File menu.

TITLE BAR — Drag anywhere in this striped area to move the entire window.

TITLE BAR ICON — Drag this little icon to move the entire window to the Trash, to another disk, or to another window. (In Mac OS 8.5.)

ZOOM BOX — Click here to make the window large enough to show all its contents.

COLLAPSE BOX — Click here to roll the window up like a windowshade so that only the title bar is showing. Click here again to re-expand the window. (In Mac OS 8.)

VERTICAL SCROLL BAR — It's white, indicating that you're seeing everything in the window (top to bottom).

SIZE BOX — Drag in any direction to make the window bigger or smaller.

WINDOW EDGES — You can move the entire window by dragging this narrow, puffy strip that runs all the way around. (In Mac OS 8.)

HORIZONTAL SCROLL BAR — It's gray, indicating that you're not seeing everything in the window (there's something off to the side). You can drag the little square from side to side to adjust your view of the window.

Macintosh HD

4 items, 887.8 MB available

Programs

OS 8 extras

System Folder

ClarisWorks

Go ahead and try out some of the little boxes and scroll bars. Click them. Tug on them. Open the window and close it again. No matter what you do, *you can never hurt the machine by doing "the wrong thing."* That's the wonderful thing about the iMac: It's the Nerf appliance.

All systems are go

In that little window diagram, you may have noticed something peculiar about the item called the *title bar icon* — as shown in the diagram, that little box is present only if your iMac has *Mac OS 8.5 or later.*

And what, you may understandably be shrieking, is *Mac OS 8.5 or later?*

Long story. Every year, Apple Computer piles neat new features onto the behind-the-scenes software that runs your computer. This backstage software was once called the *operating system.* But because everyone's in such a hurry these days, people now just call it the *OS.* (Say it "O-S," not "oss.")

The original, summer 1998 iMac models came equipped with *Mac OS 8.1* — at the time, the newest, trendiest OS around. By the end of the year, though, iMacs came with something even newer: Mac OS 8.5. (See the end of Chapter 9 for more on this topic.)

I bring up this point here because certain iMac features behave differently depending on which version you have. For example, the name of the program you're currently using is always identified in the upper-right corner of the Mac OS 8.5 screen — but not in Mac OS 8.1:

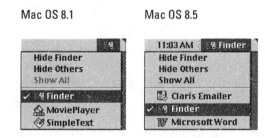

Mac OS 8.1

Mac OS 8.5

See? The *things* on the screen are pretty much the same; they've just had a makeover on *Oprah.*

In this book, I'll mostly be showing the newer look — don't let it faze you. Even with an older iMac, you'll still find everything where it's supposed to be.

Tell you what: From now on, if something I'm teaching you seems odd, look for a Mac OS 8.5 icon like the one beside this paragraph. Then you'll know you're not going crazy.

It would help, I guess, if you knew which OS version *your* iMac uses. Fortunately, finding out is easy.

Get a pencil.

See the logo in the upper-left corner of the screen? It's no ordinary logo. It's actually a menu, just like the ones you've already experienced. Point your arrow cursor tip on the apple, click the button, and watch what happens.

As with any menu, a list drops down. This one, however, includes an extremely useful command. This command is so important that it's separated by a dotted line from the mere mortal list items after it. It's *About This Computer*.

Slide the pointer down until About This Computer turns black and then click the mouse button. A window appears:

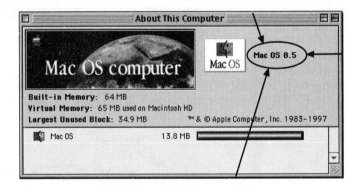

As my subtle drawn-in arrows indicate, this window reveals what version of the System software you have. The version is a number you'll need to know later in this book and later in your life. Therefore, take this opportunity to write it onto your Cheat Sheet (the yellow cardboard page inside the front cover of this book). You'll find a little blank for this information in the upper-left corner of your card, where it says, "Your System version."

When you're finished with this little piece of homework, close the About This Computer window by clicking the little square in the upper-left corner — the Close box — to make the window go away.

Double-clicking in theory and practice

All right, back to the lesson in progress. Make sure your hard-drive window is open.

So far, all of your work in the Finder (the desktop) has involved moving the mouse around. But your keyboard is useful, too. For example, do you see the System Folder? Even if you don't, here's a quick way to find it: Quickly type **SY** on your keyboard.

Presto, the iMac finds the System Folder (which happens to be the first thing that begins with those letters) and highlights it, in effect dropping it in front of you, wagging its tail.

Now try pressing the arrow keys on your keyboard — right, left, up, down. The iMac highlights neighboring icons as you do so.

Suppose you want to see what's in the System Folder. Of course, using your newfound noun-verb method, you could (1) click the System Folder to select it and then (2) choose Open from the File menu.

But that's the sissy way. Try this power shortcut: Point to the System Folder icon so that the tip of the arrow cursor is squarely inside the picture of the folder. Keeping the mouse still, click twice in rapid succession. With stunning originality, the Committee for the Invention of Computer Terminology calls this advanced computing technique *double-clicking*.

If all went well, your double-click opened a new window, showing you the contents of the System Folder. (If it didn't work, you probably need to keep the mouse still or double-click faster.)

Remember this juicy golden rule: *Double-click means "open."*

In your iMac life, you'll be asked (or tempted) to click many an item on-screen: buttons that say "OK;" tools that look like paint brushes; all manner of multiple-choice buttons. In every one of these cases, you're supposed to click *once*.

The only time you ever *double*-click something is when you want to *open* it. Got it?

Multiple windows

Now you should have two windows open on the screen: the hard-disk window and the System Folder window. (The System Folder window may be covering the first one; they're like overlapping pieces of paper on a desk.)

Try this: Click the title bar of the System Folder window (just *one* click). Drag the title bar downward until you can see the hard-drive window behind it, as shown here.

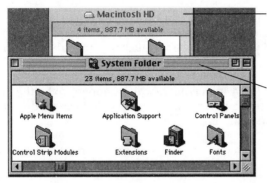

You can tell that this window is in back, because its title bar is solid light gray. Just click anywhere in the window to bring it to the front.

You know that this window is the top window, because its title bar is striped.

Take a stress-free moment to experiment with these two windows: Click the back one to bring it forward; then click the one that was in front to bring it to the front again.

Using a list view

There's one more aspect of windows that will probably make Type A person-alities wriggle with delight. Until now, you've been viewing the contents of your disk as a bunch of icons. Nice, but wouldn't it be neat to see things alphabetically?

1. **Make sure the System Folder is the active window (the one in front; "A." in the following figure).**

   We're going to use the System Folder because it's got a lot of stuff in it.

   Next, you're going to use a menu. Remember how to choose a menu command? Click the menu's name and then click the command you want in the drop-down list.

2. **Locate the View menu at the top of the screen; from it, choose "as List" (see "B." in the following picture).**

   Suddenly, the big icons are replaced by a neat alphabetical list of the window's contents (labeled here as "C.").

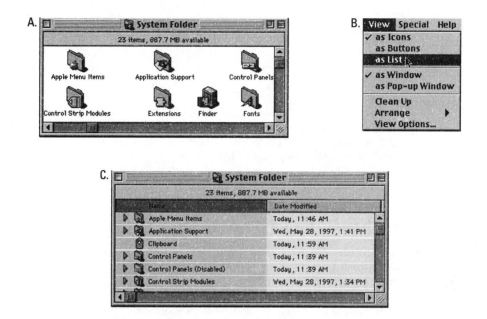

Invasion of the little triangles

When you view a window's contents in a list, each folder *within* the window is marked by a tiny triangle. The triangle points to the right.

You can open one of these folders-within-the-folder in the usual way, if you wish — by double-clicking. But it's much more satisfying for neat freaks to click the *triangle* instead. In the following figure, the before-and-after view of the Control Panels folder (inside the System Folder) shows how much more organized you can be.

When you click the triangle, in other words, your window contents look like an outline. The contents of that subfolder are indented. To "collapse," or close, the folder, click the downward-pointing triangle.

One more trick: See the words *Name, Date Modified*, and so on (at the top of the window)? Click any of these words. Instantly the iMac re-sorts everything in the window, based on the word you clicked. Example: click Size, if it's visible, and you'll see the largest files listed first.

The easiest homework you've ever had

To reinforce your budding mouse skills, here's a pathetically easy assignment: Take the iMac's own guided tour. It's easy; it's animated; and it's very,
very gentle.

To try out this self-help program, cancel your appointments for the next 20
minutes and turn off your phone's ringer. Now click the Help menu at the top
of the screen and then click Tutorial command. You'll be led softly and
sweetly through the lessons of this chapter (such as pointing, clicking, and
dragging). I'll wait right here until you're done.

Where to get help

If your tutorial-taking was successful, here's another hot tip: The iMac
stands ready to answer any other questions that may arise, thanks to its
built-in Help system. Here's how it works:

Once again, click the Help menu at the top of your screen. This time, click
the Help *command*. If you have Mac OS 8.1 on your iMac, the Mac OS Help
window appears; click the Topics, Index, or Look For button to ferret out the
answers to frequently asked questions. Once you've located a promising-
looking answer title, double-click it; the iMac actually walks you through,
step by step, whatever task you were asking about (adjusting the speaker
volume, printing, or whatever).

If you have Mac OS 8.5, on the other hand, you get a window that looks like this.

Help Viewer

Search

MacOS Help

What's New
Basics
Color accuracy
Disks
Files & programs
Internet & Networking
Memory
Monitors
Multimedia

Internet
• Connecting to the Internet and the Web
• Sharing and obtaining files over the Internet
• Finding items on the Internet
• Adjusting your Internet settings and information

Networking
• Connecting to a local network
• Sharing files with others on a network
• Getting a file from the network
• Sharing equipment over the network
• Connecting to another computer from a

You can use this Help Center in two ways. First, you can type a Help topic into the blank at the top of the window (such as **naming files** or **dialing the Internet**) — and then click the Search button. If you're having a good night, the window will then show you a list of Help pages that might contain the answer you're looking for; click the name of the topic that seems to hold some promise.

Second, you can click your way through this little Help program. In the previous illustration, see all the topics written in blue underlined type?

Of course not. This is a black-and-white book. How silly of me.

But on *your* screen, all those underlined phrases show up in blue lettering. That blueness, and that underlining, means *click me to jump to a different page*. By clicking on successive blue underlined phrases, you can often hone in on the precise Help article you're interested in.

Pit stop

Shut the iMac down now, if you want (flip back a few pages to the section "Shutting down" for complete instructions). Chapter $1^1/_2$ is something of a chalk-talk to help you understand what's really happening inside the computer's puny brain.

Top Ten Similarities between You and Your iMac

Before you move boldly forward to the next chapter, ponder the following frightening similarities between you and your computer:

1. Both are pulled out of a very special container on Day One.
2. Both have feet on the bottom.
3. Both have slots to provide adequate ventilation.
4. Both react to the movement of a nearby mouse.
5. Both sometimes crash when asked to do too much at once.
6. Both have a button on the front.
7. Both light up when turned on.
8. Both occasionally enjoy a good CD.
9. Both may be connected to a phone line for days at a time.
10. With considerable effort, both may be made to work with Microsoft Windows computers.

Chapter 1½

High-Tech Made Easy

- -

- -

How an iMac Works

I'm a little worried about sticking this chapter so close to the front of the book. Plenty of people firmly believe that the iMac has a personality — that when something goes wrong, the iMac is being cranky; and when a funny message appears on the screen, the iMac is being friendly. Don't let the following discussion of cold, metal, impersonal circuitry ruin that image for you; the iMac *does* have a personality, no matter what the wireheads say.

For the first time, you're going to have to roll up your brain's sleeves and chew on some actual computer jargon. Don't worry — you'll feel coolly professional and in control by the time it's over. Besides, it's a short chapter.

Storing things with disks

Human beings, for the most part, store information in one of two places. Either we retain something in our memory — or, if it's too much to remember, we write it down on the back of an envelope.

Computers work pretty much the same way (except they're not quite as handy with envelopes). They can either store what they know in their relatively pea-brained *memory,* which I'll cover in a moment, or they can write it down. A computer writes stuff down on computer disks.

For years, the most common kind of disk was the floppy disk. Ironically, Macintosh floppy disks aren't floppy, and they're not disks. They're actually hard plastic squares, 3½ inches on a side.

Floppy disks come in several capacities, but even the largest one holds only about 1,000 pages' worth of data. That may seem like a lot, but that's just text. Pictures, for example, take up much more space; that same floppy disk can probably hold only one or two color pictures. You can see, then, that floppies aren't very handy for storing *lots* of information. That's why they're has-beens, their careers fading faster than David Caruso's after leaving *NYPD Blue*. (And that's why your iMac can't even *accept* floppy disks unless you buy an add-on gadget; see Chapter 18 for details.)

Conceptualizing the hard disk

Fortunately, every iMac has an even better storage device built inside it — a *hard disk*. The concept of a hard disk confuses people because it's hidden inside the iMac's case. Since you can't see it or touch it, it's sort of conceptual — like beta-carotene or God, I guess. But it's there, spinning quietly away, and a hefty chunk of your iMac's purchase price paid for it.

Why all this talk of disks? Because a hard disk is where your life's work is going to live when the computer is shut off. You will, like it or not, become intensely interested in the overall health of your computer's hard disk.

Understanding memory

Okay. Now we get to the good stuff: how a computer really works. I know you'd just as soon not know what's going on in there, but this info is mental broccoli: It's good for you, and later in life, you'll be glad you were forced to digest it. If, at this point, your brain is beginning to hemorrhage, skip this section and find serenity in Chapter 2.

There's actually a significant difference between an *iMac's* memory and *your* memory (besides the fact that yours is probably much more interesting). When you turn off the iMac at night, it forgets *everything*. It becomes a dumb, metal-and-plastic doorstop. That's because a computer's memory, just like yours, is kept alive by electrical impulses. When you turn off an iMac, the electricity stops.

Therefore, each time you turn *on* an iMac, it has to relearn everything it ever knew, including the fact that it's a computer, what kind of computer it is, how to display text, how many days until your warranty expires, and so on. Now we arrive at the purpose of those disks we've been droning on about; that's where the computer's knowledge lives when the juice is off. Without a disk, the iMac is like someone with a completely hollow skull (and we've all met *that* type). If you're ever unlucky enough to experience a broken hard drive, you'll see how exciting an iMac can be without a disk: It shows a completely gray screen with a small blinking question mark in the middle. (I've met a few people like *that*, too.)

When you turn on the iMac, there's whirring and blinking. The hard disk inside begins to spin. When it hits about 4,500 rpm, the iMac starts reading the hard disk — it "plays" the disk like a CD player. It finds out: "Hey, I'm an iMac! And this is how I display text!" and so on. The iMac is reading the disk and copying everything it reads into *memory*. (That's why the computer takes a minute or so to start up.)

Memory is really neat. After something's in memory, it's instantaneously available to the computer. The iMac no longer has to read the disk to learn something. Memory is also expensive (at least compared to disks); memory is a bunch of complicated circuits etched onto a piece of silicon the size of a piece of Trident by people in white lab coats.

Because it's more expensive, Macs have far less memory than disk space. For example, even if your hard disk holds every issue of *National Geographic* ever published, you're probably only going to *read* one article at a time. So the iMac reads "The Nocturnal Nubian Gnat: Nature's Tiniest Vampire" from your hard disk, loads it into memory, and displays it on the screen. So it doesn't matter that your iMac's memory doesn't hold as much as your entire hard disk; the iMac uses the hard disk for *long-term, permanent* storage of *lots* of things, and it uses memory for *temporary* storage while you work on *one thing at a time*.

Who's Meg?

You often hear computer jocks talk about *megs*. Only rarely are they refer- ring to Meg Ryan and Meg Tilly. Meg is short for *megabyte*. So is the abbre- viation *MB*. (*Mega* = 1,000,000, and *byte* = an iota of information so small it can only specify a single letter of the alphabet.)

What's highly confusing to most beginners is that you measure memory (fast, expensive, temporary) and hard-disk space (permanent, slower) in the *same units*: megabytes. A typical iMac has 32 megs of memory (silicon chips) but 4,000 megs of hard-disk space (spinning platters).

(*Free bonus fact:* If a hard drive's size reaches 1,000 megs, it gets a new measurement name — its size is said to be one *gigabyte*. The abbreviation for one gigabyte is 1GB. Computer nerds sometimes use shorthand for this measurement — "My iMac's hard drive has four gigs" — which absolutely bewilders jazz-club musicians.)

With these vital facts in mind, see if you can answer the following paradoxi- cal dinner party question:

"How many megs does your iMac have?"

The novice's answer: "Um . . . say, have you tried those little cocktail weenies?"

The partly initiated's reply: "I . . . I think 32?"

The truly enlightened response: "What do you mean, how many megs? Are you referring to *memory* or to *hard-disk storage space?* Here, have a cocktail weenie."

Understanding RAM

Let's add another term to your quickly growing nerd vocabulary list. It pains me to teach you this word, because it's one of those really meaningless terms that was invented purely to intimidate people. Trouble is, you're going to hear it a lot. You may as well be prepared.

It's *RAM.* You pronounce it like the sheep. RAM is memory. A typical iMac has 32 megs of RAM (in other words, of memory).

Incidentally, this might be a good time to find out how much RAM *you* have. Here's how to find out.

Turn on your iMac.

Remember the menu? The fruit in the upper-left corner of the screen? Click that menu as you did in Chapter 1. Once again, point to About This Computer and then click the mouse button again.

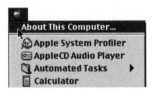

A window appears.

Why they call it RAM

You know what an *acronym* is, right? It's a bunch of initials that, together, spell out an actual word, such as M.A.D.D. or SALT Treaty . . . or RAM.

When the Committee for Arbitrary Acronyms (the CAA) ratified the abbreviation RAM, it probably stood for *Random Abbreviation for Memory*. Today, it supposedly stands for *Random Access Memory*.

Whatever *that* means.

The number labeled Built-in Memory (which I've circled in the preceding picture) is how much actual RAM your iMac has. It's generally some multiple of eight. (The total amount of usable memory, as listed on the second line, may be higher, thanks to tricks such as RAM Doubler and virtual memory. Chapter 16 explains those memory stunts in painstaking detail.)

In any case, your iMac's RAM endowment is a statistic you'll enjoy reviewing again and again. Therefore, take this opportunity to write this number onto your yellow cardboard Cheat Sheet at the front of the book. There's a little blank for this information, near where you wrote your System-software version.

Putting it all together

Now that you know where a computer's information lives, let me take you on a tour of the computer's guts. Let's get into our little imaginary Disney World tram. Keep hands and feet inside the car at all times.

When you turn on the iMac, as I noted earlier, the hard disk spins, and the iMac copies certain critical information into its memory. So far, the iMac knows only that it's a computer. It doesn't know anything else that's stored on your hard disk. It doesn't know about Nocturnal Nubian Gnats, your new screenplay, or how much you owe on your credit card — yet.

To get any practical work done, you now have to transfer the article (or screenplay or spreadsheet) into memory; in Macintosh terminology, you have to *open a file*. In Chapter 2, you'll find out how easy and idiot-proof this process is. Anyway, after you open a file, it appears on-screen. (It's *in memory* now.)

While your document is on the screen, you can make changes to it. This, of course, is why you bought a computer in the first place. You can delete a sentence from your novel or move a steamy scene to a different chapter.

(The term for this process is *word processing*.) If you're working on your finances, you can add a couple zeros to your checking-account balance. (The term for *this* process is *wishful thinking*.) All without any eraser crumbs or whiteout.

Perceptive readers who haven't already gotten bored and gone off to watch TV will recognize that you're making all these changes to what's in *memory*. The more you change the screenplay that's up on the screen, the more it's different from that *permanent* copy that's still on your disk, safe and sound.

At this point, you're actually in a pretty precarious position. Remember that memory is sustained by electricity. In other words, if your four-year-old mistakes the iMac's power cord for a handy suckable plaything and jerks it out of the wall, then the electricity stops, the screen goes blank, and all the changes you've made disappear forever. You're left with the original copy on the disk, of course, but any work you've done on it vanishes, along with anything else in the iMac's memory.

However, every software program has a simple command, called Save, that saves your work back onto the hard disk. That is, the computer *updates* the original copy that's still on the hard disk, and you're safe. Even if a sun storm wipes out all power plants in the Northern Hemisphere and your iMac goes dark, your novel or letter or spreadsheet is safe on the disk. Most people use the Save command every five or ten minutes so that their work is always up to date and preserved on the disk. (You'll learn how to use the Save command in Chapter 4.)

"I lost all my work!"

So that you'll quit worrying about it, the precariousness of memory accounts for the horror stories you sometimes hear from people who claim that they lost their work to a computer. "I was on volume Y of the encyclopedia I've been writing," they'll say, "and I lost all of it because of a computer glitch!"

Now you can cry crocodile tears and then skip back to your office with a smirk. *You* know what happened. They probably worked for hours with some document on the screen but forgot to use the Save command. Then the unthinkable happened — someone tripped on the power cord — and, sure enough, all the changes they'd made got wiped out. A simple Save command would have stored everything neatly on the hard disk.

Top Ten Differences between Memory and a Hard Disk

May you never confuse memory with a hard disk again.

1. You usually buy memory 16 or 32 megs at a time. Hard disks come in sizes like 2 gigs, 4 gigs, and on up. (A *gigabyte* is 1,000 *megabytes.*)

2. Memory comes on a little minicircuit board. A hard disk is a plastic- or metal-cased box with cables hanging out of it.

3. You can install memory only inside the computer (something you usually hire a local guru to do). A hard disk may be either inside the iMac (an *internal* drive) or in a separate box you plug into the back (an *external* drive).

4. Memory delivers information to the iMac's brain almost instantly. The hard disk sometimes seems to take forever.

5. Some disks are removable. When one fills up, you can insert a different one. (Some examples: floppy disks, Zip disks, and SuperDisk disks.) Removing RAM is a more serious proposition, generally involving a knowledgeable geek's assistance.

6. Not every computer on earth has a hard disk. (The earliest Macs used nothing but floppy disks, and pocket organizers such as the PalmPilot, Sharp Wizard, and Casio Boss have no disks at all.) But every computer ever made has memory.

7. If you listen carefully, you can hear when the iMac is reading information off a hard disk; it makes tiny frantic scraping noises. You can't tell when the iMac is getting information from RAM.

8. As a very general rule, RAM costs about $12 per meg, and hard drive space averages about 15 cents per meg.

9. Memory's contents disappear when you turn off the computer. A disk's contents stay there until you deliberately throw them away.

10. To find out how much *hard-disk space* you have left, you look at the top of a window on your desktop.

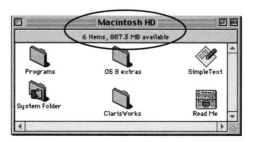

But to see how much *RAM* you have left, you must choose About This Computer from your menu to see the window shown a few pages back.

The number where it reads Largest Unused Block is roughly how much RAM you're not using at the moment. Details are in Chapter 16.

Chapter 2

Windows, Icons, and Trashes

* *

In This Chapter

▶ All about windows, folders, and icons

▶ Learning keyboard shortcuts

▶ Tips on using windows and disks to raise your social status

* *

Becoming Manipulative

All the clicking and dragging and window-shoving you learned in Chapter 1 is, in fact, leading up to something useful.

Foldermania

I've said that your hard disk is like the world's biggest filing cabinet. It's where you store all your stuff. But a filing cabinet without filing *folders* would be about as convenient to handle as an egg without a shell.

The folders on the iMac screen don't occupy any space on your hard drive. They're electronic fictions whose sole purpose is to help you organize your stuff.

Mr. Folder

The iMac provides an infinite supply of folders. Want a folder? Do this:

From the File menu, choose New Folder.

Ooh, tricky, this machine! A new folder appears. Notice that the iMac gracefully proposes "untitled folder" as its name. (Gotta call it *something,* I suppose.)

Notice something else, though: The name is *highlighted* (black). Remember our earlier lesson? Highlighted = selected = ready for you to *do* something. When *text* is highlighted, the iMac is ready for you to *replace* it with anything you type. In other words, you don't even have to backspace over the text. Just type away:

1. **Type *USA Folder* and press the Return key.**

   The Return key tells the iMac that your naming spurt is over.

   Now, to see how folders work, create another one.

2. **From the File menu, once again choose New Folder.**

   Another new folder appears, once more waiting for a title.

3. **Type *Ohio* and press Return.**

You're going to create one more empty folder. But by this time, your wrist is probably weary from the forlorn trek back and forth to the File menu. Don't you wish you could make a folder faster?

You can.

Unimportant sidebar about other menu symbols

Besides the little keyboard-shortcut symbols at the right side of a menu, you'll occasionally run into a little downward-pointing arrow, like this:

```
Font
  Avant Garde
  Bookman
  Chicago
  Courier
  Futura
  Garamond
  Geneva
  Hartel
  Helvetica
  Monaco
  Palatino
  Symbol
     ▼
```

That arrow tells you that the menu is so long, it doesn't even fit on the screen. The arrow is implying that still more commands are in the menu that you're not seeing. To get to those additional commands, carefully roll the pointer down the menu all the way to that down-pointing triangle. Don't let the sudden jumping scare you: The menu commands will jump upward, bringing the hidden ones into view.

And then there are the little black triangles pointing to the *right* (left side of the illustration). These triangles indicate that, when selected, the menu command won't do anything except offer you several *other* commands, which pop out to the side (at right in the figure):

```
Lawn                    Lawn
  Mulch      ►            Mulch      ►
  Mow        ►            Mow        ►   With Scissors
                                          Power Mower
  Re-sod ...             Re-sod ...        Hand Mower
  Dry Out ...            Dry Out ...      Riding Mower
  Trample               Trample           Flame Thrower
```

Keyboard shortcuts

Open the File menu, but don't select any of the commands in it yet. See those weird notations to the right of some commands?

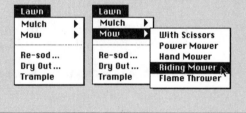

```
File
  New Folder      ⌘N
  Open            ⌘O
  Print           ⌘P
  Move To Trash   ⌘⌫
  Close Window    ⌘W

  Get Info        ⌘I
  Label           ►
  Sharing...
  Duplicate       ⌘D
  Make Alias      ⌘M
  Put Away        ⌘Y

  Find...         ⌘F
  Show Original   ⌘R
```

Get used to 'em. They're *keyboard shortcuts,* and they appear in almost every menu you'll ever see. Keyboard shortcuts let you select certain menu items without using the mouse.

Some people love keyboard shortcuts, claiming that if you're in a hurry, pressing keys is faster than using the mouse. Other people hate keyboard shortcuts, pointing out that using the mouse doesn't require any memorization. In either case, here's how keyboard shortcuts work.

When you type on a typewriter, you press the Shift key to make a capital letter, right? They call the Shift key a *modifier key* because it turns ordinary, well-behaved citizen keys like 3 and 4 into madcap symbols like # and $. Welcome to the world of computers, where everything is four times more complicated. Instead of having only *one* modifier key, the iMac has *four* of them! Look down next to your spacebar. There they are: In addition to the Shift key, one says Option, one says Ctrl, and another has a little ⌘ symbol on it.

It's that little cloverleaf — the *command key* — whose symbol appears in the File menu. Next to the New Folder command, you see ⌘-N. That means:

1. **While pressing the ⌘ key, press the N key and then release everything.**

   Bam! You've got yourself another folder.

2. **Type *Michigan* and press Return.**

   You've just named your third folder. So why have you been wasting a perfectly good afternoon (or whatever it is in your time zone) making empty folders? So you can pretend you're getting organized.

3. **Drag the Ohio folder on top of the USA Folder.**

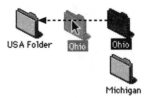

Make sure that the tip of the arrow actually hits the center of the USA Folder so that the folder becomes highlighted. The instant it turns black, let go of the Ohio folder — and watch it disappear into the USA Folder. (If your aim wasn't good, you'll now see the Ohio folder sitting *next* to the USA Folder; try the last step again.)

God never closes a window

When you opened the USA Folder, did you notice how its icon changed texture? After you double-clicked it, the icon turned dark and sort of grainy.

It's *supposed* to do that. When you double-click any icon to make its window appear, the icon itself turns into a grainy silhouette. That's your visual clue that it's been opened.

The icon won't collapse back into its normal, more attractive state until you close the corresponding window. (Can't find it? Then double-click the already-opened icon *again*. Its window will pop to the fore.)

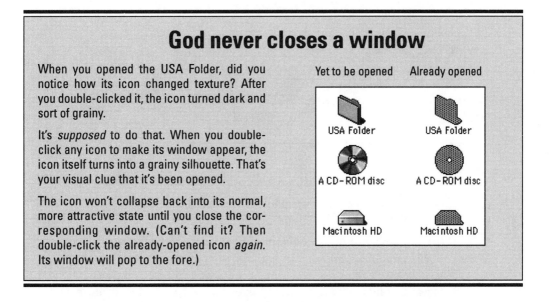

4. **Put the Michigan folder into the USA Folder in the same way — by dragging it on top of the USA Folder.**

   As far as you know, though, those state folders have *disappeared*. How can you trust me that they're now neatly filed away?

5. **Double-click the USA Folder.**

   Yep. Opens right up into a window, and there are your two darling states, nestled sweetly where they belong.

   If you were to double-click one of the *state* folders, you'd open *another* window. (Having a million windows open at once is nothing to be afraid of. If you're a neatness freak, you might feel threatened, but closing them is easy enough — remember the close box in the upper-left corner of each one?)

   Okay, so how do you get these inner folders *out* again? Do you have to drag them individually? That would certainly be a bummer if you had all 50 folders in the USA Folder.

   Turns out there are several ways to select more than one icon at a time.

6. **Click above and to the left of the Ohio folder (Step 1 in the upcoming picture) and, without releasing the mouse, drag down and to the right so that you enclose both folders with a dotted rectangle (Steps 2 and 3).**

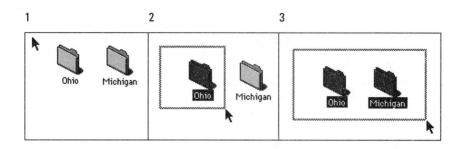

Release the mouse button when you've got both icons enclosed.

Now that you have several folders selected, you can move them en masse to another location.

7. Drag the Ohio folder outside of the USA Folder window.

The Michigan folder goes along for the ride.

This was a somewhat unproductive exercise, of course, because we were only working with empty folders. It gets much more exciting when you start working with your own documents. All of these techniques work equally well with folders and with documents.

Bonus technique for extra credit

The method of selecting several icons by dragging a rectangle around them is fine if all the icons are next to each other. But how would you select only the icons that begin with the letter A in this picture?

The power-user's secret: Click each icon *while pressing the Shift key.* As long as you're pressing Shift, you continually add additional, non-adjacent icons to the selection. (And if you Shift-click one by accident, you can *deselect* it by Shift-clicking *again.* Try it!)

You can't very well enclose each A by dragging the mouse — you'd also get all the *other* icons within the same rectangle.

How to trash something

Here's one more icon-manipulation trick you'll probably find valuable:

1. **Close the USA Folder by clicking its close box.**

2. **Drag the folder on top of the Trash can in the lower-right corner of the screen.**

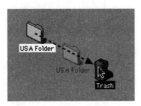

Don't let go until the Trash can actually turns black (when the tip of the arrow cursor is on it). When you do let go, notice how the Trash can bulges or overflows, a subtle reinforcement of how important it thinks your stuff is.

Anyway, that's how you throw things out on the iMac: Just drag them on top of the Trash can. (There's even a keystroke for this: Highlight an icon and then press ⌘-Delete. The chosen icon goes flying into the Trash as though it's just been drop-kicked.)

What's really hilarious is how hard Apple made it for you to get rid of something. Just putting something into the Trash doesn't actually get rid of it; technically, you've really only put it into the Oblivion Waiting Room. It'll sit there forever, in an overflowing trash can. If you needed to rescue something, you could just double-click the Trash can to open its window; then you could drag whatever-it-was right back onto the screen.

So if putting something into the Trash doesn't really delete it, how *do* you really delete it? You choose Empty Trash from the Special menu.

But even *then* your stuff isn't really gone; you get a message like this:

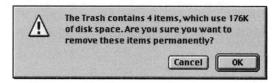

The Trash contains 4 items, which use 176K of disk space. Are you sure you want to remove these items permanently?

Cancel   OK

Click OK, and your file is finally gone.

Actually, don't tell anybody, but *even after* you've emptied the Trash, your file *still* isn't really gone forever. Programs like Norton Utilities can unerase a file that's been trashed, as long as you haven't used your iMac much since you threw away the file. That's useful to remember in case (1) you ever trash something by mistake, or (2) you're a spy.

Now you can understand why you never hear Mac owners complain of having thrown away some important document by accident — a Mac won't *let* you get rid of anything without fighting your way through four layers of warnings and red tape.

Pretty cool computer, huh?

Your basic CD-ROM crash course

You won't get far in life without knowing how to use your iMac's built-in CD-ROM drive. For example, your iMac came with such programs as MDK, Photo Soap, and a cooking how-to program. (See Chapter 6 for details on these goodies.) But they won't operate until you insert the corresponding CD that came with your computer.

To insert a CD, press the bluish, capsule-shaped button directly underneath the word "iMac" on the front of your computer. After a moment, the CD tray pops out about an inch.

With your finger, pull it out all the way. Place a CD into it — label side up — and snap the center ring down over the little sprocket in the center of the tray. (Avoid touching the underside of a CD.) Finally, push the tray shut. In a moment, the CD's icon shows up at the right side of your iMac screen.

To get the CD *out* again, don't try pressing that CD-tray button again — it won't work. (It makes the tray pop out only when the CD tray is *empty.*) Instead, click the CD's icon (on the screen) and, from the Special menu, choose Eject Disk. (Or — shortcut time — drag the CD's icon onto the Trash icon.)

The tray pops open so that you can remove the CD.

Top Ten Window, Icon, and Trash Tips

Staggering through the basics of using your iMac unattended is one thing. Shoving around those on-screen windows and icons with grace is quite another. Master the following, and then invite your friends over to watch some evening.

1. To rename an icon, click carefully on its name. Wait for a second or so, until a rectangle appears around the name. That's your cue to type away, giving it a new name. Press Return when you're done.

2. Don't forget that you can look at a window's contents in a neat list (choose "as List" from the View menu). Once in a list view, when a folder is highlighted, you can press ⌘-→ to expand it (as though you'd clicked the triangle to view its contents) and ⌘-← to collapse it again.

3. Every time you choose Empty Trash from the Special menu, the iMac asks you if you're absolutely sure. If you'd prefer to simply vaporize the Trash contents without being asked for confirmation, select the Trash icon. From the File menu, choose Get Info and then click the "Warn before emptying" check box so that the check mark (or X) disappears.

4. If you have a very important document, you can prevent it from getting thrown away by accident. Click its icon. From the File menu, choose Get Info. Turn on the Locked check box. Now, even if you put it in the Trash and try to empty the Trash, the iMac will simply tell you that there's a locked item in the Trash, which it won't get rid of.

5. To make a copy of a file, click the icon and choose Duplicate from the File menu. Or, while pressing the Option key, drag the icon into a new window or folder.

6. Isn't it frustrating to open a window that's too small to show you all its contents?

   Of course, you could spend a weekend fussing with the scroll bars, trying to crank the other icons into view. Or, by using trial-and-error, you could drag the lower-right handle (the resize box) to make the window bigger.

   There's a much quicker solution. Click the *zoom box* in the upper-right corner of the window. The iMac automatically makes the window *exactly* large enough to show all of the icons.

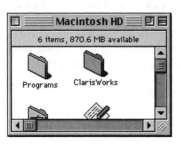

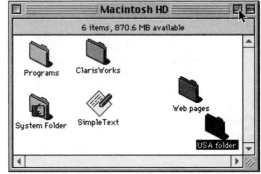

7. You don't have to be content to leave the Trash stranded way down there at the bottom of your screen. You can move it anywhere you want, just by dragging it.

   That's especially handy if you're lucky enough to have one of those screens the size of a Cineplex Odeon and don't feel like packing a week's worth of supplies every time you want to make a Journey to the Trash Corner.

8. Try this sneaky shortcut: While pressing the Control (Ctrl) key, point the cursor tip on an icon, disk, or the inside of a window. Keep the Control key pressed; if you now hold down the mouse button, a pop-up menu appears at your cursor tip, listing commands that pertain only to that icon, disk, or window.

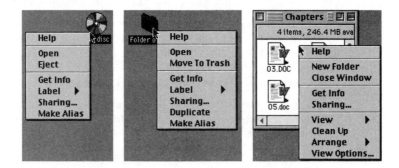

For example, if you Control-click a disk or CD, you'll be offered commands like Eject, Help, and Open. If you Control-click an icon, you get commands like Get Info, Duplicate, and Move to Trash. And if you Control-click anywhere inside a window — but *not* directly on an icon — you're offered New Folder, Sort List, and Close Window. (The geek term for this phenomenon is *contextual menus* — because the menu is different depending on the context of your click.)

9. When your life overwhelms you with chaos and random events, at least your iMac can give you a sense of control and order.

Want proof? Open a window, such as your Macintosh HD window. From the View menu, choose "as Icons." Note how messy, crude, and slovenly your icons look!

Now, from the View menu, choose View Options. In the window that appears, click Keep Arranged, like this:

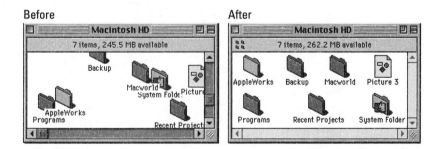

And then click OK. Now, no matter how many icons you add to this window, and no matter what size you make the window, your icons will always remain in neat alignment.

Before

After

10. You don't have to clean up your windows before you shut down the computer. The windows will be right where you left them the next time you turn on the iMac.

Chapter 3

Actually Accomplishing Something

● ●

In This Chapter

▶ What software is, for those who care

▶ Copying and pasting

▶ Desk accessories and the fruit-shaped menu they're listed in

▶ The pure, unalloyed joy of control panels

● ●

*T*he iMac is like a VCR. The software programs you install on the iMac are like the tapes you slip into your VCR. Without tapes (software), the VCR (iMac) is worthless. But with tapes (software), your VCR (iMac) can take on any personality.

A VCR might let you watch a Western one night, home movies another, and a *60 Minutes* exposé about a corrupt Good Humor man another night. In the same way, your iMac can be a typing instructor, a checkbook balancer, or a movie-editing machine, depending on the software you buy. Each piece of software — usually called a *program,* but sometimes known as an *application* — is like a different GameBoy cartridge: It makes the iMac look, feel, and behave differently. The average Mac user winds up using about six or seven different programs regularly.

Obsolescence Therapy

Your relationship with a software company doesn't end when you buy the program. First, the company provides a technical help staff for you to call when things get rocky. Some firms are great about this relationship — they give you a toll-free number that's answered immediately by a smart, helpful, customer-oriented technician. More often, though, sending out an SOS is a long-distance call . . . and a long-distance five- or ten-minute wait before somebody can help you. How can you find out how good a company's help line is? By asking around and reading the reviews in Mac magazines (such as *Macworld, MacHome Journal,* or *MacAddict*).

Like the computers themselves, software programs are continually being improved and enhanced by their manufacturers. Just as in owning a computer, owning a software program isn't a one-time cash outlay; each time the software company comes out with a new version of the program, you'll be offered the chance to get it for a small "upgrade fee" of $25 or $99, for example.

You'd think people would get fed up with this endless treadmill of expenses and just stick with the version they've got, refusing to upgrade to successive versions. Some manage it. Most people, however, succumb to the fear that somehow they'll be left behind by the march of technology and wind up forking over the upgrade fees once a year or so. Let your budget and sense of independence be your guide.

Credit Card Workout #2: Buying Software

(Credit Card Workout #1, by the way, was buying the computer.)

The iMac comes with a handsome bonus gift of software preinstalled on the hard disk. That's fortunate, because software, for the most part, is expensive.

If you decide to explore the world of Mac software beyond what came with your iMac, for example, you'll discover that the popular word-processing program called Microsoft Word sells for about $300. If you plan to do number crunching, more than 90 percent of Mac users use the Microsoft Excel spreadsheet (another $300). Want a database for handling order forms, tracking phone calls, and creating form letters? Check out the fantastic FileMaker Pro (around $200). (Try, *try* not to focus on the fact that what you *get* for that money is a 50-cent CD and a $3 manual.)

But all that's for later; for now, revel in the fact that you own one of the greats: an *integrated* program called either AppleWorks or ClarisWorks (depending upon when you bought your iMac). This single program is actually several programs mashed into one: word processor, database, spreadsheet, drawing program, and so on. (See Chapter 6, "Faking Your Way Through the Free Software.")

Where to get it

There are two places to buy software: via mail order and at a store. Unfortunately, as you'll quickly discover, today's computer stores generally offer a pathetically small selection of Macintosh software. On the other hand, mail-order companies offer thousands of choices; give much bigger discounts;

take returns after you've opened the box; and don't charge sales tax. And, of course, you don't have to fire up the old Volvo. You get your stuff delivered to your door by the next day. (The overnight shipping charge is usually $5 per order.)

The mail-order companies are called things like Mac Connection, Mac Zone, and Mac Warehouse. They all have toll-free phone numbers and Web pages (see Appendix B, "The Resource Resource," for a listing). Overnight mail-order companies like these are truly one of the bright spots in the Mac world. You can call Mac Connection, for example, until *2:45 a.m.* and get your new programs by midmorning (seven hours later). After ordering from these companies, you'll start to wish there were overnight mail-order grocery stores, gas stations, and dentists.

All right, maybe not dentists.

In the next chapter, you're going to do some word processing. As a warm-up, however, let me show you some of the basic principles of using programs on the iMac. To make sure you've got the same thing on your screen that I do, we'll start off by using the built-in programs that came with your iMac.

Your very first software

There are several *menus* across the top of the screen (remember these?). As you get to know the iMac, you'll discover that their wording changes from program to program. Right now, they say, for example, File, Edit, View, and Special; in a word processor they might say File, Edit, Font, Size, Format, and so on. The menu names (and the commands listed in those menus) are tailored to the function of the software.

El cheapo software

Once you've read Chapter 11, and you've decided it might be fun to plug your iMac into the telephone line to dial up faraway computers, you may stumble onto another kind of software: *shareware.* These are programs written by individuals, not software companies, who make their programs freely available on the Internet. You can grab them, via telephone, and bring them to your own iMac. And get this: Only the *honor system,* for heaven's sake, compels you to pay the authors the $15 or $20 they're asking for.

Sure, shareware often has a homemade feel to it. On the other hand, some of it's really terrific. You can search for the kind of shareware program you want (and also for acres of sounds, pictures, clip art, and games) on America Online and on the Internet (such as at *www.shareware.com*).

There's one menu that's *always* on your screen, though: our friend the Apple menu (the at the left edge of the menu bar). Among other things, this menu provides immediate access to some useful miniprograms known as *desk accessories*. Desk accessories are surefire, nonthreatening, and fun — perfect for your first baby steps into the world of software.

Desk Accessories

Let's start simple. Move your cursor up to the menu and choose Calculator. The Calculator pops up in a tiny window of its own.

The Calculator

Using the mouse, you can click the little Calculator buttons. The iMac gives you the correct mathematical answer, making you the owner of the world's biggest pocket calculator.

What's neat is that you can also type the keys on your *numeric keypad,* the block of number keys off to the right side of your keyboard. As you press these real keys, you can watch the on-screen keys in the Calculator window get punched accordingly. Try it out!

Take a moment to reinforce your love of windows: By dragging the *title bar* (where it says "Calculator"), move the Calculator window into a new position. If you were good and tired of looking at it, you could also make the Calculator go away by clicking its close box (in the upper-left corner, like on all windows).

But don't close the Calculator just yet. Leave it open on the screen.

The Note Pad

Now go to the menu again and this time choose Note Pad. Instantly, the world's most frill-free word processor appears on the screen.

You'll learn more about word processing in the next section. For now, we're just going to do some informative goofing around. With the Note Pad open on your screen, type a math problem, like this:

37+8+19*3-100

(In the computer world, the asterisk [*] means "times," or multiply.) If you make a mistake, press the big Delete key at the upper-right corner of your keyboard. This key means "Backspace."

Now, by dragging the Note Pad's title bar, move it so that you can see the Calculator window, too.

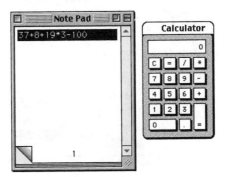

You're going to use two programs at once, making them cooperate with each other — one of the most remarkable features of the iMac.

Selecting text

This is about to get interesting.

Using the mouse, position the pointer at the left side of your equation (below, top). Press the button and drag, perfectly horizontally, to the right (middle). Release the mouse after you've highlighted the entire equation (bottom).

You've just *selected* some text. Remember in Chapter 1, when you *selected* an icon — and then used a menu command? Struggling, as always, to come up with a decent analogy, I likened this *select-then-operate* sequence to building a noun-verb sentence.

Well, it works just as well with text as it does with icons. You've now high-lighted, or selected, some text. The iMac now knows what the noun is — what it's supposed to pay attention to. All you have to do is select a verb from one of the menus. And the *verb du jour* is *Copy*.

The cornerstone of human endeavor: Copy and Paste

Choose Copy from the Edit menu.

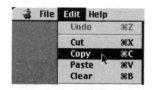

Thunder rolls, lightning flashes, the audience holds its breath . . . and absolutely nothing happens.

Behind the scenes, though, something awesomely useful occurred. The iMac looked at the selected equation and memorized it, socking it away into an invisible storage window called the *Clipboard*. The Clipboard is how you transfer stuff from one window into another and from one program into another. (Some programs even have a Show Clipboard command, in which case I take back the part about the Clipboard being invisible.)

Now then. You can't *see* the Clipboard at this point, but in a powerful act of faith, you put your trust in me and you believe that it contains the high-lighted material (the equation).

The Application menu

Do you see the tiny Note Pad icon at the right end of your menu bar? (If you have Mac OS 8.5 or later, it also *says* Note Pad.)

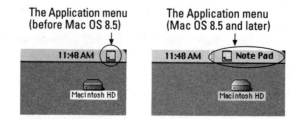

The Application menu (before Mac OS 8.5)

The Application menu (Mac OS 8.5 and later)

This icon actually represents a menu — the Application menu, of course. It lists all the programs that you have running at once. At this moment, you have *three* programs running at once: the Note Pad, the Calculator, and the famous Finder (or desktop).

You multitasking maniac, you.

Choose Calculator from the Application menu.

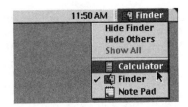

The Calculator window moves to the front, and the icon in the upper-right changes to look like a Calculator.

Those of you still awake will, of course, object to using the Application menu to bring the Calculator forward. You remember all too plainly from Chapter 1 that simply *clicking* in a window brings it to the front, which would have required less muscular effort.

Absolutely right! You may now advance to the semifinals. However, learning to use the Application menu was a good exercise. Many times in your upcoming life, the program in front will be covering up the *entire* screen. So *then* how will you bring another program forward, big shot? That's right. You can't *see* any other windows, so you can't click one to make it active. You'll have to use the Application menu.

In any case, the Calculator is now the active application. (*Active* just means it's in front.) Now then: Remember that intricate equation that's still on the iMac Clipboard? Instead of having to type an equation into the Calculator by punching keys, let's just paste it in:

1. **Press the Clear key (or the letter C key) on your iMac keyboard or click the C button on the Calculator.**

   You just cleared the display. We wouldn't want your previous diddlings to interfere with this tightly controlled experiment.

2. **From the Edit menu, choose Paste — and watch the Calculator!**

If you looked in time, you saw the number keys flashing like Las Vegas at midnight. And with a triumphant modesty, the iMac displays the answer to your math problem. (It should be 92.)

Did you get what just happened? You typed out a math problem in a word processor (the Note Pad), copied it to the Clipboard, and pasted it into a number-cruncher (the Calculator). Much of the miracle of the Macintosh stems from its capability to mix and match information among multiple programs in this way.

It's a two-way street, too. You can paste this number back into the word processor:

1. **From the Edit menu, choose Copy.**

   But wait! Something was already on the Clipboard. Where is the iMac supposed to put this *new* copied info?

   On the Clipboard, of course. And whatever was there before (your equation) gets nuked. The Clipboard contains exactly one thing at a time — whatever you copied *most recently.*

2. **From the Application menu, choose Note Pad (or just click the Note Pad window).**

   The Note Pad is now the active application.

3. **Type the following:**

   Dear son: You owe me $

   Stop after the $ sign. Move the mouse up to the Edit menu.

4. **From the Edit menu, choose Paste.**

   Bingo! The iMac pastes in the result from the Calculator (which it had ready on the Clipboard).

   Incidentally, whatever's on the Clipboard stays there until you copy something new or until you turn off the machine. In other words, you can paste it over and over again.

5. **For a second time, choose Paste from the Edit menu.**

   Another 92 pops into the window.

You don't have to use the menu to issue a command like Copy or Paste. If you wish, you can use a keyboard shortcut to do the same thing. You may remember having used the ⌘ key in Chapter 2 to issue commands without using the mouse.

And how are you supposed to remember which letter key corresponds to which command? Well, usually it's mnemonic: ⌘-P means Print, ⌘-O means Open, and so on. But you can cheat; try it right now. Click the Edit menu.

There's your crib sheet, carefully listed down the right side of the menu. Notice that the keyboard shortcuts for all four of these important commands (Undo, Cut, Copy, Paste) are adjacent on the keyboard: Z, X, C, V.

C is Copy. And V, right next to it, is Paste. (I know, I know: Why doesn't *P* stand for Paste? Answer: Because *P* stands for Print! And anyway, V is right next to C-for-Copy on your keyboard, so it *kind of* makes sense.)

Click anywhere else on the screen (to ditch the menu) and let's try it:

1. **While holding down the ⌘ key, type a *V*.**

   Bingo! Another copy of the Clipboard stuff (92) appears in your Note Pad. (In the future, I'll just refer to a keyboard shortcut like this as "⌘-V.")

2. **Press ⌘-V again.**

   Yep, that kid's debt is really piling up. He now owes you $92,929,292.

   But after all, he's your son. Why not just let him pay 10 percent down on the amount he owes you? In other words, why not *undo* that last 92 pasting?

3. **From the Edit menu, choose Undo.**

   The most recent thing you did — in this case, pasting the fourth 92 — gets undone.

Rewriting history is addicting, ain't it?

Remember, though, that Undo only reverses your *most recent* action. Suppose you (1) copy something, (2) paste it somewhere else, and then (3) type some more. If you choose Undo, only the typing will be undone (Step 3), *not* the pasting (Step 2).

Control Panels

There's one item in your menu that *isn't* a desk accessory. It says Control Panels, and all it does is open up your Control Panels folder. So what exactly *is* your Control Panels folder? It's a folder that lives inside your System Folder. It contains a bunch of icons, each of which controls some aspect of your iMac. Choose Control Panels from the menu to make the Control Panel window appear.

I'll show you around one control panel; then you can take it from there:

1. **Quickly type *DA* on your keyboard.**

   Remember this handy trick? You can select one icon in a folder just by typing the first couple of letters of its name. In this case, you get the Date & Time icon.

2. **Double-click the Date & Time icon.**

   The Date & Time control-panel window opens. This is where you set the clock — as displayed, for example, at the top right of your screen. To change the time, click a number and then type the correct number in its place.

Date & Time

Current Date   **Current Time**

`1/19/99`   `11:57:42 AM`

Date Formats...   **Time Formats...**

All right — close the Date & Time window by clicking the close box in the upper-left corner.

Top Ten Control Panel Explanations

Dozens of control panels are kicking around in your Control Panels folder. Here are a few national favorites. (Some have different names depending on when you bought your iMac.) For much more detail about all the stuff in your System Folder, see Chapter 8.

1. **Monitors & Sound** — enables you to switch your monitor among various color settings (such as *grayscale,* like a black-and-white TV, or various degrees of richness of color).

2. **Mouse** — controls how sensitive the pointer movement is. Incidentally, the pointer on the screen *always* moves slowly if you move the mouse slowly. This control panel enables you to adjust how quickly the arrow moves if you move the mouse *quickly.*

3. **Keyboard** — enables you to decide whether holding down a key should type its letter repeatedly — for example, XXXXXXXXXXX — and how fast it repeats.

4. **Appearance** — lets you decide what color "highlighting pen" you want to use whenever you drag the mouse across text. (Mac OS 8.5 offers additional options in this control panel; see Chapter 9 for details.)

5. **Map** — tells what time it is anywhere in the world. Either click to specify a location or type the name of a major city or country and click the Find button.

6. **Speech** — lets you choose a voice for the iMac to use when *talking to you* (see Chapter 19).

7. **File Exchange** or **PC Exchange** — lets your iMac use floppy disks from Windows computers (but only if you buy a floppy drive or SuperDisk drive for your iMac).

8. **Energy Saver** — lets you establish automatic shutoff times (or automatic sleep times) for your iMac, in the name of saving electricity. For example, mine is set to go to sleep if I haven't used the computer in 30 minutes.

9. **General Controls** — offers a slew of handy customizing features: how fast your cursor blinks when you're word processing, whether or not you want your System Folder protected against marauding children, and so on. Also holds the on/off switches for three of the iMac's most useful features: the Launcher (see Chapter 4), the Documents folder (Chapter 4 again), and self-hiding programs (see Chapter 8, under "General Controls").

10. **Desktop Pictures** — lets you choose a new backdrop design for your desktop. The Teddy Bears design is a particular favorite of macho computer nerds everywhere.

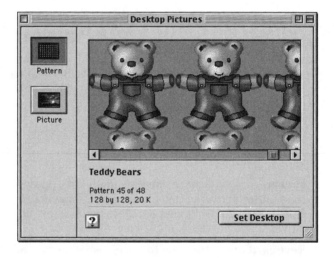

To find a pattern you like, click the arrows at either end of the horizontal scroll bar. When you see one that catches your fancy, click the Set Desktop (or Set Desktop Pattern) button.

You may also have noticed the extra button called Picture. This button lets you fill your screen with one *big* picture of your choice, instead of small, *repeated* pictures like the teddy bears.

(If you have Mac OS 8.5 or later, this entire feature has been assimilated into the Appearance control panel. There's no Desktop Pictures control panel at all. I mention that to save you the trip back to the computer store to return your iMac because you think you're missing components.)

Chapter 4

Typing, Saving, and Finding Again

· ·

In This Chapter

▶ Unlearning years of typewriter lessons

▶ Copying and pasting

▶ How to save your files so they're not lost forever

▶ You — yes, you — the desktop publisher

· ·

*L*et's not kid ourselves. Yeah, I know, you're gonna use your iMac to do photo retouching, to conquer the Internet, or to compose symphonies. But no matter who you are, what you'll probably do the *most* of is good old *word processing*.

But just because everybody does it doesn't mean word processing isn't the single most magical, amazing, time-saving invention since the microwave dinner. Master word processing, and you've essentially mastered your computer.

Your Very First Bestseller

Lucky for you, your iMac comes with a superb word-processing program. It's called AppleWorks (or ClarisWorks), and you can read about it in Chapter 6.

For this quick and dirty typing lesson, though, you may as well use a quick and dirty program: the super-budget word processor known as the Note Pad; choose its name from the menu to make it appear.

Top three rules of word processing

The first rules of typing on a computer are going to be tough to learn, especially if you've been typing for years. But they're crucial:

- ✔ **Don't press the Return key at the end of each line.** I'm dead serious here. When you type your way to the end of a line, the next word will automatically jump down to the next line. If you press Return in the middle of a sentence, you'll mess everything up.

- ✔ **Put only one space after a period.** From now on, everything you write will come out looking like it was professionally published instead of being cranked out on some noisy Selectric with a bad ribbon. A quick glance at any published book, magazine, or newspaper will make you realize that the two-spaces-after-a-period thing is strictly for typewriters.

- ✔ **Don't use the L key to make the number 1.** Your iMac, unlike the typewriter you may have grown up with, actually has a key dedicated to making the number 1. If you use a lowercase L instead, the 1 will look funny, and your spell checker will choke on it every time.

If those statements give you uncontrollable muscular facial spasms, I don't blame you. After all, I'm telling you to do things that you were explicitly taught *not* to do by that high-school typing teacher with the horn-rimmed glasses.

There are a few other rules, too, but breaking them isn't serious enough to get you fired. So let's dig in. Make sure you have a blank piece of electronic typing paper open in front of you — a new, untitled word-processing screen.

The excitement begins

You should see a short, blinking, vertical line at the beginning of the typing area. They call this the *insertion point*. It shows you where the letters will appear when you start to type.

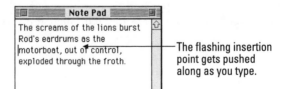

The flashing insertion point gets pushed along as you type.

All about big fat Launcher buttons

Do you recognize this thing?

If you don't see it, you can make it appear by choosing Launcher from the Control Panels command of your menu.

The Launcher is supposed to make getting into your programs easier. Studies showed that *double-clicking* an icon, as you've been thus far instructed, was beyond the technical abilities of some people. Thus the Launcher was born, where a *single* click on any icon launches (opens) a program.

The rules for using the Launcher are simple:

1. To switch to another "page" (window-full) of icons, click one of the wide text buttons at the top of the window — Applications, for example.

2. If there's some program on the Launcher window that you don't really use, you can get rid of it. While pressing the Option key, drag that sucker right to the trash. (You aren't trashing the *actual* program, wherever it may reside on your computer. You're just getting its *icon* off the Launcher window.)

3. If there's some program — or document, or folder — whose icon *isn't* on the Launcher window but should be, simply drag its icon into the Launcher window and release. A copy of that icon appears automatically, ready for subsequent one-click launching.

4. If you'd rather not have the Launcher window confronting you at all every morning, choose Control Panels from the menu. Double-click the control panel called General Controls. Click the check box called "Show Launcher at system startup" to turn it off.

Type the upcoming passage. If you make a typo, press Delete, just like you would Backspace on a typewriter. *Don't* press Return when you get to the edge of the window. Just keep typing, and the iMac will create a second line for you. Believe. *Believe.*

The screams of the lions burst Rod's eardrums as the motorboat, out of control, exploded through the froth.

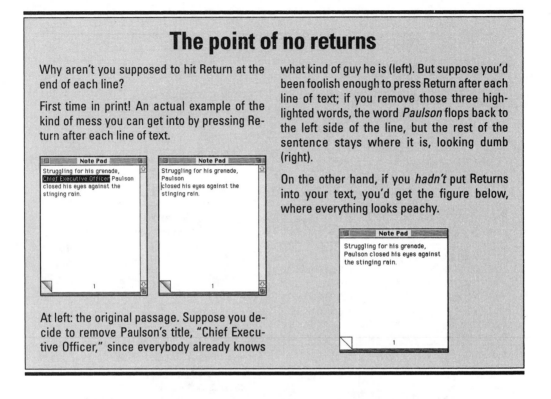

The point of no returns

Why aren't you supposed to hit Return at the end of each line?

First time in print! An actual example of the kind of mess you can get into by pressing Return after each line of text.

At left: the original passage. Suppose you decide to remove Paulson's title, "Chief Executive Officer," since everybody already knows what kind of guy he is (left). But suppose you'd been foolish enough to press Return after each line of text; if you remove those three highlighted words, the word *Paulson* flops back to the left side of the line, but the rest of the sentence stays where it is, looking dumb (right).

On the other hand, if you *hadn't* put Returns into your text, you'd get the figure below, where everything looks peachy.

See how the words automatically wrapped around to the second line? They call this feature, with astonishing originality, *word wrap*.

But suppose, as your novel is going to press, you decide that this sleepy passage really needs some spicing up. You decide to insert the word *speeding* before the word *motorboat*.

Remember the blinking cursor — the insertion point? It's on the screen even now, blinking calmly away at the end of the sentence. If you want to insert text, you have to move the insertion point.

You can move the insertion point in two ways. First, try pressing the arrow keys on your keyboard. You can see that the up- and down-arrow keys move the insertion point from line to line, and the right- and left-arrow keys move the insertion point across the line. Practice moving the insertion point by pressing the arrow keys.

If the passage you want to edit is far away, though (on another page, for example), using the arrow keys to move the cursor is inefficient. Your fingers would be bloody stumps by the time you finished. Instead, use this finger-saving technique:

1. **Using the mouse, move the cursor (which, when it's near text — looks like this: I) just before the word *motorboat* and click the mouse.**

   The I-beam changes to the insertion point.

   This is as confusing as word processing ever gets — there are *two* little cursors, right? There's the blinking insertion point, and there's this one I, which is called an *I-beam* cursor.

   In fact, the two little cursors are quite different. The blinking insertion point is only a *marker,* not a pointer. It always shows you where the next typing will appear. The I-beam, on the other hand, is how you *move* the insertion point; when you click with the I-beam, you set down the insertion point.

   In other words, editing stuff you've already typed, on the Macintosh, is a matter of *click and then type.*

2. **Type the word *speeding.***

   The insertion point does its deed, and the iMac makes room on the line for the new word. A word or two probably got pushed onto the next line. Isn't word wrap wondrous?

Editing for the linguistically blessed

So much for *inserting* text: You click the mouse (to show the iMac *where*) and then type away. But what if you need to delete a bunch of text? What if you decide to *cut out* the first half of our sample text?

Well, unless you typed the challenging excerpt with no errors, you already know one way to erase text — by pressing the Delete key. Delete takes out one letter at a time, just to the left of the insertion point.

Deleting one letter at a time isn't much help in this situation, though. Suppose you decide to take out the first part of the sentence. It wouldn't be horribly efficient to backspace over the entire passage just so you could work on the beginning.

No, instead you need a way to edit any part of your work, at any time, without disturbing the stuff you want to leave. Once again, the Macintosh method, noun-then-verb, saves the day. Try this:

1. **Using the mouse, position the I-beam cursor at the beginning of the sentence.**

   This takes a steady hand; stay calm.

2. **Click *just* to the left of the first word and, keeping the mouse button pressed down, drag the I-beam cursor — *perfectly horizontally,* if possible — to the end of the word *as.***

   As you drag, the text gets highlighted, or *selected.* You've done this once before, in your copy-and-paste lesson.

   The screams of the lions burst Rod's eardrums as the speeding motorboat, out of control, exploded through the froth.

If you accidentally drag up or down into the next line of text, the highlighting jumps to include a big chunk of that additional line. Don't panic; without releasing the mouse button, simply move the cursor back onto the original line you were selecting. This time, try to drag more horizontally.

If you're especially clever and forward-thinking, you'll also have selected the blank space *after* the word *as.* Take a look at the previous illustration.

All right, in typical Mac syntax, you've just specified *what* you want to edit by selecting it (and making it turn black to show it's selected). Now for the verb:

1. **Press the Delete key.**

   Bam! The selected text is gone. The sentence looks pretty odd, though, since it doesn't begin with a capital letter.

2. **Using the mouse, position the cursor just before (or after) the letter *t* that begins the sentence and drag the cursor sideways across the letter so that it's highlighted.**

   the speeding motorboat, out of control, exploded through the froth.

Here comes another ground rule of word processing. See how you've just selected, or highlighted, the letter *t?* The idea here is to capitalize it. Of course, using the methods for wiping out (and inserting) text that you learned earlier, you could simply remove the *t* and type a *T.* But since you've selected the *t* by dragging through it, replacing it is much easier.

3. Type a capital *T*.

The selected text gets replaced by the new stuff you type. That, in fact, is the fourth ground rule: *Selected text gets replaced by the new stuff you type.* As your iMac life proceeds, keep that handy fact in mind; it can save you a lot of backspacing. In fact, you can select 40 pages of text so that it's all highlighted and then type *one single letter* to replace all of it. Or you could *select* only one letter but replace it with 40 pages of typing.

Take a moment now for some unsupervised free play. Try clicking anywhere in the text (to plant the insertion point). Try dragging through some text: If you drag perfectly horizontally, you select text just on one line (below, left). If you drag diagonally, you get everything between your cursor and the original click (below, right).

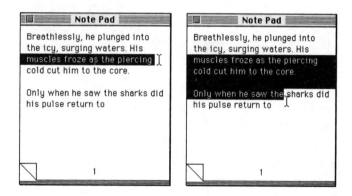

You *deselect* (or, equally poetically, unhighlight) text by clicking the mouse. Anywhere at all (within the typing area).

Here's about the most fabulous word-processing shortcut ever devised: Try pointing to a word and then double-clicking the mouse! You've easily selected *exactly* that word without having to do any dragging.

As you experiment, do anything you want with any combination of drags, clicks, double-clicks, and menu selections. It's nice to know — and you might want to prepare a fine mahogany wall plaque to this effect — that *nothing you do using the mouse or keyboard can physically harm the computer.* Oh, sure, it's possible to erase a disk or wreck one of your documents or something, but none of that requires a visit to a repair shop. You can't *break* the computer by playing around.

A word processing rule-ette

You know, by now, that your mouse pointer looks like this — I — whenever it's near text. And you know, by now, that you use this cursor to *click* wherever you want to type next.

But suppose you want to add some words way down the page, like this:

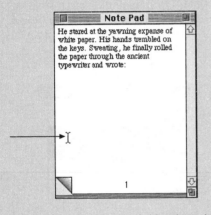

You'll discover pretty quickly that the Macintosh won't let you type there. The rule is: You can click your cursor anywhere on the page *that already has typing on it*. But if you try to click down *below*, in the white space, you're out of luck; the blinking insertion-point cursor simply jumps back up to the end of what you've already typed. In its ornery way, the Macintosh enforces its own rule of writing: No jumping ahead, bub.

Of course, you *can* skip down the page if you want some words to appear there. But you have to *type your way* down the page first. That's why God invented the Return key. Press it over and over again until your little insertion-point cursor is blinking merrily away at the bottom of the page — or wherever you tell it to go — and *now* start typing.

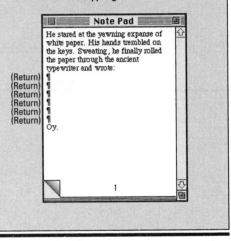

Puff, the Magic Drag-N-Drop

You kids today, with your long music and loud hair! You don't know how lucky you are! Why, when I was your age, if I wanted to rearrange a couple of words, I'd have to *copy and paste them!*

But not anymore. Nowadays, you can move text around on the screen just by *pointing* to it! This profoundly handy feature is known as Macintosh *drag-and-drop.*

Unfortunately, drag-and-drop doesn't work in every program, but it works in most of the biggies: the Note Pad; AppleWorks/ClarisWorks; Microsoft Word (5.0 or later); WordPerfect (3.5 or later); SimpleText; America Online (3.0 or later); FileMaker; Mariner Write; Nisus Writer (5.0 or later); and so on.

1. **Launch a program that offers drag-and-drop.**

   If you've been following along with the chapter already in progress, just remain in ClarisWorks/AppleWorks where you've already been. Press the Return key a couple of times to move into an empty part of the page.

2. **Type up two phrases, as shown here:**

3. **Highlight *Eyes of blue*.**

   You've done this before: Position the insertion-point cursor just to the left of the word *Eyes* and *carefully* slide directly to the right, highlighting the sentence (below, left).

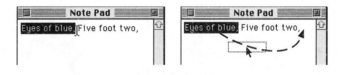

4. **Now position the arrow cursor right smack in the middle of the blackened phrase — hold down the mouse button — and *drag* the arrow to the end of the line (above, right).**

   When your arrow is correctly positioned at the end of the line, you'll see the new insertion point appear there.

5. **Release the mouse!**

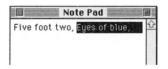

   As you can see, you've just *dragged* the first phrase into position after the second phrase! Cole Porter would be very grateful for your correcting his lyrics.

But wait — there's more! Once you've mastered the art of dragging text around your screen, the sky's the limit! To wit:

- ✔ If you press the *Option* key while you drag some highlighted text, instead of *moving* that phrase, you actually make a *copy* of it, as shown here:

- ✔ You can actually drag text *clear out of the window* and into another program — for example, from AppleWorks into the waiting Note Pad. (The Note Pad is a stripped-down, cheapie word processor found in your menu.)
- ✔ You can also drag text clear out of the window and *onto the desktop.* When you release the mouse, you'll see that your little drag-and-dropped blurb has turned into a *text clipping,* as shown here:

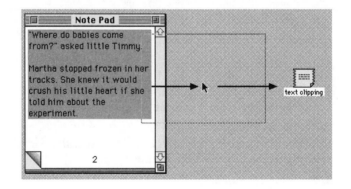

Next time you need that blob of text, you can point to the text clipping and drag it back into your word-processing program, and — presto! — the text appears there, exactly as though you'd typed it again.

Now if they'd only work it out so we could edit our *printouts* using drag-and-drop. . . .

Form and Format

For your next trick, it's time to graduate from the Note Pad to a true word processor. Close the Note Pad window. Open your hard drive; open the Applications folder; open the AppleWorks folder (or ClarisWorks folder, if that's what your iMac came with); and double-click the AppleWorks (or ClarisWorks) icon.

After a moment, the AppleWorks welcome screen appears, listing six kinds of work you might want to do: Database, Spreadsheet, and so on. Double-click the one called Word Processing to open up a new, blank sheet of electronic typing paper. Now you're ready for the lesson.

One of the most important differences between a typewriter and its replacement — the computer — is the sequence of events. When you use a typewriter, you set up all the formatting characteristics *before* you type: the margins, the tab stops, and (for typewriters with interchangeable type heads) the type style.

But the whole point of a word processor is that you can change anything at *any* time. Many people type the text of an entire letter (or proposal or memo) into the iMac and *then* format it. When you use a typewriter, you might discover, after typing the entire first page, that it's *slightly* too long to fit, and your signature will have to sit awkwardly on a page by itself. With an iMac, you'd see the problem and nudge the text a little bit higher on the page to compensate.

Word processing has other great advantages: no crossouts; easy corrections that involve no whiteout and no retyping; a permanent record of your correspondence that's electronic, not paper, and so it's always easy to find; a selection of striking typefaces — at any size; paste-in graphics; and so on. I think it's safe to say that once you try processing words, you'll never look back.

The return of Return

With all the subtlety of a Mack truck, I've taught you that you're forbidden to use the Return key *at the end of a line*. Still, that rectangular Return key on your keyboard *is* important. You press Return at the end of a *paragraph* and only there.

To the computer, the Return key works just like a letter key — it inserts a *Return character* into the text. It's just like rolling the paper in a typewriter forward by one notch. Hit Return twice, and you leave a blank line.

Seeing the unseen

I said that Returns are *usually* invisible. However, every time you press the Return key, the iMac actually does plop down a symbol onto your screen. Same thing with the space bar. Same with the Tab key.

Virtually every word processor lets you see these markings. In AppleWorks or ClarisWorks,

choose Preferences from the Edit or Tools menu to access the Show Invisibles (or View Nonprinting) option. In any case, the result looks something like this:

♦   "Alison—my·god,·not·that!·Anything·but·that!"¶

♦   But·it·was·too·late.·She·had·already·disappeared.¶

The point of Return, then, is to move text higher or lower on the page. Check out this example, for instance.

```
█¶                          ¶
¶                           Dearest·Todd,¶
¶                           ¶
¶                           I·have·never·loved·so·much·as·I·did·last·
Dearest·Todd,¶              night.·Imagine·my·joy·as·I·watched·you·
¶                           plunch·your·shining·scimitar·into·the·
I·have·never·loved·so·much·as·I·did·last·   greasy·flesh·of·that—that—hideous·thing·
night.·Imagine·my·joy·as·I·watched·you·     from·the·deep.¶
plunch·your·shining·scimitar·into·the·      ¶
greasy·flesh·of·that—that—hideous·thing·    Unfortunately,·the·IRS·has·determined·
from·the·deep.¶             that·you·failed·to·file·returns·for·the·years·
¶                           1982–1986.·They·have·asked·that·I·notify·
Unfortunately,·the·IRS·has·determined·      you·of·¶
that·you·failed·to·file·returns·for·the·years·
1982–1986.·They·have·asked·that·I·notify·
you·of·¶
```

Return characters move text down on the page. So, if you want to move text up on the page, drag through the blank space so that it's highlighted (above, left); of course, what you've really done is select the usually invisible Return characters. If you delete them, the text slides up the page (right).

Combine this knowledge with your advanced degree in Inserting Text (Remember? You *click and then type*), and you can see how you'd make more space between paragraphs or push all the text of a letter down on the page.

Appealing characters

Another big-time difference between word processing and typing is all the great *character formatting* you can do. You can make any piece of text **bold,** *italic,* underlined, all of these, and more. You also get a selection of great-looking typefaces — only a few of which look like a typewriter. By combining all these styles and fonts randomly, you can make any document look absolutely hideous.

Here's the scheme for changing some text to one of those character formats: noun-verb. Sound familiar? Go for it:

1. **Select some text by dragging through it.**

   Remember you can select a single word by double-clicking it; to select a bunch of text, drag the cursor through it so that it turns black. You've just identified *what* you want to change.

   Each word processor keeps its Bold, Italic, and Underline commands in its own specially named menu; in ClarisWorks/AppleWorks, they're in the Style menu. (In Microsoft programs, the Bold, Italic, and Underline commands may not be in a menu at all. Instead, you may have little buttons labeled **B,** *I,* or U at the top of your screen.)

2. **From the Style menu, choose Bold.**

   You've just specified *how* you want to affect the selected text.

You can apply several of these formats to the same text, too, although you won't win any awards for typographical excellence. Try changing the typeface also; the various fonts are called things like Chicago, Geneva, Times, and so on. Changing fonts works the same way: Select text and then choose the font.

And sizes — same deal: Select some text and then choose a type size from your word processor's Size or Font menu. The font sizes are measured in points, of which there are 72 per inch. Works out nicely, too — a typical iMac monitor has 72 *screen* dots per inch, meaning that 12-point type on the screen really *is* 12-point.

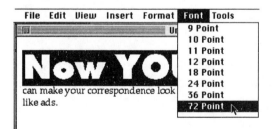

Before you know it, you'll have whipped your document into mighty handsome shape.

Formatting paragraphs

Whereas type styles and sizes can be applied to any amount of text, even a single letter, *paragraph formatting* affects a whole paragraph at once. Usually these styles are easy to apply. To select a paragraph, you don't have to

The efficiency zealot's guide to power typing

Because you *can* format text after you've typed it doesn't mean you *have* to. Most power-users get used to the keyboard shortcuts for the common style changes, like bold and italic. They're pretty easy to remember: In nearly every word-processing program, you get bold by pressing ⌘-B and italic with ⌘-I.

What's handy is that you can hit this key combo just *before* you type the word. For example, without ever taking your hands off the keyboard, you could type the following:

He stared at the **Delinquent Birds** folder. No: it *was not* happening!
↑ ↑ ↑ ↑
⌘-B ⌘-B ⌘-I ⌘-I

In other words, you hit ⌘-B once to turn bold *on* for the next burst of typing, and ⌘-B again to turn it off — all without ever having to use a menu. (You do the same with ⌘-I.)

highlight all the text in it. Instead, you can just click *once,* anywhere within a paragraph, to plant the insertion point. Then, as before, choose the menu command that you want to apply to that entire paragraph.

Her heart pounding, she looked toward the door. It swung open with a creak. The stench hit her first—an acrid, rotting swamp smell. She covered her mouth with the blood-soaked handkerchief and stepped backward, her naked back pressed hard against the fourposter.

Left-justified

Her heart pounding, she looked toward the door. It swung open with a creak. The stench hit her first—an acrid, rotting swamp smell. She covered her mouth with the blood-soaked handkerchief and stepped backward, her naked back pressed hard against the fourposter.

Right-justified

Her heart pounding, she looked toward the door. It swung open with a creak. The stench hit her first—an acrid, rotting swamp smell. She covered her mouth with the blood-soaked handkerchief and stepped backward, her naked back pressed hard against the fourposter.

Fully justified

Her heart pounding, she looked toward the door. It swung open with a creak. The stench hit her first—an acrid, rotting swamp smell. She covered her mouth with the blood-soaked handkerchief and stepped backward, her naked back pressed hard against the fourposter.

Centered

This figure shows some of the different options every word processor provides for paragraph formatting — left-justified, right-justified, fully justified, and centered.

You can control paragraphs in other ways, too. Remember in high school when you were supposed to turn in a 20-page paper, and you'd try to pad your much-too-short assignment by making it two-and-a-half spaced? Well, if you'd had an iMac, you could have been much more sneaky about it. You can make your word-processed document single-spaced, double-spaced, quadruple-spaced, or any itty-bitty fraction thereof. You can even control how tightly together the letters are placed, making it easy to stretch or compress your writing into more or fewer pages.

Take this opportunity to toy with your word processor. Go ahead, really muck things up. Make it look like a ransom note with a million different type styles and sizes. Then, when you've got a real masterpiece on the screen, read on.

Working with Documents

It might terrify you — and it should — to find out that you've been working on an imaginary document. It's only being preserved by a thin thread of streaming electrical current. It doesn't exist yet, to be perfectly accurate, except in your iMac's *memory*.

You may recall from the notes you took on Chapter $1^1/2$ that memory is fleeting. (Specifically, I mean *computer* memory, but if you find a more universal truth in my words, interpret away.) In fact, the memory is wiped away when you turn the iMac off — or when somebody's trip over the power cord turns it off *for* you. At that moment, anything that exists on the screen is gone forever.

Therefore, almost every program has a Save command. It's always in the File menu, and its keyboard shortcut is always ⌘-S.

When you save your work, the iMac transfers it from transient, fleeting, electronic memory onto the good, solid, permanent disk. There your work will remain, safely saved. It will still be there tomorrow. It will still be there next week. It will still be there ten years from now, when your computer is so obsolete that it's valuable again.

Therefore, let's try an experiment with your ransom note document on the screen. From the File menu, choose Save.

Uh-oh. Something weird just happened: The iMac presented you with a box full of options. It's called a *dialog box,* because the computer needs to have a little chat with you before proceeding.

When you see this box, what the iMac mainly wants to know is: "Under what name would you like me to file this precious document, Massssster?"

And how do you know this? Because in the blank where it says "Save as," a proposed title is highlighted (selected already). And what do you know about highlighted text? *Anything you start typing will instantly replace it.*

The iMac, in its cute, limited way, is trying to tell you that it needs you to type a title. Go ahead, do it: Type *Ransom Note*.

At this point, you could just click the Save button. The iMac would take everything in perilous, fleeting memory and transfer it to the staid, safe hard disk, where it would remain until you're ready to work on it some more.

However, a bunch of other stuff lurks in this dialog box. Especially since this is the Numero Uno source of confusion to beginners, I think a tour of the Save File box is in order.

Navigating the Save File (and Open File) box

You've already learned about the way your computer organizes files: with folders and with folders *in* folders. Remember this little exercise from Chapter 2, where you put state-named folders inside the USA Folder?

Well, all the complicated-looking stuff in the Save File box is a miniature version of that same folder-filing system. Suppose you see this when you're trying to save your file:

Look at the open-folder "menu" (in a rectangle above the list). It tells you that you're viewing the contents of the USA Folder. In other words, if you click the Save button, you'll file your new Ransom Note document in the USA Folder, mixed in among the state folders.

But suppose that you want to file the Ransom Note document in one of the state folders. You already know how you open a folder — by double-clicking it — so you'd point to Alaska, for example, and double-click.

Now the open-folder "menu" above the list says *Alaska,* and you can see the stuff inside the Alaska folder. Some names are dimmed because they're all *documents;* the only things whose names are black in this dialog box are folders. (The iMac wants to know where you want to put your new document. Because you can't very well store one document inside *another* document, the names are grayed out and unavailable, and only the folder names are black and available.)

Okay. So now you're viewing the contents of the Alaska folder. What if you change your mind? What if you decide that the ransom note should really go in the World folder — the one that *contains* the USA Folder?

You must retrace your steps. That's what the little folder menu is all about (where it now says *Alaska*). They call this doohickey a *pop-up menu:* It's a menu, but it's not at the top of the screen. The small black triangles beside the name Alaska tell you: "Click me!"

Sure enough, when you click the word Alaska, you see the list of all the nested folders you had to travel through to get here. This is where things get a little weird: The list is *upside-down* from the path you took!

In other words, if you were in the Finder instead of in this Save File dialog box, you'd have started at the desktop level (the colored background). You'd have double-clicked the hard-disk icon (probably called Macintosh HD) to open its window. Then you'd have double-clicked the World folder to open that, and the USA Folder inside of *that,* and finally the Alaska folder. If you look at the preceding menu picture, you'll see that, sure enough, your entire folder path is listed. You can view the entire hierarchy of folders — as long as you get used to the fact that the list is upside-down, and the outer levels (the hard disk and the desktop) are listed at the bottom.

Therefore, if you wanted to file the ransom note in the World folder (below, right), you'd simply slide down the pop-up menu list and choose World (below, left).

Then, at long last, when you're viewing the contents of the folder you want to save the file in, you can name your file and click the Save button.

For the purposes of following along with this exercise, double-click a folder — any folder — to store your file in. Type a name for your file, such as *Ransom Note,* in the blank where it probably now says "untitled." And then click Save.

Your file gets snugly tucked away into the folder whose contents you're viewing. Want proof, O Cynic? All you have to do is choose Finder from the Application menu. Remember, the Application menu is the icon at the upper-right side of the screen. It lists all the programs that are running at once.

When you choose Finder, our friends the folders, windows, and Trash can pop up. If you wanted to make sure your file really exists, and it really got put where you wanted it, you could now double-click your hard drive icon

Worrywarts' corner

From the way I've described the terrifyingly delicate condition of a document that's on the screen (that you haven't saved to disk yet) — that is, precariously close to oblivion, kept alive only by electric current — you might think that closing a window is a dangerous act. After all, what if you forgot to save some work? Wouldn't closing the window mean losing that critical memo?

Not really — if you try to close a document, the iMac won't *let* you proceed until it asks you whether you're *sure* you want to lose all the work you've done. It will say something like:

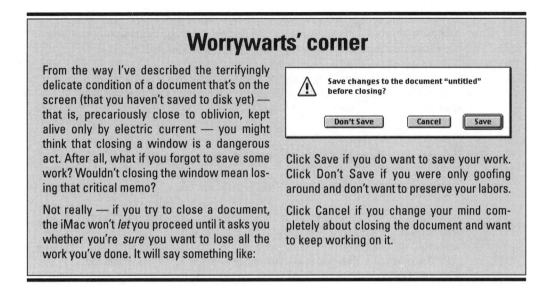

Click Save if you do want to save your work. Click Don't Save if you were only goofing around and don't want to preserve your labors.

Click Cancel if you change your mind completely about closing the document and want to keep working on it.

(Macintosh HD) and then double-click your way through folders until you found it. In our example, your ransom note would be in the World folder:

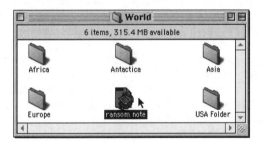

 Why are we kicking this absolutely deceased horse? Because the same folder-navigation scheme (where you see an upside-down list of nested folders) is used for *retrieving* files you've already created. You need to know how to climb up and down your folder tree, as you'll see in a moment, if you ever want to see your files again.

Closing a file, with a sigh

You've created a ransom note. It's got all kinds of text and formatting. You've saved it onto the disk so that it'll be there tomorrow. In a moment, you'll get a chance to prove it to yourself.

Switch back into AppleWorks (or whatever word processor you've been using) by choosing its name from the upper-right application menu. Click the close box in the upper-left corner of the window. Once.

In the iMac's universal language of love, clicking the small square up there means *close the window,* as you'll recall. If all went well, the window disappears.

How to find out what's going on

This gets sort of metaphysical. Hold onto your brain.

Just because you closed your *document* doesn't mean you've left the *program*. In fact, if you pull down the Application menu at the right side of the screen, you'll see that the word-processing program is, in fact, still running. (It's the one with a check mark beside it — such as ClarisWorks or AppleWorks or Microsoft Word.)

You could bring the Finder to the front by choosing its name from the Application menu — without exiting the word processor. They both can be running at the same time, but only one can be in front.

In fact, that's the amazing thing about a Macintosh. You can have a bunch of programs all open and running at once. The more memory your iMac has, the more programs you can run simultaneously.

What gets confusing is that one program (say, your word processor) may be active, but you'll *think* you're in the Finder. After all, you'll see your familiar icons, Trash, folders, and so on. You need to understand that all this is simply *shining through* the emptiness left by your word processor, which has no windows open at the moment. If a window *were* open, it would cover up the desktop behind it.

Right now, for instance, I realize that it's hard for you to believe that you're using a word processor, when there are no words on the screen. But you have several clues as to what program you're using.

CLUE #1: The first command in the Apple menu always identifies the program you're in.

CLUE #2: The menu titles are different in each program.

CLUE #3: In Mac OS 8.5 and later, the program you're in is named here.

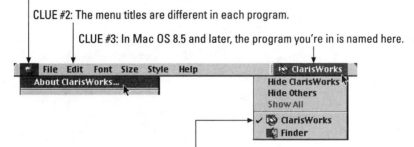

CLUE #4: The check mark in the Application menu indicates the program you're in.

For the moment, I want you to stay in your word-processing program.

Getting It All Back Again

Okay. You've typed a ransom note. Using the Save command, you turned that typing on your screen into an icon on your hard disk. Now it's time for a concept break.

Crazy relationships: Parents and kids

Two kinds of files are lying on your hard disk right now: *programs* (sometimes called *applications*) and *documents*. A program never changes; it's like a Cuisinart on your kitchen counter, sitting there day after day. Documents are what you *create* with a program — they're the coleslaw, crushed nuts, and guacamole dip that come out of the Cuisinart. You pay money to buy a program. After you own it, you can create as many documents as you want for free.

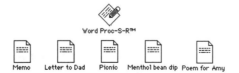

For example, you could use the Word Proc-S-R program (above, top) to create all the different word-processing documents below it and thousands more like them. If you love analogies as much as I do, you can think of the application as the mommy and the documents as the kiddies.

Two easy ways to avoid losing stuff

This business about the "Save Where?" dialog box is, as anybody will tell you, the most confusing thing about the Macintosh. After years of experience, a few professional beginners have adopted one of the following cheats — and they never lose another file.

Cheat 1:

Whenever you save a file, and you're faced with the Save dialog box, *click the Desktop button first*. Only then should you click the Save button.

Go ahead, ask it. "What's the point?"

Easy: When you're done working for the day, and you return to the desktop, you won't have to wonder what folder your document's icon fell into. Your new file will be sitting right there, *on the desktop*, in plain sight.

At this point, it's child's play to drag the icon into the folder you *want* it in.

Cheat 2:

So many people complained that they couldn't find documents that they had saved that Apple invented the Documents folder. It sits on your desktop, usually just below your hard drive, like at left.

To make yours appear, choose Control Panels from your menu. Double-click General Controls. In the lower-right corner of the resulting window, select Documents folder (to turn it on) or one of the other choices (to turn it off). Close all the windows you've just opened.

From now on, every time you save a file — or try to open one — you'll always be shown the contents of the Documents folder.

The contents of the special magnet folder will be in your face at all times. You'll never wonder where some file went — it'll always be right in your Documents folder.

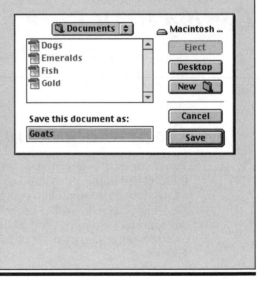

Here's what their family relationships are like:

- ✔ Double-click the *program* icon when you want to open a brand-new, untitled, clean-slate document.

- ✔ Double-click a *document* icon to open that document. Unbeknownst to you, double-clicking a document simultaneously opens the program you used to create the document.

Double-click a
document to
open it . . .

Memo

Word Proc-S-R™

. . . and the Mac automatically
launches the corresponding program
that gave it birth, even if it's buried
in a folder somewhere.

Fetch: How to retrieve a document

Let's pretend it's tomorrow. Yawn, stretch, fluff your hair (if any). You find
out that the person you've kidnapped actually comes from a wealthy Rhode
Island family, and so you can demand much more ransom money. Fortunately, you created your ransom note on the iMac, so you don't have to
retype anything; you can just change the amount you're demanding and
print it out again.

But if you've been following the steps in this chapter, then there's *no* document on the screen. You're still *in* your word-processing program, though
(or should be; look for the check mark in the Application menu). So how do
you get your ransom note file back?

Like this:

1. From the File menu, choose Open.

A dialog box appears. You probably remember dialog boxes — in fact,
you probably remember this one. It looks just like the Save dialog box,
where you were asked to give your document a title. This one,
navigationally speaking, works exactly the same way:

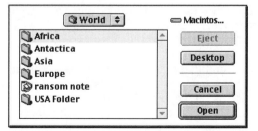

Unfortunately for my efforts to make this as instructional as possible, if
you've been following these steps, your ransom note is staring you in
the face right now. It's in whichever folder you saved it into. The iMac is
nice that way — it remembers the most recent folder you stashed

something in and shows you that location the next time you try to save or open something.

If you want to emerge from this experience a better person, pretend that you can't find your ransom note. Pull down the pop-up menu and jump to your hard-disk level (below, left). Now the display changes to show you the contents of your hard disk (below, right).

And from here, you know how to get back into the World folder, don't you? Correct — double-click the World folder, and you're right back where you started.

2. Double-click the ransom note.

This is what you've been working up to all this time. The ransom note appears on your screen in its entirety. Now, at last, you can edit it to your heart's content.

Save Me Again!

To continue this experiment, make some changes to your document. Once again, you have to worry about the fact that your precious work only exists in a fragile world of bouncing electrons. Once again, turning the iMac off right now means you'll lose the *new* work you've done. (The original ransom note, without changes, is still safe on your disk.)

Therefore, you have to use that trusty Save command each time you make changes that are worth keeping. (For you desk potatoes out there, remember that ⌘-S is the keyboard shortcut, which saves you an exhausting trip to the menu.) The Save dialog box will *not* appear on the screen each time you use the Save command (as it did the first time). Only the very first time you save a document does the iMac ask for a title (and a folder location).

As mentioned in Chapter 1½, you've probably heard horror stories about people who've lost hours of work when some glitch made their computers crash. Well, usually it's their own darned fault for ignoring the two most important rules of computing:

Rule 1. Save your work often.

Rule 2. See Rule 1.

"Often" may mean every five minutes. It may mean after every paragraph. The point is to do it a lot. Get to know that ⌘-S shortcut, and type it reflexively after every tiny burst of inspiration.

Now you know how to start a new document, edit it, save it onto the disk, reopen it later, and save your additional changes. You know how to launch (open or run) a program — by double-clicking its icon. But now you have to learn to get out of a program when you're finished for the day. It's not terribly difficult:

Choose Quit from the File menu.

If the word processor was the only program you were running, then you return to the Finder. If you were running some other programs, then you just drop down into the next program. It's as though the programs are stacked on top of each other; take away the top one, and you drop into the next one down.

How to Back Up iMac Files

Duty compels me to keep this chapter going just long enough to preach one other famous word of advice to you: Back up.

To *back up,* or to *make a backup,* means to make a safety copy of your work.

The importance of being backed up

When you're in the Finder, the documents you've worked on appear as icons on the hard disk. Like any of us, these disks occasionally have bad hair days, go through moody spells, or die. On days like those, you'll wish you had made a *copy* of the stuff on the hard disk so your life won't grind to a halt while the hard disk is being repaired.

You know the cruel gods that make it rain when you forget your umbrella? Those same deities have equal powers over your hard disk and an equal taste for irony. That is, if you don't back up, your hard disk will *certainly* croak. On the other hand, if you back up your work at the end of every day or every week, nothing will ever go wrong with your hard disk, and you'll mumble to yourself that you're wasting your time.

Life's just like that.

Where's the floppy drive?

Many Mac users back up their work by copying their important icons onto floppy disks. Unless your computer-store salesman was a fast-talking slimeball, however, it should be no surprise to you by now that your iMac *doesn't have* a built-in floppy-disk drive.

There are three reasons the iMac doesn't have a floppy drive. All of them have to do with the changing times (and making the iMac inexpensive):

- ✔ In the olden days, newly purchased software came on a floppy disk. Today, almost all new software comes on a CD. And your iMac *does* have a CD player.

- ✔ In the olden days, you needed floppy disks so that you could transfer files to a friend or coworker. These days, you'd probably just send your file by e-mail or over a network cable. (The iMac *does* do e-mail and networking.)

- ✔ In the olden days, you'd use floppy disks to make a safety copy of your work. These days, a floppy's too small to hold much more than a chapter's worth.

Still, you're going to need to make safety copies of your work *somehow*. Some iMac fans use the Internet as a giant backup disk, a trick described in Chapter 11. Others make safety copies of their work by copying them to *another* computer, a scheme described in Chapter 10.

But many break down and *buy* a disk drive for the iMac. You can buy a doodad that accepts floppy disks, or a Zip-disk or SparQ-disk reader, or a gadget that accepts floppy disks *and* much larger disks. (All these gizmos are described in Chapter 18.)

If you've bought and connected such a disk drive, the next section is for you. If not, skim the following with a look of detached bemusement.

How to insert a disk

Take your first disk (floppy, SuperDisk, Zip, or whatever). You're going to slip it into your extra-purchase disk drive *metal side* first, *label side* up. Put the disk into the disk drive *slot.* Keep pushing the disk in until the disk drive gulps it in with a satisfying *kachunk.*

If it's a brand new floppy disk, or not a Macintosh disk, you'll probably see this message:

Go ahead. Click Initialize. You're then asked to name the disk; type a name, click OK, and then wait about 45 seconds while the iMac prepares the disk for its new life as your data receptacle.

If it's *not* a new disk, its icon shows up on the right side, just beneath your hard-disk icon.

To see what's on the disk, double-click the icon. As you've no doubt tired of hearing repeated, a *double-click* on a disk icon *opens* its contents window.

How to copy stuff onto a disk

Here's how you copy files onto a disk — floppy, Zip, SparQ, SuperDisk, or whatever. We'll assume that you've already inserted a disk.

1. **Double-click your hard-disk icon to open its window.**

2. **Drag your document icons on top of the floppy-disk icon.**

That's it. On a Macintosh, making a copy of something is as easy as dragging it to the disk you want it copied onto. You can also drag something into the disk's *window* (instead of onto its *icon*).

You can also, incidentally, drag things *from* a floppy (or other kind of disk) *to* your hard drive.

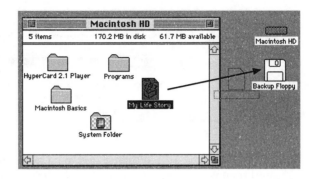

You can make as many copies of a file as you want without ever experiencing a loss of quality. You're digital now, kids.

How to get a disk out again

Okay, so you've made a backup copy of your fourth-quarter report, or you've just copied a new program onto your hard disk. Now what? How do you get the disk out? And if you've inserted a CD-ROM disc into your iMac, how do you get *it* out again?

Just click the disk icon on the screen — and then, from the Special menu, choose Eject Disk. The disk — floppy, Zip, CD, whatever — pops out of the iMac (or its disk drive) automatically.

Want a more exciting method? Try this: Drag a disk's icon *to the Trash can!* Yes, yes, I *know* it looks like you're erasing the entire disk. It looks that way to *every* first-time Mac user. But you're not — instead, the disk just pops out of the slot.

When the disk is too shy to come out

Every now and then, you'll be stuck with a disk or CD that won't come out of the drive, even if you've tried the usual ways of ejecting it.

In that case, turn the iMac off. While pressing the mouse button down continuously, turn it on

again. Keep the mouse button pressed until the Trash can appears.

And if *that* doesn't pop the disk out, straighten a paper clip. Push it slowly but firmly into the tiny pinhole to the right of the drive slot. That'll shove out the disk or CD no matter *what.*

Mac OS 8.5 and later: Super-Find!

In the illustration of the Find window you may have noticed two other interesting-looking places to click: a tab that says Find by Content and one that says Search Internet.

See, the trouble with the traditional Find command is it searches only the *names* of your files. If you wrote a 253-page thesis on Wombat Worship Societies, but you accidentally *named* that file "Gift Ideas for Marge," you could search for "Wombat" from now until doomsday without turning up the file.

It would be different, however, if the Find command were smart enough to search for words *inside* your documents. That's exactly what the Find by Content thing does (in Mac OS 8.5 and later).

But before you can use this feature, the iMac must be allowed to create its own private card-catalog of your hard drive. This process is called *indexing* — spending a couple of hours analyzing every single document you've got. To make this happen, click the "Search by Content" tab of the Find window; click the Index Volumes button, click the name of your hard drive, click Create Index, and then go out to see a nice long movie (such as *Titanic II: The Return*). (If you're *really* into your computer, you could teach yourself to use the Schedule button, which makes your iMac do this kind of thing in the middle of the night, unattended.)

When it's over, you'll be able to use the Find by Content thing to look for words inside your files. (You'll need to let the iMac update that index from time to time to keep it current; fortunately, each index-updating takes only 10 minutes or so.)

The final tab of the Find program, Search Internet, isn't nearly as complicated. It does require, however, that you have an Internet account (see Chapter 11). Once you're hooked up, you can type something into this Find blank, wait a few minutes, and be shown a list of every World Wide Web page that matches your search request. Not bad for a hunk of software, eh?

When What Was Found Is Now Lost

Okay. You've practiced saving and retrieving files. Yet still it happens: You can't find some file you were working on.

This is nothing to be ashamed of! Thousands of people lose files every day. But through the intervention of caring self-help groups, they often go on to lead productive, "normal" lives.

Here's what to do: Sit up straight, think positive thoughts, and press ⌘-F. Or do it the long way: Choose Find File, or Sherlock (if you have Mac OS 8.5), from your menu.

On the screen, you see the Find box: your personal electronic butler who's prepared to spend the next few seconds rummaging through the attics, garages, and basement of your iMac. (This illustration is what the Mac OS 8.5 Find program looks like; the window is simpler in Mac OS 8.1.)

```
┌──────────────────────── Find ────────────────────────┐
│ ┌ Find File ┐┌ Find by Content ┐┌ Search Internet ┐   │
│                                                        │
│  Find items [ ⌐ on "Macintosh HD"    ◆] whose    [?]  │
│                                                        │
│   [name      ◆][ contains     ◆][ fish            ]   │
│                                                        │
│   [ More Choices ] [ Fewer Choices ]        [ Find ]  │
└────────────────────────────────────────────────────────┘
```

Type a few letters of the missing file's name. (Capitals don't matter, but
spaces do!) Then click the Find button (or press Return).

A new window appears, listing everything on your hard drive whose name
contains what you looked for. At this point, you can perform any of the
following stunts.

When you're finished playing with the Find File thing, choose Quit from its
File menu (or press ⌘-Q).

Double-click an icon to open it. Or drag it someplace — onto the desktop,
maybe, or even directly to the Trash. To open the window a file's in, click
the icon and press ⌘-E.

```
┌──────────── Items Found: name contains "fish" ────────────┐
│                    Items Found: 8                          │
│  Name            │ Kind          │ Date Modified │ Size │  │
│ A Fish of a Different Color  folder       8/18/98, 11:33...  —    │
│ 3 Fish, 4 Fish, Dinosaur Fish  SimpleText te... 8/18/98, 2:13 PM  8K │
│ A Fish of My Own   SimpleText te... 8/18/98, 2:13 PM  8K    │
│ Fish Bowl        ClarisWorks ...  8/24/97, 4:00 PM  124K    │
│ name contains "fish"                                        │
│  ⌐ Macintosh HD                                            │
│     📁 New Book Projects                                    │
│        📁 Doomed to Failure                                 │
│           📁 Pseudo-Victorian                               │
│              📄 A Fish of My Own                            │
└────────────────────────────────────────────────────────────┘
```

This area shows you where the file is, no matter how many folders deep it's
buried. You can double-click a folder, too, to open it.

Top Ten Word-Processing Tips

1. Select a word by double-clicking — and then, if you keep the mouse down on the second click and drag sideways, you select additional text in complete one-word increments.

2. Never, never, never line up text using the spacebar. It may have worked in the typewriter days, but not any more. For example, you may get things lined up like this on the screen.

   1963   **1992**   **2001**
   Born   Elected President Graduated college

   Yet, sure as death or taxes, you'll get this when you print.

   1963 **1992**   **2001**
   Born   Elected President   Graduated college

   So instead of using spaces to line up columns, use *tab stops* instead.

3. You can select all the text in your document at once by using the Select All command (to change the font for the whole thing, for example). Its keyboard equivalent is almost always ⌘-A.

4. Don't use more than two fonts within a document. (Bold, italic, and normal versions of a font only count as one.) Talk about ransom notes!

5. Don't use underlining for emphasis. You're a typesetter now, babe. You've got *italics!* Underlining is a cop-out for typewriter people.

6. The box in the scroll bar at the right side of the window tells you, at a glance, where you are in your document.

   By dragging that box, you can jump anywhere in the document.

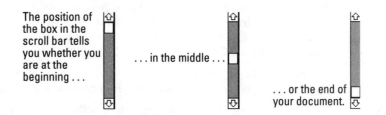

The position of the box in the scroll bar tells you whether you are at the beginning . . . . . . in the middle . . . . . . or the end of your document.

You can move around in two other ways.

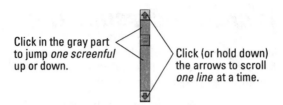

Click in the gray part to jump *one screenful* up or down.

Click (or hold down) the arrows to scroll *one line* at a time.

7. You've already learned how to *copy* some text to the Clipboard, ready to paste into another place. Another useful technique is to *cut* text to the Clipboard. Cut works just like Copy, except it snips the selected text out of the original document. (Cut-and-paste is how you *move* text from one place to another.)

8. It's considered uncouth to use "straight quotes" and 'straight apostrophes.' They hearken back to the days of of your typewriter. Instead, use "curly double quotes" and 'curly single quotes' like these.

   You can produce curly double quotes by pressing Option-[(left bracket) and Shift-Option-[for the left and right ones, respectively. The single quotes (or apostrophes) are Option-] (right bracket) and Shift-Option-], for the left and right single quotes, respectively. But who can remember all that? That's why every word processor (AppleWorks, ClarisWorks, Word, and so on) has an *automatic* curly quote feature, which is a much better solution.

   (On the other hand, don't type curly quotes into an e-mail message; they come out as bizarre little boxes and random letters at the other end.)

9. If there's an element you want to appear at the top of every page, like the page number, don't try to type it onto each page. The minute you add or delete text from somewhere else, this top-of-the-page information will become *middle*-of-the-page information. Instead, use your word processor's *running header* feature — it's a little window into which you can type whatever you want. The program automatically displays this info at the top of each page, no matter how much text you add or take away. (There's also such a thing as a *running footer,* which appears at the *bottom* of the page.)

10. You know how to select one word (double-click it). You know how to select a line (drag horizontally). You know how to select a block of text (drag diagonally through it). By now, you're probably about to reach Selection-Method Overload.

    But none of those techniques will help when you want to select a *lot* of text. What if you want to change the font size for *ten pages'* worth?

    Instead, try this two-part tip: First, click at the *beginning* of the stuff you want to highlight so that the insertion point is blinking there.

    Now scroll to the *end* of what you want to highlight. Hold down the *Shift key* with one hand and click the mouse with the other. Magically, everything between your original click and your Shift-click gets highlighted!

Chapter 5

A Quiet Talk about Printers, Printing, and Fonts

- -

In This Chapter

▶ The different kinds of printers and how much they cost

▶ How to hook up and start printing

▶ The truth about fonts

- -

*Y*ou, gentle reader, are fortunate that you waited until now to get into the Mac. You completely missed the era of *dot-matrix* printers, whose printouts were so jagged that they looked like Dante's *Inferno* written in Braille.

The purchase of a printer for your iMac constitutes Credit Card Workout #3, and it probably falls into one of two categories: *laser printers* and *inkjet printers.*

Inkjet printers

The least expensive kind of printer is called an *inkjet*. Hewlett-Packard (HP) makes a line called DeskJets; Epson makes some terrific color-printing models known as the Stylus Color series. A typical inkjet looks like this.

Inkjet printouts are so good that they almost match a laser printer's. The printers are small, lightweight, and almost silent. You can feed all kinds of nonliving things through them: tagboard, envelopes, sheet metal, whatever. And they cost less than $300, even for ones that can print in color. (If you have a color inkjet, and you want to print out photographs, you can buy fancy shiny paper for this — correction: *expensive* fancy shiny paper — that make the printouts look almost like actual photos.) Some HP and Epson injkets have USB connectors (see Chapter 10) that plug directly into the iMac; if you have a different brand (that's designed for older Mac models), you can plug it into the iMac with an adapter, such as an iPort or Farallon iPrint (see Appendix D).

So what's the catch? Well, they're inkjet printers. They work by spraying a mist of ink. Therefore, the printing isn't laser-crisp if your stationery is even slightly absorbent, and you have to replace the ink cartridges fairly often. Note, too, that inkjet-printed pages smear if they ever get the least bit damp, making them poor candidates for use during yacht races.

Still, inkjet printers are so compact, quiet, and inexpensive that they're hard to resist, especially if you want to print in color.

Laser printers

If you can afford to pay something like $900 for a printer, some real magic awaits you: *PostScript laser printers*. Don't worry about the word *PostScript* for now. Just look for the word PostScript in the printer's description, as though it's some kind of seal of approval.

Tales of dpi

Why have America's scientific geniuses invented all these different kinds of printers?

In a word, they're on a quest for higher *dpi.* That stands for "dots per inch," and it measures the quality of a printout. We're talking about *tiny* dots, mind you — there are about 100 of them clumped together to form the period at the end of this sentence. Clearly, the more of these dots there are per inch, the sharper quality your printouts will have.

A typical inkjet printer, such as a DeskJet, sprays 360 or even 720 dpi onto your paper. Old laser printers manage 300 dpi, and today's generally do 600 dpi. Those Epson color inkjet printers, if you use the expensive glossy paper, actually manage 1,440 dpi. Photos printed by a 1,440 dpi printer *look* like photos, let me tell you.

Pretty good, you say? Yeah, well, so's yer ol' man — this book was printed on a *2,400* dpi professional printer!

A PostScript printer, like HP's LaserJet series or Apple's discontinued (but ubiquitous) LaserWriters, can print any text, in any style, at any size, and at any angle, and everything looks terrific. These laser printers can also print phenomenal-looking graphics, like all the diagrams in Macintosh magazines and the weather maps in *USA Today*. They're quick, quiet, and hassle-free; most can print envelopes, mailing labels, and paper up to legal-size (but not tagboard). They're also much bigger and bulkier than inkjets, as you can see by this example.

If you can afford a PostScript printer, get it. If you're a small-time operation — a home business, for example — get the cheapest PostScript laser printer you can find. Almost all laser printers between $800 and $1,400 have exactly the same quality printouts.

Just remember that laser printers, while superior to inkjets for *black-and-white* quality, aren't what to buy if you want color. Sure, you can *buy* a color laser printer — for several thousand dollars — but the printouts aren't even as realistic as color *inkjet* printers' printouts.

How to Print

I'm going to assume that you've happily purchased a printer. If it's already hooked up, and you've made some successful printouts already, fast-forward to the end of this section.

If you bought an Epson or other inkjet, you may need to buy the cable (printer-to-iMac), too. Run this cable from the printer to one of the iMac's USB jacks (see Chapter 10). Of course, you also need to plug your new appliance into a power outlet.

Laser printers usually don't come equipped with cables either. After having collected your hundreds of dollars for a laser printer, printer companies have charitably recognized that this machine may wind up being *shared* among several different computers. Therefore, laser printers are designed to be *networked.*

In the case of the iMac, this means that you connect a laser printer, if it's "Ethernet compatible" (most laser printers are) to the iMac's *Ethernet* jack (see Chapter 10). And if it's an old laser printer that doesn't have an Ethernet jack, see the sidebar "Old lasers, new iMacs."

The Chooser: Where iMac meets printer

When you first plug a printer into the iMac, it's not smart enough to notice that it's got a new friend; you have to *tell* it. Therefore, after the iMac is connected to the printer, turn on both machines. If your printer came with a CD containing installation software — most inkjets do — insert it and follow the installation instructions.

Now choose Chooser from the menu. It looks something like this:

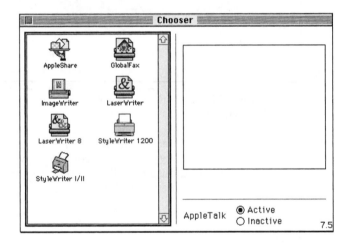

The icons that appear in the left half of the window depend on which *printer drivers* are in your System Folder. A printer driver is a little piece of software that teaches the iMac how to communicate with a specific printer. Its name and its icon match the printer itself, as you can tell, sort of, from the preceding figure.

> ✔ *If you have a laser printer:* If you see a printer driver icon in the Chooser window that matches your printer, you're in luck! Click it. If you don't see your specific model named, try the LaserWriter 8 icon. Either way, if your printer is turned on, you should see its actual name show up in the *right* side of the Chooser window, as shown here; click the printer's name. (Make sure AppleTalk is turned on; the on/off switch is at the bottom of the Chooser window.)

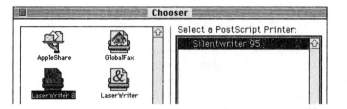

If the names of *several* printers show up on the right, you're either part of an office network with several printers or you're an unexpectedly wealthy individual. Congratulations. Click the one you want to print on.

Old lasers, new iMacs

If you're trying to make an older laser printer (one that doesn't have an Ethernet jack) connect to your iMac, start by buying an adapter that lets it connect to the iMac, such as an iPort or Farallon iPrint LT adapter (see Appendix D).

You'll also need one or two *PhoneNet* connectors. (These doo-dads are actually sold under many different brands, but PhoneNet is by far the most famous.) What's great about PhoneNet-type connectors is that you string ordinary *telephone wire* between them. If you decide to move your printer into the next room,

no big deal — just buy a longer piece of phone wire from Radio Shack.

With an iPrint LT: Plug the iPrint's Ethernet cable into the iMac's Ethernet jack, plug the PhoneNet connector into the printer, and connect the iPrint and the PhoneNet connector with a piece of telephone wire.

With an iPort: Plug one PhoneNet connector into the back of the printer and the other into the printer port on your iPort. Then connect the connectors with a piece of phone wire.

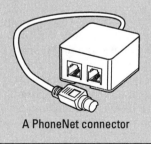

A PhoneNet connector

✔ *If you have an inkjet that didn't require an iMac adapter:* Click the inkjet's icon; that's it.

✔ *If you're using an iPrint adapter:* Open your AppleTalk control panel. Make sure Ethernet is selected from the pop-up menu (and when you're asked if you want AppleTalk turned on, say yes). Now return to the Chooser and click the icon of the kind of printer you want, as described in the previous three paragraphs.

When you close the Chooser, you get a soon-to-be-annoying alert message. It tells you (as if you didn't know) that you've just changed to a new printer. Just ignore it and click OK.

You've just introduced the iMac to its new printer. All this is a one-time operation, by the way. Unless you have to switch printers or something, you'll never have to touch the Chooser again.

Background printing

In the Dark Ages of the 1980s, when you printed something, the printer's soul took over your Mac's body. You couldn't type; you couldn't work; you couldn't do anything but stare at the sign on the screen that said, "Now printing." It was a dark and stormy era, a time of wild and rampant coffee breaks. Only when the paper came out of the printer were you allowed to use your computer again.

Since then, some clever engineer at Apple figured out how to allow *background printing*. When you use this handy feature, the iMac sends all the printing information, at a million miles per hour, into a *file* on your hard disk. It then immediately returns its attention to you and your personal needs.

Then, quietly, behind the scenes, the iMac shoots a little bit of that file to your printer at a time. It all happens during the microseconds between your keystrokes and mouse clicks, making it seem as though the iMac is printing in the background. In time, the printer receives all the information it needs to print, the paper comes gliding out, and you've been able to keep working the whole time. This simultaneous-processing bit can slow down your iMac, but it's a great feature to remember when it's 1:55 pm and the meeting starts at 2:00 and you haven't printed your outline yet.

The on/off switch for Background Printing is buried, and it's different on every printer, but I'll do my best. When you choose Print from an iMac program's File menu, you get a dialog box like the one shown in the following illustration. If it's an Epson printer, click the tiny second-from-right icon, which I've circled in the upcoming illustration. If it's some other printer, look for a pop-up menu that contains a Background Printing command.

Either way, you'll wind up with an on/off switch for Background Printing. Click accordingly.

After all that: How you actually print

Suppose that your printer is finally plugged in and, via the Chooser, has been introduced to the iMac. The moment has arrived: You'd actually like to *print* something.

Make sure whatever you want to print (a ClarisWorks or AppleWorks document, for example) is on the screen. From the File menu, choose Print. A dialog box appears; it looks different depending on your printer, but this one is typical of what you see if you have an Epson color printer.

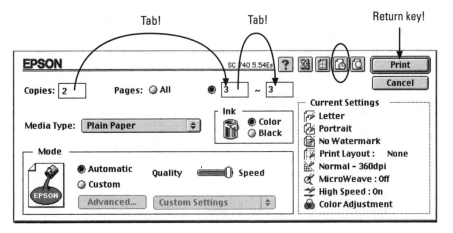

For 95 percent of your life's printouts, you'll completely ignore the choices in this box and simply click the Print button.

For the other 5 percent of the time, the main thing you do in this dialog box is tell the iMac which pages of your document you want it to print. If you just want page 1, type a *1* into *both* the From and To boxes. If you want page 2 to the end, type *2* into the From box and leave the To box empty. (The From: and To: blanks in the Epson dialog box don't have *From:* and *To:* labels, but they're there. They're the two unlabeled boxes, in the preceding illustration, where *3*'s have been typed in.)

Specify how many copies you want by clicking and typing a number in the Copies box.

Using the Tab key in dialog boxes

Now would be a good time, I suppose, to mention what the Tab key does in dialog boxes. Suppose you want to print *two* copies of page 3. Instead of using the mouse to click in each number box on the screen, you can just press Tab to jump from box to box.

Therefore, you'd just type **2** (in the Copies box); press Tab and type **3** (in the From box) and press Tab and type **3** again (in the To box), as shown in the previous illustration. And the mouse just sits there gathering dust.

Anyway, after you're done filling out the options in this box, you can either click the Print button *or* press the Return key. (Pressing Return is always the same as clicking the outlined button.) The iMac should whir for a moment, and pretty soon the printout will come slithering out of your printer.

This handy shortcut — using the Tab key to move around the blanks and pressing the Return key to "click" the OK or Print button — works in *any* dialog box. In fact, any time you ever see a button with a double-thickness outline, as shown in the preceding illustration, you can press the Return key instead of using the mouse.

Canceling printing

If you want to interrupt the printing process, ⌘-period does the trick — that is, while pressing the ⌘ key, type a period. Several times, actually. Even then, your printer will take a moment (or page) or two to respond.

A shortcut for multiple-printer owners

As often happens in democracies, the rich sometimes carry special influence. In the case of the Mac, the early 1990s saw the uprising of the powerful People With More Than One Printer lobby (the PWMTOP, as it's known in insider circles). These people — usually people in an office where several different printers are hooked up — resented having to lumber off to the Chooser each time they wanted to redirect their printouts from one printer to another. They asked Apple to come up with some easier method of switching.

Apple complied. When you first turned on your iMac, you may have noticed an icon that matches your printer sitting out *on the desktop,* as shown below.

To create more of these, the PWMTOP members simply select corresponding icons in the Chooser; each time they do so, another printer's icon shows up on the desktop. Thereafter, these lucky folk can direct a printout to a particular printer just by dragging the document's icon onto the appropriate printer icon, like this:

If, on the other hand, you use only *one* printer, this desktop printing thing is a waste of your memory, disk space, and screen space. Here's how you can turn it off:

1. From the menu, choose Control Panels.

2. Double-click the one called Extensions Manager (if you see something called Conflict Catcher, open that instead).

   You should now see a list of a million computer-looking control panels and *extensions,* as they're called. (More about these in Chapter 15.) Click all the ones with the word *Desktop Printing* or *Desktop Printer* in them to turn them off (so that they're no longer highlighted or checked off).

3. Restart your iMac.

Now you can throw away any printer icons that still appear on your desktop (which now probably have a big X through them).

Now *that's* what I call a grass-roots campaign against the rich!

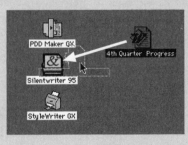

Top Ten Free Fun Font Factoids

The various *fonts* (typefaces) listed in the Font menus of your programs (such as ClarisWorks or AppleWorks) are amazing. They look terrific on the screen and even better when printed, and they're never jagged-looking like the computer fonts of the early days. You may not realize it, but your fonts are a special kind of idiot-proof, jaggy-free, self-smoothing font that looks great on any printer at any size: *TrueType* fonts.

If you work in the professional printing or graphic design industry, by the way, you may hear about a competing kind of font known as *PostScript* fonts: If you're truly interested in learning about the differences and history of these warring font types, check out a book like *Macworld Mac Secrets*; for now, let's just say that TrueType fonts — the kind that came on your iMac — are easier to manage, handle, and install.

Here are ten examples of the kind of fun you can have with your fonts:

1. Want more fonts? You can, of course, *buy* them. Your friendly neighborhood mail-order joint, like those listed in Appendix B, are only too happy to sell you CD-ROMs crammed with new fonts:

   Those on a budget, however, can still get tons of great fonts. Dial up America Online or the Internet (see Chapters 11 and 12), for example, and help yourself to as many fonts as your typographical taste buds can tolerate. (On America Online, use keyword *filesearch;* on the Internet, try *www.shareware.com*; either way, search the resulting page for "fonts.")

2. To install a new font, quit all your programs (if you're running any). Drag the font-file icon (shaped like a suitcase) on top of the System Folder icon. (Do *not* drag it into the open System Folder *window*. Do not drag it to the Trash can. Do not collect $200.)

System Folder · Yer Basic Font Suitcase · Yer Basic Font Suitcase

   You'll see a message alerting you that the iMac is going to install the font for you. Just smile, wave, and click OK.

3. Want to see where your fonts live? Open your System Folder and then open the Fonts folder therein. You'll see a list of your fonts in a window. To see what a font looks like, double-click its suitcase icon. You'll get a window showing the individual font sizes, like Times 10 and Times 18; double-click one. A little window opens, displaying a few words to live

by (such as: "Cozy lummox gives smart squid who asks for job pen"), displayed in the font you're investigating.

4. To remove a font, open your Fonts folder (as described in the previous paragraph). Then just drag the offending font — or its entire suitcase — out of the window. Put it onto the desktop. Or put it into some other folder — or right into the Trash can.

5. There are two kinds of people: those who place everything into two categories and those who don't. Among fonts, there are two basic types: *proportional* fonts, where every letter gets exactly as much width as it needs, and *monospaced* fonts, where every letter is exactly the same width, as on a typewriter. What you're reading now is a proportional font; notice that a W is much wider than an I.

Your iMac comes with two monospaced fonts: Courier and Monaco. All the others are proportional.

And who the heck cares? You will — the moment somebody sends you, perhaps by e-mail, some text that's supposed to line up, but doesn't. For example, this table that arrived by e-mail:

```
From:      IntenseDude
To:        pogue@aol.com

Hello, David! Here are the prices you asked about:

Item              Features              Price
----              --------              -----
Seinfeld Statuette       Removable hairpiece       $25.00
Baywatch digital watch    Surfboard sweep-second hand  $34.50
"60 Minutes" bowtie       Mike Wallace autograph       $65.75
E.R. BandAid Pak™          100 per box              $ 9.85
```

All you have to do is highlight this text and change it to, say, Courier, and everything looks good again!

```
From:        IntenseDude
To:          pogue@aol.com

Hello, David! Here are the prices you asked about:

Item                     Features                   Price
----                     --------                   -----
Seinfeld Statuette       Removable hairpiece        $25.00
Baywatch digital watch   Surfboard sweep-second hand $34.50
"60 Minutes" bowtie      Mike Wallace autograph     $65.75
E.R. BandAid Pak™         100 per box               $ 9.85
```

6. From the File menu, choose Page Setup. The Page Setup dialog box offers a handful of useful options — whether you want the paper to print lengthwise or the short way, for example, or how much you want your document enlarged or reduced.

The Paper pop-up menu near the middle, however, offers one of the most useful controls. If yours says "US Letter Small," your laser printer leaves a half-inch margin all the way around the page, chopping off any part of your printout that extends into it. If that bothers you, choose US Letter from that pop-up menu (and to make your change permanent, hold down Option as you click OK). From now on, your laser can print to within a quarter-inch of the edge of the paper.

7. If you've got iMac OS 8.5 or later, you've got the slickest font trick yet at your disposal. It goes like this:

   From your menu, choose Control Panels. Double-click the one called Appearance, and click the tab that says Fonts. Turn on the option called "Smooth all fonts on screen."

   Now revisit your word processor (or any other program, for that matter). Notice that the edges of your typed letters are drawn with softer and smoother edges, making your entire computer look as though it's an elegantly designed ad.

Before

The Staten Island Fairy

A true story in nine chapters

Once upon a time there was a water sprite named
Tia. She lived in New York, near the harbor where

After

The Staten Island Fairy

A true story in nine chapters

Once upon a time there was a water sprite named
Tia. She lived in New York, near the harbor where

8. In AppleWorks, ClarisWorks, Word 98, and some other word processing programs, you can actually see the names of the fonts in your font menu *in* those typefaces, like this:

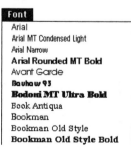

Problem is, how are you supposed to read the names of *symbol fonts* — fonts where every "letter" is actually a symbol or little picture (such as Zapf Dingbats)? Easy. Hold down the Shift key as you pull down the Font menu. Now every font *doesn't* show up in its own typeface — they're all in the usual menu font now.

The Dogcow

No iMac book would be complete without at least a passing acknowledgment of the Dogcow. To see him, choose Page Setup from the File menu.

His name, need I point out, stems from the fact that nobody can precisely figure out what kind of animal he is. In the inner sanctum of Apple Computer Corporation, it is said that, late at night, you can hear the sound made by the Dogcow: Moof!

---

9. Want to look good the next time you're hanging out with a bunch of type geeks? Then learn to bandy about the terms *serif* (pronounced SAIR-iff) and *sans serif* (SANNZ sair-iff).

   A serif is the little protruding line built onto the edges of the letters in certain typefaces. In the *serif font* pictured in the top example here, I've drawn little circles around some of the serifs.

Terrif serifs
Sans-serif

   A *sans serif* font, on the other hand, has no little protuberances, as you can see by their absence in the little square (in the lower example above). Times, Palatino, and the font you're reading are all serif fonts. Helvetica, Geneva, and the headlines in most newspapers are sans serif fonts. And that information, plus 32 cents, will buy you a first-class U.S. postage stamp.

10. This one's techy, but it's good.

    When the iMac prints, it matches the placement of each word *exactly* according to its position on the screen. Trouble is, the iMac's screen resolution isn't that good — it's only 72 dots per inch instead of 300 or 600 dpi (the usual for printers). As a result, you sometimes get weird spacing between words, especially between **boldface** words (see the bottom-left printout on the following page).

    The solution: When you print, turn on the Fractional Character Widths feature. This makes words look a little bit cramped on the screen (top right in the figure on the next page) but makes your printouts look *awesomely* professional (bottom right).

	Fractional Widths OFF	Fractional Widths ON
On the screen:	**Bullwinkle's Little Secret**	**Bullwinkle's Little Secret**
In the printout:	**Bullwinkle's Little Secret**	**Bullwinkle's Little Secret**

So how do you find this magical feature? In WordPerfect and Word 5, it's in the Page Setup box (File menu). In Word 98, choose Preferences from the Tools menu and click the Print tab. In AppleWorks/ClarisWorks, Fractional Widths is one of the Preferences (Edit menu). Try keeping it off when you're typing and on when you print.

Part II
Software Competence

"Great! It comes with Quicken. Now maybe we can figure out where all the money around here is going."

In this part . . .

The next three chapters introduce you to the *software* that came with (or can be added to) your iMac.

After all, without software, your iMac is little more than an art object — cool-looking, to be sure (especially the transparent mouse and power cord), but not much help when it's time to write a letter.

Chapter 6

Faking Your Way Through the Free Software

In This Chapter

▶ Faking your way through AppleWorks (ClarisWorks)

▶ Impersonating a Quicken Expert

▶ Good Cooking, Kai's Photo Soap, MDK, PageMill, and Nanosaur

*T*his chapter is a survival guide for stranded-on-a-desert-island, filling-in-for-Mr.-Big, my-son's-at-school-but-I-need-to-print-out-something, the-computer-just-arrived-but-the-board-meeting-is-in-two-hours, in-a-computer-store-to-try-something-but-don't-know-how-it-works situations.

Macintosh users are notorious for not reading their software manuals. They're actually belligerently *proud* of the fact that they never read manuals. Of course, two years down the line, one user will look at another user's techniques and intone, astounded, "I never knew it could do *that!*"

But in the case of you and your iMac, I took pity; I'm well aware that you got next to nothing in the way of manuals with your computer. In this chapter, I'll do what I can to give you a crash course in the programs that came with your iMac; in the next chapter, I'll lead you through the next programs you're most likely to use: Microsoft Word and Microsoft Excel.

About AppleWorks

AppleWorks is Swiss Army Knife software. (AppleWorks, by the way, was formerly known as *ClarisWorks,* but in this chapter I'll simply call it AppleWorks, because saying "AppleWorks/ClarisWorks" three times per paragraph would drive you quietly postal.) Just look at all you get, even if you don't know what they are yet: a word processor, a database, and a spreadsheet. Now, how much would you pay? But wait — you also get a graphics program that can even serve as a basic page-layout system. And if you order now, you even get a little telecommunications program — absolutely free!

All these modules are neatly bundled into a single integrated program. You can write a letter and put a graphic in it or design a flyer that has a little spreadsheet in it and so on. Chances are good that you and AppleWorks will get to know each other very, very well in the coming months.

Launching AppleWorks

Double-click the AppleWorks icon.

After the logo disappears, you're asked to decide what you want to accomplish. Because you'll face this decision every time you use this program, a rundown may be in order here. If my Executive Summaries don't quite do the trick, don't sweat it; you'll be introduced to each of these modules in this chapter.

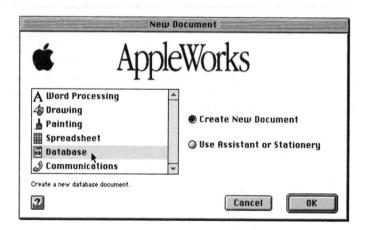

Word Processing: You know what a word-processing document is: something that you type: a memo, a novel, a ransom note.

Drawing: This is a *drawing program*. In this kind of document, you toy around with lines, shapes, and colors to produce such important visuals as logos, maps, and Hangman diagrams.

Painting: This is a painting window. *Painting* is another way of making graphics. But unlike the Drawing mode, where you can create only distinct circles, lines, and squares, the Painting tools lets you create shading, freeform spatters, and much more textured artwork.

Spreadsheet: A computerized ledger sheet, almost exactly like Excel (described in the next chapter). Crunches numbers: Calculates your car's mileage per gallon, your bank account, how much of the phone bill your teenage daughter owes, that kind of thing.

Database: An electronic index-card file. You type in your lists — household expenditures; record collections; subscriber list to *Regis & Kathie Lee!* magazine — and the program sorts them, prints them, finds certain pieces of info instantly, and so on.

Communications: You rarely need this kind of program. It's useful primarily for dialing up local "electronic bulletin boards" (a rapidly fading memory, thanks to the much zestier Internet) and hacking your grades on the school's computer.

To make AppleWorks strut its stuff, I'll show you how to create a thank-you letter. But not just *any* thank-you letter — this is going to be the world's most beautiful and personalized *form letter*. You're going to merge a list of addresses into a piece of mail, creating what appear to be individually composed letters; thus the technoid term for what you're about to do is *mail merge*.

Yeah, yeah, I hear ya: Form letters aren't exactly what you bought a computer to create. Follow along anyway. This exercise will take you through most of AppleWorks, and you'll brush up against some features that *will* be useful to you.

Your first database

Suppose that you just got married. You were showered with lovely gifts. And now it's your task to write a charming thank-you note to each of your gift givers. You'll begin by typing a list of the gift givers. The ideal software for organizing this kind of information is a *database*.

Therefore, double-click the word Database, as shown in the previous illustration.

Don't be alarmed. The screen that now appears may look complicated, but it's actually not so bad — it simply wants to know what *blanks* you'll be wanting to fill in for each person in your list (name, address, gift type, and so on).

You're about to type names for these blanks (which the program calls *fields*). As always, if you make a typo, just press the Delete key to backspace over it. Here we go:

1. **Type *First Name* and press the Return key.**

   Pressing Return is the same as clicking the Create button.

2. **Type *Last Name* and press Return.**

3. **Type *Address* and press Return.**

   See how you're building a list?

4. **Type *Gift* and press Return.**

5. **Type *Adjective* and press Return.**

   In this blank, you'll eventually type a word that describes the glorious present that this person gave you.

6. **Finally, type *Part of House* (you'll see why in a moment) and press Return.**

   Your masterpiece should look something like this.

7. Click the Done button in the lower-right corner.

The dialog box goes away.

When you see what you've created, things should make a little bit more sense. You've just created the blanks (oh, all right, *fields*) to fill in for each person in your list.

First Name	
Last Name	
Address	
Gift	
Adjective	
Part of House	

Data entry time

This is important: To fill in the fields of a database (like this one), just type normally. To advance from one field to the next — from First Name to Last Name, for example — *press the Tab key*. Do *not* press the Return key, as every instinct in your body will be screaming to do. You'll discover why in a moment. (You can also move to a new field by clicking in it, but the Tab key is quicker.)

So here goes:

1. Make sure that you can see a dotted-line rectangle for each field, like the ones in the preceding figure; if not, press the Tab key.

The little blinking cursor should be in the First Name blank. (If it's not, click there.)

2. Type *Josephine* and then press the Tab key to jump to the Last Name field.

First Name	Josephine
Last Name	
Address	
Gift	

3. Type *Flombébé* and, again, press Tab.

(See the sidebar "Accent heaven" to find out how you make those cool little accents.) Now you're in the Address blank.

Accent heaven

Ah, mais oui, mon ami. C'est vrai, c'est la vie, c'est le résumé.

I know what you're thinking: What a smooth, sophisticated guy to be able to speak French like that! Thank you.

But you're also thinking: How did he get those cool accent marks? Very easily — and you, having been smart enough to choose an iMac over all its inferior competitors, can do it, too.

The iMac has a ton of these special characters. Look at your keyboard — I bet you don't see © or ™, or •, or ¢, or any other useful symbols that Mac people use all the time. That's because they're hidden. The secret that unlocks them is . . . the Option key.

It works like the Shift key: While pressing Option, you type a key. Here are some popular ones:

To Get This . . .	Press Option and Type This . . .
©	g
™	2
ç	c
¢	4
¡	1
£	3
•	8
®	r
†	t

What's nice to know is that you have a complete built-in cheat sheet that shows these symbols' locations on the keyboard. It's the Key Caps desk accessory, which is in your menu.

Open it up and take a look. Now try pressing the Option key.

So that's where all those little critters live!

Anyway, there's one more wrinkle to all this. A few symbols, called *diacritical marks* (that's not a computer term; it's a proofreading one, I think) can be placed over any letter. They include the markings over this ü, this é, this è, and so förth. Because the iMac doesn't know ahead of time which vowel you're going to type, creating these marks is a two-step process:

1. While pressing Option, type the key as shown here.

To Get This . . .	Press Option and Type This . . .
é	e
ü	u
è	`
ñ	n
î	i

When you do this, nothing will happen. In other words, no marking appears on the screen — until you do Step 2.

2. Type the letter you want to appear under the diacritical marking.

Only now does the entire thing — letter and marking — appear on the screen. So if you think about it, typing the six-letter word résumé requires eight keystrokes. *C'est formidable, ça!*

4. **Type *200 West 15th Street*.**

   Ready to find out what the Return key does? Go ahead and press Return. Notice that you don't advance to the next blank; instead, the program thoughtfully makes this box bigger so that there's room for another line of address.

First Name	Josephine
Last Name	Flombébé
Address	200 West 15th Street
Gift	New York, NY 10010
Adjective	
Part of	

   If you ever hit Return by *mistake,* intending to jump to the next blank (but just making this blank bigger), press the Delete key.

5. **Go ahead and type *New York, NY 10010* and then press Tab.**

   And don't worry that the second line of the address immediately gets hidden. The information you typed is still there.

6. **Type *acrylic sofa cover* (and press Tab); *practical* (and press Tab); and *living room* (and stop).**

You've just filled in the information for your first gift sender. So that this won't take all day, let's pretend that it was what they call an *intimate* wedding, and you received gifts from only three people.

But let's see — we need a new set of fields, don't we? Come to think of it, wouldn't life be sweeter if there were a computer *term* for "set of fields"? By gumbo, there is! A set of fields is called a *record*.

I wouldn't bother with that term if it didn't crop up in the next instructions:

1. **From the Edit menu, choose New Record.**

   A new record ("set of fields") appears, and you're ready to type the second person's information.

2. **Type anything you want, or copy the example below, but remember to press Tab at the end of each piece of information.**

   (Oh, and if you want a second line for the address, press Return. Make up a town and state; you're a creative soul.)

First Name	Suzie
Last Name	Khiou
Address	1 Doormouse Ave.
Gift	Harley
Adjective	expensive
Part of	garage

3. **Choose New Record from the Edit menu again and type a third set of information, perhaps along these lines.**

Fabulous! You're really cooking now.

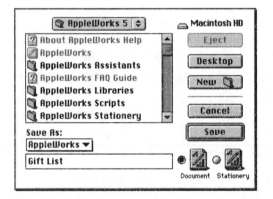

4. **As a final wise step, choose Save from the File menu and type** *Gift List* **as the name of your database into the Save As text box.**

5. **Click Save to preserve your database on the hard disk.**

You've just created your first database. Having gone through the tedium of typing in each little scrap of information the way the iMac wants it, you can now perform some stunts with it that'd make your grandparents' jaws drop. You can ask the iMac to show you only the names of your friends whose last names begin with Z. Or only those who live in Texas. Or only those whose gifts you've categorized as *fabulous*. See the sidebar "Finding and sorting in AppleWorks databases" for details.

Finding and sorting in AppleWorks databases

After you've got some data typed into an AppleWorks database, you can manipulate it in all kinds of fun and exciting ways. Choose Find from the Layout menu to get what appears to be a blank record. Type what you're looking for into the appropriate blanks. For example, if you're trying to find everybody who lives in zip code 90210, you'd fill out the Find dialog box as you see it in the figure below. Then click the Find button. After about one second, you'll be returned to normal view, where you'll see the results of your search.

This is important — AppleWorks is *hiding* the records that *didn't* match your search requirements. You haven't lost them; they're just out of sight until you choose Show All Records from the Organize menu. You can prove this to yourself by consulting the little book at the left side of the screen. It will say "Records: 22 (194)." That means that AppleWorks still knows there are 194 addresses in your mailing list, but only 22 have zip code 90210 (and they're all attractive teenage models on a major TV show).

	First Name	
	Last Name	
1	Address	90210
	Gift	
Requests: 1	Adjective	
	Part of House	
Find from
○ Visible
● All
☐ Omit
[Find]

Forming the form letter

Next, you're going to write the thank-you note. At each place where you want to use somebody's name (or other gift-related information), you'll ask AppleWorks to slap in the appropriate info.

1. **Choose New from the File menu.**

   Again, you're asked to choose the kind of document you want.

2. **Double-click Word Processing.**

   You get a sparkling new sheet of electronic typing paper. You'll start the letter with the address, of course. Yet the address will be different on each letter! This is where mail-merging is handy.

3. **From the File menu, choose Mail Merge.**

   When the little window appears, you'll see your database name, Gift List, prominently displayed.

4. **Double-click Gift List to tell AppleWorks that it's the database you want to work with.**

   Now a strange-looking window appears:

   In the scrolling list you see the *Field Names* from your database. Here's how it works.

5. **Point to First Name and double-click.**

   See what happened? The program popped a placeholder for the First Name right into your letter. When you print, instead of *<<First Name>>*, it will say *Josephine*.

6. **Type a space; in the Mail Merge window, point to *Last Name* and double-click; press Return to begin a new line of the address; then point to the Mail Merge window again and double-click *Address*.**

   Before you continue typing, you may want to drag the little Mail Merge window off to the right of your screen as best you can. (To move the window, drag its title bar.) You're going to want to see both it and your typing simultaneously.

7. **Press Return a couple of times and then type *Dear,* followed by a space.**

8. **Point to the words *First Name* in the Mail Merge window, as you did a moment ago; double-click; then type a comma.**

   Your letter should look something like this.

```
«First Name» «Last Name»
«Address»

Dear «First Name»,
```

This is where it gets good.

9. **Press Return a couple of times and then type *I nearly cried when I unwrapped the incredible,* followed by a space.**

10. **Double-click the word *Gift* in the Mail Merge window.**

11. **Continue typing the following: *you gave me for my wedding. It is far and away the most* (and now double-click Adjective in the Mail Merge window) *gift I will ever receive.***

```
«First Name» «Last Name»
«Address»


Dear «First Name»,

I nearly cried when I unwrapped the incredible «Gift» you gave me for my wedding. It
is far and away the most «Adjective» gift I will ever receive.
```

Are you getting the hang of this? At each place where you want AppleWorks to substitute a piece of information from your Gift List database, you insert a little *<<placeholder>>*.

To see the last field name, Part of House, you may need to use the Mail Merge window's scroll bar. Then finish the letter as follows.

12. **Type *It will look sensational in the* (double-click Part of House in the Mail Merge window) *of our new home.***

13. **Press the Return key twice and finish up like this: *I had to write this personal note to you and you alone, so you'd know how much I treasure your gift above all the others. Love, Marge***

```
«First Name» «Last Name»
«Address»


Dear «First Name»,

I nearly cried when I unwrapped the incredible «Gift» you gave me for my wedding. It
is far and away the most «Adjective» gift I will ever receive.

It will look sensational in the «Part of House» of our new home.

I had to write this personal note to you and you alone, so you'd know how much I
treasure your gift above all the others.

Love, Marge
```

Miss Manners would go instantly bald in horror if she thought you were about to send out a letter that says *Dear First Name.* But through the miracle of computers, when these letters are printed, it'll be impossible to tell that each one wasn't typed separately.

Save from the File menu. Type *Thank-You Letter* in the Save As text box and click Save.

The graphics zone: Designing a letterhead

To show you how AppleWorks can tie everything together, let's whip up a quick letterhead in the Drawing module.

Choose New from the File menu. Our friend, the New Document dialog box, appears. This time, double-click the word Drawing.

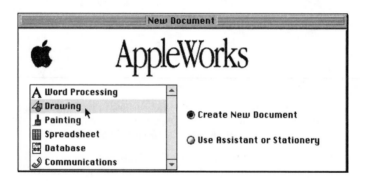

AppleWorks shows you its drawing window. The grid of dotted lines is there to give things a nice architectural look; it won't appear in the finished printout.

See the tool icons on the left side of your screen? They're pretty much covered in the section on drawing programs in the preceding chapter. Now then:

1. **Click the Text tool — it looks like a letter A — and release the mouse button; then move your cursor onto the drawing area and drag across the screen, as shown here.**

2. **Use the Font menu and choose Times; use the Size menu and choose 24 Point.**

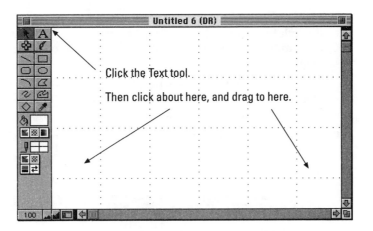

3. **Type three spaces and then a long dash (to make a long dash, hold down the Shift and Option keys and type a hyphen); type *A Very Personal Note;* type another long dash and then three more spaces.**

4. **Press the Enter key so that handles appear around your text; using the Alignment submenu of the Format menu, choose Center.**

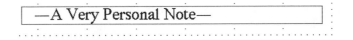

Finally, you'll add that elegant white-lettering-against-black look that shows up on so many corporate annual reports. At the left side of your screen, there's a set of odd-looking icons. Find the one immediately below the tiny pouring paint can icon, as shown by the arrow in this illustration (left).

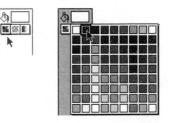

This icon is actually a pop-out palette (right).

5. **Click the paint-can icon but keep the mouse button pressed so that the palette appears (preceding figure, right); drag carefully to the right until the pointer is on the solid black square; release the mouse.**

You've just used the Fill palette to color in the entire text block with black. Which is just great, except that now the text is a solid black rectangle! To fix the problem, you need to make the text *white*.

6. **From the Text Color submenu of the Format menu, choose White (ta-da!).**

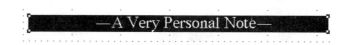

Of course, while you're in the Drawing mode, you could actually do some graphics . . . you could use any of the other drawing tools to dress up your logo. You could draw a box around this letterhead. You could rotate the whole thing 90 degrees. You could make all kinds of insane diagonal stripes across it. You could choose, from the File menu, Library — and select any of the "libraries" full of ready-to-use graphics (flags, stars, flowers, and so on) worthy of dragging into your drawing as an aid to the artistically challenged.

Keep those creative possibilities in mind when it comes time to design your real letterhead.

For control freaks only: The View buttons

Before you leave the drawing window, cast your eyes upon the lower-left corner of the screen. There you'll find this odd-looking array of controls.

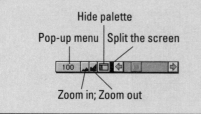

Hide palette

Pop-up menu | Split the screen

Zoom in; Zoom out

As you can tell, AppleWorks/ClarisWorks makes blowing up your work extremely easy. (Obviously, I mean *magnifying* it; *destroying* it is up to you.) A quick click on either of those little mountain buttons makes the artwork smaller or larger. Or jump directly to a more convenient degree of magnification by using the percentage pop-up menu (where it says 100 in the figure to the left). You're not changing the actual printed size — only how it's displayed on the screen.

The return of Copy and Paste

All that remains is for you to slap this letterhead into your mail-merge letter:

1. **Using the Arrow tool, click your letterhead; from the Edit menu, choose Copy.**

   Now you need to return to your word-processing document. Here's a quick way to pull it to the front.

2. **From the Window menu, choose Thank-You Letter (WP).**

   (*WP* stands for Word Processing document; *DB* stands for Database; DR stands for Drawing; and *PT* stands for Painting.)

   Your letter springs to the fore.

3. **From the Format menu, choose Insert Header.**

   (A *header* is an area at the top of every page, above whatever text you've typed. In this case, it looks like an empty text area.)

4. **From the Edit menu, choose Paste.**

   Et voilà . . . your graphic pops neatly into the header.

You've actually done it: combined a database, a word processor, and a drawing program in a single project! For a real kick, click the Print Merge button. It's on the little floating mail merge windowette that should still be on the screen. Watch how the program automatically replaces actual names for the <<*placeholders*>> on the screen.

Other Cool Stuff AppleWorks Does

The little form-letter thank-you note example was only one example of AppleWorks' power. It left plenty of features unexplored, however. For example . . .

A little paint

If you've been following along, you haven't yet tried the Painting window. By this time, I trust that you know how to get there: Choose New from the File menu and then double-click the word Painting.

Suddenly, you're in a pixel-blitzing wonderland, where you can create all kinds of "painted" artwork. This kind of artwork has pros and cons. The pro is that you can change the color of *every single dot* on the screen (instead of just making circles, lines, rectangles, and text, which is all that you can do in the Drawing window). The con is that you can't move or resize something in a painting after you've laid down the "paint" (which you *can* do in the Drawing window).

A little slide show

One of the strangest and most delicious things people can do with an iMac is make slide shows. These can be self-running (a new "slide" every four seconds, say). They can be controlled by you (a new slide every time you click the mouse button). Most of all, they can be really impressive-looking to your friends.

All you need to do is choose New from the File menu; select Use Assistant or Stationery; and double-click the Assistant called Presentation. Now AppleWorks asks you a series of questions, such as what kind of message you want to present, what style of slide background you want, and so on. When you're finished answering, you've got a terrific-looking slide show on the screen. Use the scroll bars to move among the slides, changing the (forgive the term) dummy text on each slide to say what you want it to say.

Other assistants

While we're on the topic of Assistants, remember that AppleWorks beats the pants off most other programs when it comes to creating certificates, press releases, address books, to-do lists, and so on. The key, after choosing New from the File menu, is to select the Use Assistant or Stationery button, as shown here.

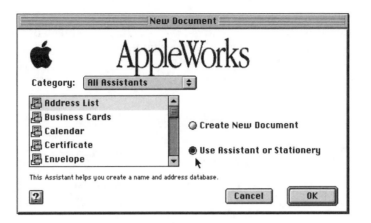

Experiment with the pop-up menu at the top of this screen; some of the most useful ready-made documents (which they call *stationery*) are hiding in here.

A little spreadsheet

AppleWorks also does *spreadsheets* — which is to say, electronic ledger books that automatically recalculate any numbers you type. For a complete workout, read about Microsoft Excel in the next chapter, which is almost identical to the AppleWorks spreadsheet window.

Quicken

Quicken, another free program you got with your iMac, is the ultimate checkbook program. Of course, calling Quicken a checkbook program is slightly understating the case, like calling AT&T a phone company or calling O.J. Simpson a former football player. As you'll discover, Quicken can really be the cornerstone of your entire bank account, credit card, tax, investment, and otherwise financial empire.

The category concept

When you first launch Quicken, it asks you to name the file in which you'll keep all of your financial info. In the same dialog box where you type a name, Quicken makes you choose a set of *categories* before you do anything else — either Home or Business. When it's time to do your taxes; when you want to see where your money's going; when you want to plan ahead for next year; in all of these cases, Quicken can show you a snapshot of your current financial status, organized, as always, by *category*. It's a great system.

Pick Home, Business, or both to start you off, depending on how you're going to be using Quicken, to get past the opening screen or two. (You can always make up your own categories later.)

When you arrive at this screen, grab your bank account statement.

```
┌────────────────────────────────────────────────────────────────┐
│                        Set Up Account                            │
│ ┌─ Account Type ─────────────────────────────────────────────┐ │
│ │ ● Bank                         ○ Liability                  │ │
│ │   Use for checking, savings, or money   Use for items you owe, such as a loan │ │
│ │   market accounts.                      or mortgage.        │ │
│ │                                                             │ │
│ │ ○ Cash                         ○ Portfolio                  │ │
│ │   Use for cash transactions or petty cash.  Use for brokerage accounts, stocks, │ │
│ │                                         or bonds.           │ │
│ │                                                             │ │
│ │ ○ Asset                        ○ Mutual Fund                │ │
│ │   Use for valuable assets such as your home.  Use for a single mutual fund. │ │
│ └─────────────────────────────────────────────────────────────┘ │
│                                                                  │
│   Account Name:  [                ]     ☐ Hide in lists          │
│                                                                  │
│   Description:   [                  ]                            │
│     (optional)                                                   │
│                                                                  │
│  [ Enable Online Services ]    [ Notes ]   [ Cancel ]  [ Create ]│
└────────────────────────────────────────────────────────────────┘
```

Fill in what you want to call this account. *Money-Grubbing Corporate Bank Vermin* is fine, except that it won't fit. *Savings* or *Checking* is a more common title.

The Register

At last you're permitted to see the Face of Quicken: the Register window.

Type in the opening balance — in other words, the ending amount on your last bank statement.

```
┌──────────────────────────── Checking: Register ─────────────────────┐
│ Date   │ Number │ Payee/Category/Memo │ Payment │Clr│ Deposit │Balance│
├────────┼────────┼─────────────────────┼─────────┼───┼─────────┼───────┤
│3/20/99 │ Num    │ Opening Balance     │ Payment │ ✓ │5,000.00 │5,000.00│
│        │ ▦  ▼   │ [Checking]    ▼ Memo│ Split   │   │Shortcuts ▼│     │
│3/20/99 │        │                     │         │   │         │       │
│        │        │                     │         │   │         │       │
│        │        │                     │         │   │         │       │
│        │        │                     │         │   │         │       │
│ [ Record ] [ Restore ]    Sort by: Date ▼   Balance Today:  $5,000.00 │
│                                              Balance 3/20/99: $5,000.00│
└──────────────────────────────────────────────────────────────────────┘
```

Type the date and final amount of your last bank statement, as shown above.

This Register window may look like any normal iMac window, but that's like saying that a jalapeño looks like any normal salad component. There are 1,000 Handi-features to make typing information fast and easy. To wit:

- ✔ **Change the date by pressing the + and – keys on your keyboard.** Most of The Quicken Experience involves recording money you've spent and money you've made. The first stage of each typing binge is to set the date. Just click there, and then make the date advance or retreat by using + and – ; the longer you hold down the key, the faster the number changes.

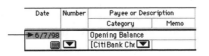

Date	Number	Payee or Description	
		Category	Memo
►6/7/98		Opening Balance	
		[Citi Bank Che	

Neater yet — after you've clicked the Date blank, you can also type **t** for today's date, **m** or **h** for the beginning or ending date of the **m**ont**h**, or **y** or **r** for the beginning or ending date of the **y**ea**r**. Isn't that adorable?

- ✔ **Press Tab to jump from column to column.** Press *Shift*-Tab to jump *backwards* through the blanks. You can get by for months without ever needing the mouse.

- ✔ **Don't bother tabbing to the cents place; just hit the decimal.** When you're typing in a dollar amount, leave off the $ sign and just type a decimal point (period) in the usual place. Quicken's smart enough to put the dollars and cents on opposite sides of the dividing line.

- ✔ **If Quicken recognizes something you're typing, it'll finish the phrase for you.** You do *not* need to type *Metropolitan Light, Power, and Water Authority of Northern California* every time that you cut a check for utilities. By the time you've typed *Metrop,* Quicken will have filled in the rest of the payee for you (assuming that you've typed it before).

  If Quicken guesses *wrong,* just keep typing. Quicken will remove its guess.

- ✔ **After entering a transaction, press Return.** Quicken sets you up with a new blank line, ready to receive the next scrap from your envelope of receipts. Oh, yeah — it also does all the math for you and updates the bottom line at the bottom of the window.

Just another $10,000 day

Now that you've got your register set up, the rest of Quicken is simplicity itself. Suppose that you made a bank deposit today — your weekly paycheck plus the first installment from a lottery you won. (I like to use examples that everyone can relate to.)

Click in the bottom row of the ledger, which is blank. (There's *always* one blank line at the bottom of the register. If you don't see it, maybe you need to scroll down using the scroll bar at the right side.) Use the + and – keys, naturally, to adjust the date (or type **t** for today).

Then type a description of today's event — in this case, *Paycheck and Lottery #1.* Press Tab.

Now type in the *total* amount of your bank deposit — paycheck plus prize money. If this weren't a dual-source deposit, you'd be done — but you're not. Here's where it gets really neat.

See the little *Split* button in the Payment column? Click it. A stack of subblanks appears, in which you can break down your total transaction amount:

When you click the Split button, this sub-list appears.

The Category must be on the Category list — generic labels like Tax, Auto, or Insurance.

The Memo can be anything you want.

You've got to choose a category for this part of the split. For the paycheck, no sweat — it would be Salary. If you type the letters *Sa,* Quicken will recognize where you're headed, and it will fill in the rest of the word. (Alternatively, you can press ⌘-L, for *list,* to see Quicken's complete list of categories. You can double-click anything on that list to make it fill in the Category blank here. Or you can choose a category name from the pop-up menu — the tiny black down-pointing triangle at the right edge of the Category blank.)

Press Tab. Then type, for the paycheck, a memo. Anything you want. Or nothing. Press Tab again.

Now enter the amount of the paycheck. In this case, you work as a tollbooth operator for a remote and impoverished township in a debt-ridden South American country, so you make only 49 cents per week. Type *.49*. Press Tab.

Creating a new category

Now you're supposed to enter the category for your lottery money. Yet oddly enough, Quicken doesn't come with a Lottery Winnings category. You're going to need to make it up.

Suppose that you decide to call this category *Prizes*. Type that and then press Tab — and Quicken will tell you that you've colored outside the lines.

> Can't find category 'Prizes'. Would you like to select from the list, or set it up?
>
> [Cancel]   [Set Up]   [Select]

Fortunately, Quicken also offers you the easy way out. Click Set Up. Now you can create your new financial category.

> ▦ ▦ **Set Up Category** ▦ ▤
>
> Category: Prizes
>
> Description: [   ]
> (optional)
>
> ┌ **Type** ─────────────────
> ● Income
> ○ Expense   ☑ Tax-related
>
> [Cancel]   [Create]

When coming up with a name for your new category, think general. Think tax time. Don't create a category called *Beige leatherette camera case, that one with the tassels*. Instead, the IRS would probably be content to see *Equipment* or something.

In the case of the lottery winnings, make sure that you specify the Type — Income — and that, God knows, it's tax-related. In other words, this little baby is definitely going to find a place on your 1040 form. Groceries, on the other hand, will not.

Click Create. You return to your entry, where Prizes is now accepted as a legit category name. Tab over to the Memo blank, type something like **First installment,** and you're done. Quicken has already entered $10,000 into the Amount blank to make the split amounts match the grand total.

To close up the Split window, click the Close Split button (or press ⌘-E).

More typical examples

Another great candidate for the Split window: credit-card payments. Suppose that you write a check to pay this month's credit-card bill. (Most people have a separate Checking account, which you can create by choosing New Account from the File menu.)

Choose Write Checks from the Activities menu. You get this representation of America's most recognized piece of paper.

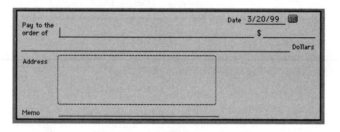

Start typing the payee's name. As you know by now, if Quicken recognizes the name, the program will complete the typing for you. Press Tab and then type in the amount.

This time when you press Tab, you get to see one of the slickest features ever. If you typed *$432.45,* Quicken writes out, in longhand English, *Four hundred thirty-two and 45/100* on the second line.

Tab your way into the Address box and type the mailing address (pressing *Return* after each line, *not* Tab). Then Tab to the Memo blank and type your account number. And *now* (egg roll, please) — choose Memorize from the Edit menu. From now on, when you start to make a check out to *Citib,* Quicken will fill in the payee name *and* the address *and* the account number!

Checking: Write Checks

Pay to the order of	Citibank Visa
Date	3/20/99
$	432.45

Four hundred thirty-two and 45/100***************************** Dollars

Address: Citibank Visa
Box 8201
Hagerstown, MD 21278

Memo: 4128 654 982 65548 965

Category _____ ▼ Split

Record Restore

Balance Today : $5,000.00
Balance 3/20/99: $5,000.00

Before you hit Return (or click Record), it's a good idea to note what this credit-card payment *covers*. Just as you did before, click the Split button at the bottom of the check window. Now your expenditures are logged safely in case of disaster (such as fire, flood, or April 15).

The category payoff

The point of all this categorizing, of course, comes at year-end (or any other occasion where a financial snapshot is required). Quicken does some amazing number crunching.

At tax time, for example, choose Reports from the Reports & Graphs command in the Activities menu. Double-click, say, Category Summary. Plug in the year's starting and ending dates; instantly, you've got a detailed breakdown to hand your tax guy (or yourself, as the case may be). The graphs are equally impressive. (Choose Graphs from the Reports & Graphs command.)

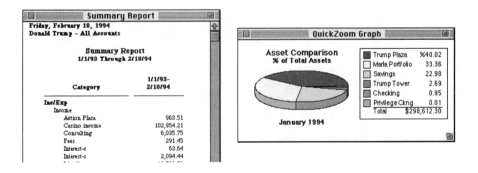

Summary Report

Friday, February 18, 1994
Donald Trump - All Accounts

Summary Report
1/1/93 Through 2/18/94

Category	1/1/93– 2/18/94
Inc/Exp	
Income	
Action Plaza	963.51
Casino income	102,954.21
Consulting	6,035.75
Fees	291.45
Interest-c	63.64
Interest-s	2,094.44

QuickZoom Graph

Asset Comparison
% of Total Assets

Trump Plaza	%40.02
Marla Portfolio	33.36
Savings	22.98
Trump Tower	2.69
Checking	0.95
Privilege Ckng	0.01
Total	$298,612.30

January 1994

Reconciling for the nonaccountant

Like many of us out in America Land, there was a time when I, too, occasionally failed to compare my checkbook with the bank statement each month. But trusting the bank's computers can be dangerous; they *do* make mistakes. In my six years of using Quicken, I've caught my bank with its computerized hands in my tiller twice — $45 the first time and $200 the second!

Anyway, here's how this feature (called *reconciling*) works. With your bank statement in front of you, choose Reconcile from the Activities menu. Fill in the closing balance from the bank statement; fill in any interest your money earned, too, as well as any finance charges those filthy usurers charged you.

GrubberBanc International
Acct. #2348-45-388573-23984-2238-499835-98857-6637

Opening balance: $9384.23
Closing balance: $6504.22

3/23/99	DEPOSIT	$345.34
3/29/99	CHECK 398	433.98
4/4/99	CHECK 399	89.32

Checking: Reconcile Startup

1. Enter the following information from your bank statement.

Beginning Balance: 5,000.00   As of: 3/20/99

Ending Balance: 6,504.22   As of: 4/23/99

2. Enter any service charge or interest amounts from your statement. Quicken will add transactions for those amounts to your register.

	Amount	Date	Category
Service Charge:	0.00	3/20/99	
Interest Earned:	12.54	3/18/99	Interest Earned

[Cancel]   [**Start**]

Click OK. Now the fun begins. Read down the transactions listed on your bank statement. Each time that you find one that matches a listing in Quicken's Reconcile window, click it in the Reconcile window so that a check mark appears next to it. Keep going until you've accounted for everything on the statement.

Almost always, Quicken will show transactions that your bank statement doesn't. That's normal. It means that your life didn't stop on the 15th of the month (or whenever the bank's cutoff date for your statement was). The items you're seeing are transactions you've made since the day the statement was printed and mailed.

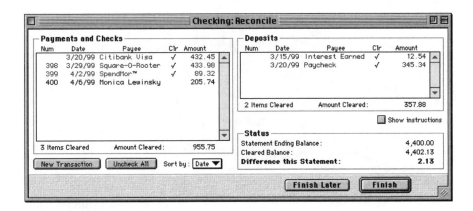

If the statement has extra items

But what if the bank lists some deposit or payment that Quicken doesn't know about? In most cases — forgive me — this is your mistake; you probably forgot to record something in Quicken. (Or, as they say in the biz, PBKC: *problem between keyboard and chair*.) On the other hand, as I've noted, once in a blue moon, you'll catch a genuine bank mistake.

If you notice discrepancies as you go, use one of these two techniques:

> ✔ **Double-click any transaction listed in Quicken's Reconcile window.**
> You'll be teleported directly to the Register entry for that item so that
> you can read the description and try to get more information. For
> example, if you have two different entries for "New co-op in St. Tho-
> mas," the odds are pretty good that you entered it twice. Unless you
> truly did buy two, delete one of them (by using Delete Transaction in
> the Edit menu).

> ✔ **Pull the Register window to the front.** If you discover a transaction on
> the statement that you forgot to plug into Quicken during the month,
> click the New Transaction button and type it in. Then return to the
> Reconcile window and click it off.

What's *supposed* to happen is that the Difference this Statement line (see the previous illustration) winds up at zero. If it does, click OK and bask in the warm sunny feeling of Quicken's little congratulatory message.

If the Difference this Statement doesn't come out to zero, you can either squirm for another 20 minutes trying to find out why your computer doesn't match the bank's, or you can take the fatalistic approach and click the OK button.

Going electronic

In general, adulthood is a joy. I've got to admit, though, that bill-paying is one of the serious downsides of having to grow up.

As it turns out, though, one of the iMac's most remarkable benefits is *automatic bill paying* — using Quicken in conjunction with your bank. For this service, you usually pay $7 or 10 per month — unless you choose a bank, such as Citibank, that doesn't charge at all.

In return, you gain a remarkable feature: When you enter a check in your Quicken registry, it becomes a reality! Quicken, at the end of your session, dials a phone number, transmits your check information, and instructs the bank to issue a check to the payee (or, if you're paying a company, to make an electronic transfer), without any further effort on your part.

There are no envelopes, no stamps, and much less record-keeping. The real point here, though, is that e-banking saves money (and not just in postage). For example, you can input the payment the day your bill arrives, but the check doesn't get *sent* (by your bank) until the date you specify. Suppose that your credit-card, mortgage, utilities, phone bill, cable TV, car payments, and Internet account bills total about $3,500 a month. If that money earns 5 percent interest in the bank, in the three weeks between a bill's arrival and the due date, it could have racked up $10.02 in interest! Yes, $120.24 a year is what you *give away* to those money-grubbing corporations if you pay promptly. Do it electronically, and that's $120 a year in cold, hard cash you save.

Setting up the electronic check-paying thing in Quicken takes a little bit of effort, and you'll have to wait for some special codes (from your bank) in the mail. But going through the setup is well worth it — electronic banking is like a gift of four hours (and $10) per month with no strings attached.

In that event, Quicken creates a new entry in your register called, ahem, Balance Adjustment. Try, *try* not to think of it as shouting in huge capital letters, *"This is where you screwed up, you numerically incompetent clod!"* every time that you look at it for the rest of your life.

In my experience, by the way, the temptation to simply accept the discrepancy is much greater when it's in your favor.

Photo Soap, Good Cooking, PageMill, & Company

Your iMac also comes with the Williams-Sonoma Guide to Good Cooking; Kai's Photo Soap; MDK; Nanosaur; Adobe PageMill (recent-vintage iMacs only); and much more. In fact, somebody could probably write an entire book just on the software that comes with an iMac. *(Now there's an idea! —* Ed. *Don't even think about it. —* Auth.)

Here's a crash course. You'll find each of these programs in the Applications folder, which is on your hard drive. Also note: Except for Nanosaur and PageMill, the CD containing the program must be *in the iMac* whenever you want to use the program. For example, you can't launch Photo Soap unless the Photo Soap CD is inserted into the iMac.

Williams - Sonoma Guide to Good Cooking

This CD is gorgeous, richly photographed, and saliva-inducing — it's got 1,000 illustrated recipes in a searchable electronic card catalog.

The main WS Guide screen is a photo of several books: Glossary, Recipe Finder, Menu Planner, Recipe Index, and Favorite Recipes. For best results, try the Recipe Finder, which lets you search for specific recipes among the 1,000 available on the CD, like this.

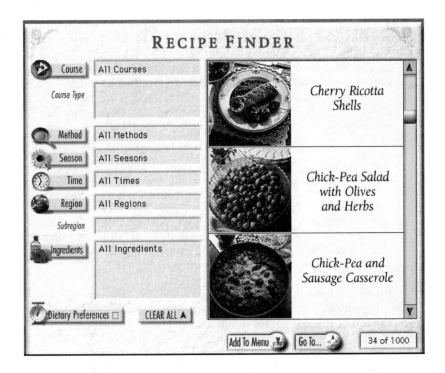

The other highlight of the CD is the Glossary. Not only is it a treat for the eye, but many of the entries also feature actual *movies* that play right on your screen, illustrating how to carve meat, fold calzones, and perform other mission-critical techniques.

MDK

I can't tell you what MDK stands for. I can, however, tell you that it's a dazzling 3-D adventure game.

You control your guy, Kurt, by pressing keys on the keyboard (the arrow keys to move, for example, the Control key to fire your gun, and so on). Press the F1 key on your keyboard to view a full cheat sheet of the key-strokes that make MDK go. If you make it to the very end — via arenas, corridors, freefalls, streams, and just generally blowing up scary-looking customers who wander by — congratulations. If you get stuck, visit *www.playmatestoys.com/pie/mdk/mdkfaq.htm* on the Web (see Chapter 12) for some hints and tips.

Kai's Photo Soap

The purpose of this strange, confusing, wonderful program is to fix photos: remove redeye from snapshots, repair tears or specks from existing photos, fix over- or underexposure, and so on. If you don't have a digital camera or scanner as a source of photos, you can still have fun wreaking havoc on the sample pictures included with the program.

When you launch the program, you'll feel distinctly disoriented; this program's design is like no other Macintosh program. There are no menus at the top of the screen, for one thing.

The concept: You're supposed to bring a photo into the program and then repair it in a succession of "rooms" (different screens), each of which handles one kind of fixing. To view the list of different "rooms," point to the word Map at the top of the screen, as shown here.

Then click the name of the screen you want to visit next. Here's what they do:

- ✔ **In** — A "home-base" view where you choose a photo to transmogrify. Click the File button (top left) to view your hard drive's contents so that you can double-click a photo file to work with. If you're feeling particularly organized, you can also drag your photos around into "albums" on this screen.

- ✔ **Prep** — Drag the horizontal and vertical lines, as shown above, to chop off excess edges of a picture. The various buttons on the left side of the photo can flip it mirror-image or upside-down; the Enhance button on the right side fixes over- or underexposure. And the scale slider at the lower-right enables you to make the picture larger or smaller (although you'll see the difference only when you print).

- ✔ **Tone** — On this screen, you can adjust the brightness and contrast levels of the whole photo — or just parts of it. Use the weird-looking, three-slider doodad below the photo to set up the effect you'd like. (They correspond to intensity, brightness, and contrast.) If you'd like to apply these effects to only a *part* of the photo, click the ribbed left side of the photo frame and then click the picture of painting tools. You'll be offered a couple of paintbrush icons that, when clicked and then dragged across your photo, apply your tone changes only to the parts that the brush touches. (The eraser *removes* the tone changes.)

- ✔ **Color** — This screen adjusts the intensity and hue of the colors in your photo. Again, don't miss the ribbed "drawer" of painting tools at the left edge of the photo; these brushes let you apply the color shifts only where you drag.

✔ **Detail** — In this room, you can perform astonishing transformations to your photo — or ruin it completely. The Sharpen and Smooth modes bring the picture into, or out of, focus; the Red Eye heals the red-pupil effect in flash photos; Heal fixes tears and blotches; and Clone lets you duplicate an element of the photo, thus turning twins into triplets, for example. (To use this last feature, click once to indicate *what* you want to duplicate; click again to indicate *where* you want the copy placed — and begin painting.)

After clicking one of these effect buttons, your cursor becomes target-shaped so that you can click *where* on the photo you'd like to operate. (The program automatically enlarges the photo to actual size as you dab away.)

✔ **Finish** — In this final room, you can add predrawn, colorful frames or accent graphics to your finished photo. Click the Backgrounds, Edges, or Objects buttons to summon corresponding palettes filled with choices. (Double-click the edge of a palette to make it go away again.) This "room" is also where you'll find Save and Print buttons, thus preserving your edge-cropped, tone-shifted, color-tweaked, rip-fixed, twin-cloned, frame-added photo for future generations.

In most of the rooms, you'll find three important consistent elements. The magnifying glass, when selected, lets you click your photo to enlarge it for detail work (or Option-click to zoom out). The weird-looking remote-control thing (in the lower-right) offers access to many of the program's overall options (such as whether you'd like an extra-large cursor or the normal iMac one). And the Help button summons explanations of the tools.

When on a Help screen, don't miss the ribbed slots at the left side of the screen, as shown above. As you point to these tabs with your mouse, you're offered a selection of Help topics — including the all-important Exit Help button (at the bottom), without which you'd be stuck in Help mode forever.

Speaking of being trapped in a software room for eternity, by the way: In the absence of menus, you may wonder how the heck you're supposed to *leave* this program, neato though it is. *Solution:* Press ⌘-Q, the universal iMac shortcut for the Quit command.

Nanosaur

This stunning, 3-D dinosaur shoot-'em up is all about violence, noise, and wiping out endangered species. Kids adore it.

Just press the arrow keys to move your little dino around, and press the space bar to fire little dino-bullets. (I'm resisting a pun about dino-might here.) Check out the help screen (which appears just after you launch the program) to view the complete keystroke list. You can turn off the sound (or press the + and – keys to adjust the volume), but don't do so until you've admired the way Nanosaur capitalizes on the iMac's "3-D" sound feature.

PageMill

Adobe PageMill, our final software of this evening's presentation, comes with the second wave of iMacs, those sold after November 1998 (it replaces MDK).

And what, you may ask, is a page mill? It's a program that lets you make your *own* World Wide Web pages, like those illustrated in Chapter 12. That's the beauty of the Internet: *Anyone* can be represented equally. *Your* personal Web page can be just as prominent on the Web as, say, the Web pages of Sony, General Motors, or the Seinfeld Fan Club. Maybe you have a small business you'd like to promote; maybe you want far-flung relatives to be able to see your new baby pix; or maybe you just want the world to know what you had for breakfast. With programs like Adobe PageMill (or its rival, Claris Home Page), creating a home page of your own requires no knowledge of foreign languages (such as computer code); if you've got something to say to the world, you can now stake your claim to a piece of property with frontage on the information superhighway.

The blank canvas

A Web page is made up of several different components: a couple of pictures, say, plus some writing. A solemn word of advice: In your forays into Web-page making, keep all these Web-page files together on your hard drive in a single folder.

It's all HTML to me

Behind the scenes, Web pages don't look like Web pages. If you open one in a word processor, even a *blank* Web-page document contains enough geeky gobbledygook to curl your toes:

```
<HTML>  <HEAD>
<META NAME="GENERATOR"
   CONTENT="Adobe PageMill 3.0
   Mac">
<TITLE>Untitled Document</TITLE>
   </HEAD>
<P></P>
```

```
</BODY>
   </HTML>
```

What you're reading is a computer language called *HTML*, or Hypertext Markup Language. Fortunately, today's Web-page-making programs (such as PageMill) hide all of this nerdspeak from you. I mention HTML only so that you won't panic if you happen to stumble onto some of it when PageMill isn't looking.

You start your Web experiment, then, by creating a new folder on your desktop in which to store all the parts of your magnum opus. Call it "Web Page folder" or something similar.

Before you begin making your page, figure out what's going to be *on* it. If graphics are involved — and I certainly hope they will be, since the Web is all about pretty pictures — create them in a graphics program like Photoshop or ClarisWorks/AppleWorks, or grab them from a digital camera or scanner (see Chapter 18). (If, when you save your finished graphics, the iMac gives you a choice of *file format* for your finished pix, choose *JPEG* for photos, and *GIF* is best for non-photos like logos and cartoons.)

As you design, remember that *big* graphics and *multiple* graphics make your Web page take much longer to appear on your visitors' screens, so design judiciously. Put your finished graphics files into your Web Page folder.

Creating a new, blank page

When you double-click the PageMill icon, you get a shiny, new, blank canvas on which to proclaim yourself to the world. In the blank white strip at the top of the window, type a title for your page (such as *Bullwinkle's Home Page*); once this page is on the Web, this name will appear at the top of your visitors' screens. Now choose Save from the File menu and give a name to your PageMill document — that is, its icon on your hard drive.

PageMill proposes adding *.html* at the end of your document's name. Welcome to the World Wide Web, where, in the spirit of open-hearted fairness, even the users of non-Macintosh computers are allowed online. Because some of those computers are, shall we say, *differently abled,* names of files must meet some very rigid standards. For example:

- ✔ **Thou shalt not put spaces in the names of files.** If you feel the absolute need to put a space in the file name of a Web page, use the underline key (shift-hyphen) in place of the spaces, as in "Big_Gray_Poodle.gif" or "Space,_the_final_frontier.html."

- ✔ **Every file name shalt end with a suffix.** In other words, a GIF picture should have the letters *.gif* at the end of its name, JPEG should end *.jpeg,* and a Web-page document (the kind you're making in PageMill) should end *.html* — for example, *Bullwinkle's_Home_Page.html.*

Meet your toolbar

PageMill's toolbar is crammed with useful gimmicks, most of which are just shortcuts for the menu commands. If you point to some control without clicking, a pop-up yellow label helpfully identifies what you're pointing at. For purposes of this experiment, for example, you'll use these toolbar icons:

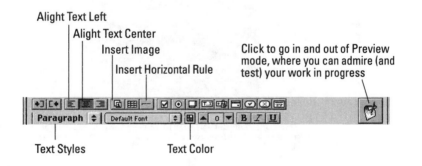

Alight Text Left
Alight Text Center
Insert Image
Insert Horizontal Rule
Click to go in and out of Preview mode, where you can admire (and test) your work in progress
Text Styles
Text Color

Add the text

At the moment, your blank document is surprisingly drab for the supposedly colorful world of the Internet. Instead of that sickly gray background color, let's choose something that won't look quite so much like a prison cell. See the Inspector panel, the little floating window off to the right of your screen? From the Background pop-up menu, choose the White color. Ahh . . . much better.

Designing a Web page is something like designing a nice magazine layout. Most Web pages start, therefore, with a headline. Inspect, for the moment, the Text Styles pop-up menu on your toolbar. See the list of Heading types?

This pop-up menu offers you a list of various canned text styles: Heading styles are big and bold; Definition List is small and indented; and so on. For now, choose Largest Heading. Now click the Center Align Text toolbar icon. Type the headline for your Web page.

The page isn't the only thing that can be colorized, by the way. You can change the color of your text, too. Highlight some of the words in your headline and choose from the Text Color pop-up menu on the toolbar.

Hanging pictures

Adding pictures to pages to your Web page is simple. Just click the Insert Image button on the toolbar. In the Open dialog box, find, and double-click, the graphics file you'd like to slap onto your Web page. (You can also paste in a picture you've copied from another program, such as AppleWorks.) The image appears right there on your Web page, as shown in the following illustration.

If you click the pic, handles appear, which you can use to change the picture's size. Keep the Shift key pressed as you drag to avoid distorting the image.

A little separation

Back to our Web-page-in-progress: Press Return a couple of times. Click the Align Text Left button on the toolbar. Start typing; now's your chance to spill your guts — as much guts as you'd like to spill in front of a 200-million-person audience, that is.

When you want to introduce a new topic, you might consider drawing a horizontal line between paragraphs. To do so, press Return, and then click the Insert Horizontal Rule button on the toolbar; a 3-D looking line appears on your page, as shown at the bottom of the previous figure.

Linking up

That's certainly enough creativity for one afternoon. From here on in, you can rely on the creativity of *others,* by creating *links* from your Web page to other peoples' pages. This linking thing, of course, is what the World Wide Web is all about.

Suppose your Web page continues with this common phrase: "If you've enjoyed this Web page, I owe it all to *The iMac For Dummies,* which showed me how to do it. Click here to visit Pogue's Pages."

Highlight the text you want to serve as the link; the idea is for it to turn *blue and underlined,* like the blue, underlined phrases on millions of Web pages all over the universe. Blue underlining tells the visitor: *Click me to move to a different Web page!*

Then, in the "Link To:" strip at the bottom of the window, type the target Web address, like this:

Highlighted text to become the link.

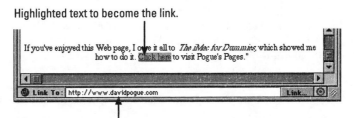

The Web page you're linking to.

After typing the Web address, press Return; you've just created your first Web link. If somebody's looking at your Web page and clicks the "Click here" phrase, their screen will soon fill with *my* Web page.

Getting published

Unfortunately, getting your Web page *on* the Web is almost as much work as *creating* your page. The good news is that America Online, plus nearly every Internet access company, offers free space to put up your Web pages. The bad news is that putting your pages up forces you into encountering such geeky terms as *FTP* and *server.*

If you have an America Online subscription, use keyword: MYPLACE. From here, click the Go To My Place button, click Upload, find your various Web Page Folder files, and transmit them, one at a time, to AOL. (The instructions you'll find at keyword: MYPLACE are much more detailed.) Then start telling your friends your Web page address: It's *http://members.aol.com/skibunny* (substitute your own screen name for *skibunny*).

If you have a direct Internet account instead of AOL, call the access company (or visit its Web page) for instructions on posting your Web page. And set aside a whole Saturday; the process gets a little technical. Your Web page address will usually be something like *http://www.earthlink.com/~skibunny,* where *skibunny* is you and *earthlink.com* is the name of your Internet access company.

When it's all over, you, my friend, will be a Web publisher — circulation: 200 million!

Top Ten Programs Not in the Top Ten

For your shopping pleasure and entertainment: a double handful of neat programs that are often discussed at techno-savvy cocktail parties. ("Hi there, baby. Want to come up and see my FreeHand printouts?")

Plug alert: If these additional programs interest you, then so might *MORE Macs For Dummies* (IDG Books Worldwide, Inc); its "Faking Your Way Through Eight More Programs" covers many of them.

1. **FreeHand** or **Illustrator.** Primo, powerful, professional, pricey PostScript graphics programs. Be prepared to read the manual.

2. **Photoshop.** AppleWorks' painting window on steroids. A stunning, pro-level photo painting program, capable of fantastic transparency effects or undetectably painting your in-laws right out of the family portrait.

3. **Chronos Consultant.** A gorgeous, fast, feature-filled address-book/calendar program. Stores your names, addresses, e-mail addresses, appointments, and even dials the phone for you.

4. **Microsoft PowerPoint.** It's called *presentation software.* Enables you to quickly and easily assemble slide shows — graphs, bullet charts, colorful diagrams — with a choice of many rich, unified color schemes. Print the slides onto slides or transparencies or use the iMac itself to give a slide show.

5. **PageMaker** or **QuarkXPress.** These are what's known as *page-layout* programs — something like a cross between a word processor and a graphics program. They're designed to help you design flyers, newsletters, magazines, and so on, complete with photos, boxed mini-articles, headlines, and so on.

6. **FileMaker.** A database. A heck of a lot like the AppleWorks database you used in this chapter, actually, but considerably beefed-up, ready for running your business, CD collection, or gambling operation.

7. **Myst** and its sequel, **Riven.** Reason enough to justify the invention of the CD-ROM player (which you need for these CDs). Spectacular visual treats and darned addictive wordless mysteries.

8. **Claris Emailer.** If you use America Online or the Internet primarily for e-mail, this program is a godsend. In the middle of the night (or in the middle of whatever part of the day you specify), it quietly dials up your account, fetches all the waiting messages, and hangs up, offering you a neat list of all the messages. You can answer them at your leisure, without being online; at its *next* dialing time, it'll send your replies, and the cycle begins again. Makes organizing and filing your e-mail 1 million times easier and can even act as an e-mail answering machine while you're away. (Eudora and Outlook Express are similar but can't get your mail from America Online — only from the Internet itself.)

9. **InfoGenie.** A sizzlingly fast Rolodex program. Can pull up one person's card out of 2,000 in less than half a second. Can even dial the phone if you have a modem. Easier to use than a hairbrush.

10. **Premiere.** This is the program for making your own digital QuickTime movies right on the screen. And what's QuickTime? Like the man said: digital movies right on the screen. See Chapter 19.

Chapter 7

Cozying Up to Microsoft Word and Excel 98

• •

In This Chapter

▶ Word-processing mastery in Word 98

▶ Number-crunching heaven in Excel 98

▶ So many features, so little time

• •

*Y*our iMac was thoughtful enough to come equipped with several planeloads of free software, as documented in Chapter 6.

As superb as ClarisWorks (or AppleWorks) is, however, you don't find many copies of it kicking around at General Motors or Sony Corporation. No, the business world sneers at such simple, easy-to-use software; instead, corporate Planet Earth has adopted a different set of programs as its choice of What We're All Gonna Use — a suite of programs called Microsoft Office 98. (Microsoft Office refers to a cluster of three programs: Word, for word processing; Excel, for number crunching; and PowerPoint, for making slide shows.)

These Microsoft programs don't come free with the iMac — they're an extra purchase. But just in case you find yourself working for a company where Word and Excel are the Bread and Butter, I'd better show you the ropes in these programs.

As you go, meanwhile, rejoice in one nifty aspect of these programs: Microsoft has somehow worked things so that the Office files you create on your Macintosh open just beautifully on Windows computers. (Windows is a technologically inferior but far more common kind of computer operating system.) And vice-versa. You don't have to convert, translate, or otherwise adapt your Word, Excel, and PowerPoint files when transferring them from Mac to Windows or back again — an enormous savings of time and hassle if you collaborate with non-iMac users.

Microsoft Word 98

You've already absorbed most of the basics of word processing (in Chapter 4). Word 98, which is actually a very good program, has a few fancy features worth learning, though (and does some basic things in interesting ways).

Views

To start a new document, double-click the Microsoft Word icon. (***Hint:*** Never move the Microsoft Word icon out of its Microsoft Office 98 folder; if you do, it will politely decline to operate. If you really want to put the Word icon somewhere else on your hard drive, make an *alias* of it, as described in Chapter 9, and move *that*.)

You arrive at a blank screen. Go ahead and start typing your Oscar-winning screenplay. Use the usual word processing techniques (Delete to backspace, drag through text to select it, don't press Return at the end of each line, and so on) to whip it into shape.

You'll discover, though, that your piece of paper appears to be endless, as though it's delivered on a never-ending roll of Bounty. That's because you're in *Normal view,* where you never see a page end. (The end of a page is symbolized by a thin dotted line, but you sort of have to watch for it.)

If you want to see a more accurate display of what you'll get when you print, choose Page Layout from the View menu. Now you clearly see where each page ends, and you get to see things like page numbers and multiple columns.

Page break

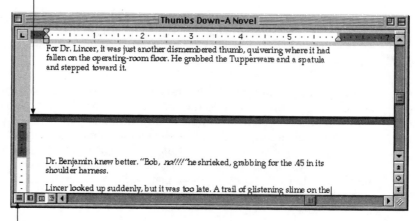

Back to Normal view

The View menu also contains commands for *Online Layout view,* which just makes the page narrower so that your text looks more like a magazine article; *Outline view,* a bizarre realm where you can rearrange your headings by dragging them; and *Master Document,* which only one person in America understands, and he's out of town until the 25th.

Finally, there's *Print Preview,* an absolutely vital and useful view. (Just to make sure that the program isn't too easy to use, they've put the Print Preview command in the *File* menu, not the View menu with the other views.) In Print Preview, you get to see the entire page — in fact, two side-by-side pages — no matter what size monitor you have.

To change the margins

Print Preview also provides the easiest way to adjust the margins. See the rulers at the top and left edges of the page? Position your cursor *carefully* over the spot where the white and dark gray strips of the ruler meet. Wait for the arrow cursor to change its shape into a double-headed arrow — and then drag to change the margins. (Remember that you're adjusting the margins for *all* the pages when you do this.)

Drag to change the page margins (only when cursor is a double-headed arrow)

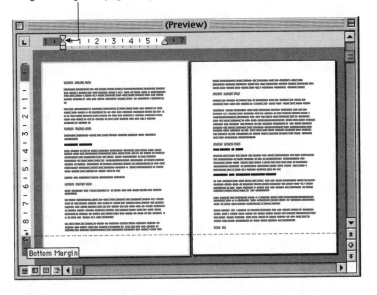

You can also, by the way, change the margins by choosing Document from the Format menu. A dialog box appears into which you can specify what you want for the top, bottom, left, and right margins. Specifying margins by typing numbers isn't as much fun as dragging the margins manually, but it does leave less margin for error. *(Dear Editor: That's the dumbest pun in the whole book. Let's make sure it gets taken out before the book is actually published, okay? Love, David.)*

Invasion of the toolbar people

Toolbars are strips of icon buttons, each of which does exactly the same thing as one of the menu commands. When you first install Word 98, you get these two toolbars (called, respectively, the *Standard* and *Formatting* toolbars). Here are what a few of the most useful buttons do.

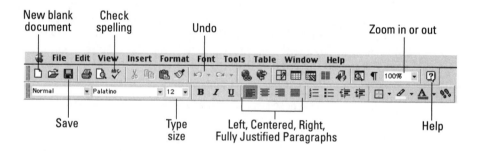

For the most part, the Standard toolbar controls the *program* (like opening, saving, and printing your work), and the Formatting toolbar controls *formatting* — the size of type, the style (bold or italic), the font, and so on. To do formatting, you *first* have to select some text you've already typed by dragging through it.

If you ask me, the most useful settings are the B, I, and U (for Bold, Italic, and Underline) buttons in the middle of the Formatting toolbar. You can glance at them and know immediately what formatting the next letters you type will have. The font and size controls (toward the left side) are useful, too, after you figure out that you have to click the downward-pointing triangle to change the setting.

A Microsoft joke that says a lot

How many Microsoft software programmers does it take to change a light bulb?

None. They just declare darkness to be the standard.

Formatting paragraphs

In the middle of the Formatting toolbar are icons that make changes to an entire paragraph at a time — and remember, a "paragraph" is anything you've typed that ends with a Return. Before you can use these controls, you must first *select the paragraphs you want to change*!

Nine out of ten novices surveyed find this concept hard to get used to. If you want to make one paragraph centered, just click anywhere in it — and then click the Center icon in the middle of the Formatting toolbar. If you want to affect several paragraphs but not the whole memo, drag through them before clicking the icon.

The point is to remember the Macintosh mantra: Select, then apply. Select, then apply. Select, then apply . . .

Toolbar bedtime

Fortunately, you can summon toolbars that pertain to every conceivable word processing task. Unfortunately, turning on a lot of them has one small downside: It doesn't leave you any room to *type*.

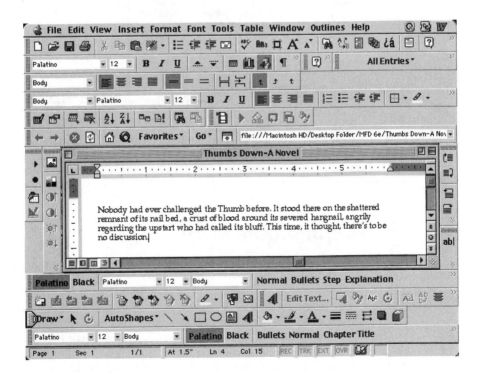

Fortunately, you can make them come and go as your whims dictate. The scheme for doing so is pretty simple: From the View menu, from the Toolbars submenu, choose the name of the toolbar you want to disappear (if it has a check mark) or reappear (if it doesn't).

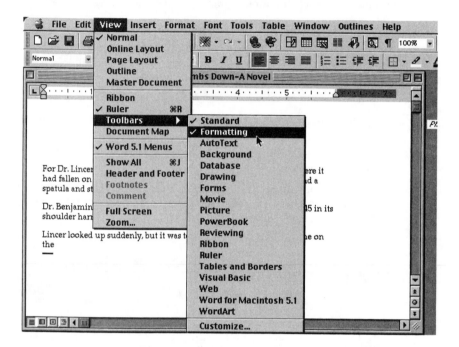

Don't let your self-esteem take a hit if you decide to turn off all of the toolbars. Thousands of people have *all* of these strips turned off. Without these strips, using Word is almost exactly like using a typewriter, and that's 100 percent okay.

Be careful on the strip

And here you thought we'd finished talking about all Word's toolbars and strips. No such luck.

Word's most hazardous feature, as far as you, Most Honorable Newcomer, are concerned, is its *selection bar*. This is a very, very skinny, invisible stripe up the left side of the window. You'll know when your cursor has inadvertently wandered in there because your arrow pointer will suddenly start pointing to the *right* instead of left. (This narrow vertical slice is in every version of Word.)

You may find this impossible to believe, but Word's left-margin strip was not, in fact, designed out of pure foaming malice toward new iMac users. It's actually supposed to make editing your work easier by providing some text-selecting shortcuts. Here are a few favorites.

Shortcut 1: Select one line of text by clicking in the selection strip.

Shortcut 2: To select a paragraph instantly, double-click in the selection strip. (Or triple-click anywhere inside a paragraph.)

Shortcut 3: To select the entire document, triple-click in the selection strip. (Do this when you want to change the font for the entire memo, for example.)

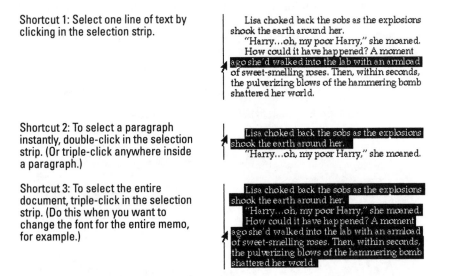

Checking your spelling, grammar, and vocabulary

Word 98 has this funny quirk of checking your spelling and grammar *all the time*. The instant you type a boo-boo, Word lets you know with a colored, wavy underline.

You could, of course, rely on your years of schooling, experience, and quiet can-do attitude to correct such mistakes yourself. Or you could take the easy way out: While pressing the Control key, click (and hold the mouse button down) on the wavy-underlined word. A special pop-up menu appears, sprouting directly out of your cursor, offering — get this — suggestions for correcting the misspelled word! (You can also spell-check your entire document by choosing Spelling from the Tools menu.)

If the wavy line is green, Word is suggesting that your *grammar* could stand improvement; its suggestions (when you Control-click the sentence) aren't always terrific improvements over your original, but they're sometimes worth considering.

And speaking of Control-clicking: That same trick works on words that *aren't* underlined. The resulting pop-up menu shows, among other commands, a Synonyms command that actually lists synonyms for the word you clicked — the perfect cheat for the vocabularically impaired.

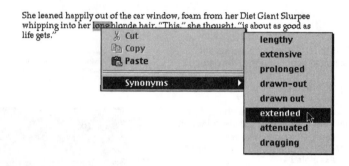

Killing the "Choose a template" box

One of Word's most annoying tics is that whenever you want a new document, it presents you with a list window offering you such preformatted layouts as Thesis, Weekly Time Sheet, and Brochures 1 and 2. Well, that's terrific — too bad for the 98 percent of us who just want to type up a gosh-darned letter.

Fortunately, you can eliminate this annoying obstacle to getting on with your work day. Instead of choosing New from the File menu, just press ⌘-N — instant blank document.

Single-spaced or double?

If you wonder why millions of Mac fans quietly grumble about Microsoft's mediocrity, here's a classic example: There's no easy way to change your document from single-spaced to double-spaced.

Anyway, here's what you have to do: From the Format menu, choose Paragraph. In the dialog box that appears, click Indents and Spacing. You should now see the tiny pop-up menu that lets you control spacing — not just Single and Double, but even "1.5 lines" or any number of lines you type into the box.

Page numbering

To add page numbers to your document, choose Page Numbers from the Insert menu. A neat little dialog box appears where you can specify where you want the page number to appear: top, bottom, left, or right — and whether you want a number to appear on page 1.

How to kill superfluous commands

Unless you're trying to crank out the next Sears catalog on your iMac or something, chances are good you won't be needing indexing, auto-hyphenation, and other abstruse options in Word.

Removing a command you never use is incredibly easy. While pressing ⌘ and Option together, press the minus (hyphen) key. Your cursor turns into a big fat minus sign! Handle your mouse with care, now — it's a loaded weapon. Any menu command that you touch will disappear from the menu!

Here's a partial listing of the commands I nuked from my Word 98 menus. Depending on how far you intend to let Word take you, you may want to augment this list (or leave some of these alone):

- **File menu:** Open Web Page, Save as HTML, Versions, Properties.
- **Edit menu:** Paste Special, Go To, Publishing, Links, Object.
- **View menu:** Master Document, Online Layout.
- **Insert menu:** Frame, Field, Caption, Cross-Reference, Index and Tables, Text Box, Movie, Frame, Object, Hyperlink.
- **Format menu:** Drop Cap, Style Gallery, Text Direction, Background, Object.
- **Tools menu:** Language, Merge Document, Protect Document, Revisions, Macro, Templates and Add-Ins.
- **Table menu:** Almost everything.

And, by the way, you're not removing these commands from the *program* — you're simply removing them from the menu listings. If you ever want to restore Word's menus to their original condition, choose Customize from the Tools menu. In the dialog box that appears, scroll down, click Menu Bar, and then click Reset. (And when Word asks if you're sure, click OK.)

Getting help — and goofy animations

This crash course in Word 98 has been brought to you by People With Very Little Spare Time. But if you're going to get into Word's more advanced features — you know, putting boxes around paragraphs, automatic indexing, outlining, making tables — you'll need to consult the Word 98 manual. It's electronic, built right into the program, saving you years' worth of paper cuts. From the Help menu, choose Microsoft Word Help. If he's not already on your screen, the dancing Mac (known as Max) appears in his little movie window, like this.

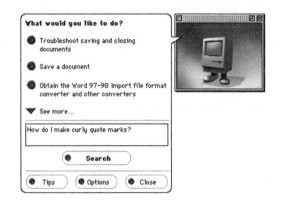

What would you like to do?

● Troubleshoot saving and closing documents

● Save a document

● Obtain the Word 97-98 Import file format converter and other converters

▼ See more...

How do I make curly quote marks?

(● Search)

(● Tips) (● Options) (● Close)

Into the little Search blank, type whatever you'd like help with (such as "margins" or "green text") or even a question (such as "How do I make an outline?"). Then click Search. After a moment, you'll be shown a list of help topics; click one to read all about it. Word's not always brilliant at providing answers — but every now and then, it'll surprise you.

And speaking of Max, the animated doodad: Public opinion is evenly divided on this little guy. Half the world thinks he's kinda cute; the other half considers taking a sledge hammer to their screens.

If he bugs you, click the tiny close box in the upper-left corner of his window and watch him wave goodbye forever. If he charms you, hold down the Control key, click his window, and choose Animate! from the pop-up menu that appears. Each time you do so, Max will perform another little stunt for you, such as dismantling himself, putting on glasses, going to sleep, and so on.

Who *said* computers don't make us more productive?

Excel 98

If you're not familiar with a *spreadsheet,* get psyched — even if you only use 1 percent of its features, Excel can really be a godsend. It's for math, finances, figuring out which of two mortgage plans is more favorable in the long run, charting the growth of your basement gambling operation, and other number-crunchy stuff.

Starting up

Double-click the Excel icon. A blank spreadsheet appears on your screen. It's a bunch of rows and columns, like a ledger book. The columns have letters, and the rows are numbered. Each little rectangular cell is called, well, a *cell*. It's referred to by its letter and number: A1, for example.

To type a number into a cell, click the cell with the mouse and begin typing. You can do your typing (and editing) in the cell itself, but notice that all the action is duplicated in the editing strip at the top of the window. When you're done typing or editing, press Enter.

Formatting numbers and text

As you enter numbers, don't bother to format them with dollar signs, decimal points, and all that jazz. Formatting can be applied later. For example, you could enter the following numbers, each of which has a different number of decimal places (below, left). Now drag vertically through them with the pointer (below, right).

By now, you can probably say it in your sleep: In the world of Mac, you select something first and then act on it . . . *Select and then apply* . . . After the numbers are selected, you can format them all with dollar amounts in one fell swoop. See the little dollar-sign button on the lower toolbar at the top of the screen? (If you don't, open the View menu, choose Toolbars, and choose Formatting from the submenu.) Click that $ icon.

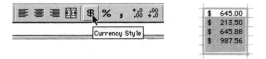

Instantly, Excel formats all the selected numbers as dollar amounts. Notice how it adds zeros (or rounds off excess decimal places) as necessary.

Spreading the sheet

Now it gets good. If you've been fooling around so far, erase everything you've done. Drag the cursor diagonally through whatever you've typed and then choose Clear from the Edit menu (and All from the submenu). We're gonna start you off freshlike.

Click in cell B3. (That's column B, row 3; a spreadsheet is like a good game of *Battleship*.) Type in *1969*.

To jump into the next cell to the right, press Tab. Or press the right-arrow key. (You move to the *left* by pressing *Shift*-Tab or the left-arrow key.) In any case, enter *1979*. Repeat until you've filled in the years as shown below.

You move *down* a row by pressing Return or the down-arrow key. Shift-Return moves you up a row and so does the up-arrow key. (There's a certain twisted logic to this, isn't there?)

You can also jump to any cell by clicking it, of course. Now then: Go wild. With these navigational commands under your belt, type in the text and numbers as shown below. (Frankly, it doesn't make any difference *what* numbers you type. I made them all up anyway.)

	A	B	C	D	E	F
1						
2						
3		1969	1979	1989	1999	
4	Quarter 1	1234	2345	4567	7899	
5	Quarter 2	3123	2396	3556	3488	
6	Quarter 3	120	1589	6455	122	
7	Quarter 4	2000	3225	5353	8441	
8						
9	TOTALS:					
10						
11						
12						

Want to make the top row boldface, as shown in the preceding figure? Drag the cursor through the years. Now click the B button on the toolbar at the top of the screen. If you haven't guessed, **B** means **Bold**, and *I* means *Italic*. (And I *mean* italic!)

Creating automatically calculating cells

Here comes the juicy part. Click the Totals row, under the 1969 column of numbers. Click the funny Σ button on the top toolbar, as shown here.

That's the AutoSum button, and it's some button.

In the formula bar at the top of the screen, you'll see that Excel has entered `=SUM(B3:B8)`.

In English, the program is trying to say: "The number I'll enter into the cell you clicked (Total) is going to be the sum of . . . well, I suppose you mean the numbers directly *above* the cell you clicked — cells B3 down to B8." Isn't it smart to guess what you mean?

Well, smart, but not quite smart enough — because you *don't* want the number 1969 included in the total! So you can override Excel's guess by showing it which numbers you *do* want totaled . . . by dragging through them. Try it. While the dotted-line rectangle is still twinkling, drag vertically through the four cells *below* 1969. Then press Enter.

Neat, huh? Excel automatically totals the four numbers you selected. But that's only the half of it. Now click one of the cells below the 1969 heading — and *change the number*. That's right; type a totally different number. (And press Enter when you're done typing. You always need to press Enter to tell Excel you're done working in a cell.) Voilà — the total *changes* automatically!

This is the origin of the phrase "What-if scenario." You can sit here all day, fiddling with the numbers in the 1969 column. As soon as you change a number and press Enter, the total updates itself. That's why it's so easy to compute a mortgage at 10 percent for five years and see if it's better than one at 8 percent for seven years (or whatever).

Fill right, feel right

Now then. You have three other columns to contend with. Do you have to redo the Σ business each time? Nope. You've already explained to Excel how the Total row should work: It should add up the four numbers above it, *not* including the year at the top of the column.

So you could just take that magic total cell (B9 in the preceding picture) and *copy* it into the three cells to its right. Excel is smart enough to add up the right numbers in each column. (No, it won't put the *1969* total into each cell.)

Of course, you could use the regular Copy and Paste commands — but that's too tedious. Use the Fill Right command instead. Drag through the Totals row, starting with the 1969 total and extending through the three other years' total cells.

Then press ⌘-R — or do it the long way: From the Edit menu, choose Fill and choose Right right from its submenu. Bingo! Excel 98 intelligently copies the *formula* from the first cell into the other cells, totaling each column automatically. You may as well know that there's also a Fill Down command, used when you want to copy a formula to a series of cells *below* the one that contains it.

From here to infinity

Using the standard math symbols (+, –, / [for division], and * [for multiplication]), you can build much more complicated autocalculating cells than the simple SUM function described in "Creating automatically calculating cells." For example, you can use nested parentheses and the whole works. To make a cell calculate how many hours are in ten years, for example, you'd click on it. Then you'd type =**(24*365)*10** and press Enter. The formula always has to begin with the equal sign, but otherwise your equations can be as complicated as you want.

You can have formula cells that work with numbers from *other* formula cells, too — in the example above, you could create a Grand Total cell that would sum up the 1969, 1979, 1989, and 1999 totals automatically. There are even a few dozen more complex formula elements — financial, statistical, math, and time functions — listed in the Paste Function command (Edit menu), if you're into that kinky stuff.

Making a chart

There are a zillion options for charting, too, but here's the quick-and-dirty approach.

Drag through the table you created earlier — just the data part, not the totals in the bottom row. After this section is highlighted, click the Chart Wizard button, as shown here.

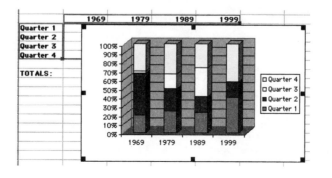

Now a dialog box appears, filled with amazing-looking examples of every kind of chart you've ever seen: bar, pie, line, area, Perot, and so on. Click the kind you want. In fact, you could spend several more hours here, tweaking every little chart option — but for this example, simply clicking the Finish button is enough.

When the dialog box disappears, a charming little chart pops up. (If it's charmingly covering up your numbers, hold down the cursor inside an empty part of the graph and drag it into a new position.) Double-click an individual bar (or other piece of the chart) to adjust the colors and styles for that element.

Excel also has outlining, drawing tools, macros, a database function, and probably a convenient toaster-oven . . . but this was supposed to be a crash course. If you want those frills, you'll have to actually put your nose in the manual.

Chapter 8

System Folder: Trash Barge of the iMac

• •

• •

*T*here it sits. Only one folder on your hard drive looks like it — or acts like it. It's the System Folder, which holds software that the iMac needs for itself. Every Mac has a System Folder. (Correction: Every *functioning* Mac has one.) Yours probably looks like any other folder, except that it's called System Folder and its icon has a tiny, special logo in the middle:

System Folder

Do it right now: Double-click your System Folder to open it. (Your System Folder is in your main hard-drive window.) Now click the zoom box, the tiny square in the inner top-right corner of the System Folder window, so you can see as much of the System Folder contents as possible. As a matter of fact, move your mouse up to the View menu and choose "as List." That should put everything into a neat list.

Just *look* at all that junk! *You* sure as heck didn't put it there — what's it *doing* there?

Who else would be utterly mad enough to say the following in public? *Half the stuff in your System Folder is worthless.* It's designed for power users, or people in big corporate networks, or superweenie jet-propulsion scientists and their Mensa-qualifying 8-year-old offspring. Meanwhile, these files are taking up room on your hard drive.

The System Folder Trashfest

Here's a wonderful, worth-the-price-of-the-book-right-there list of everything in your typical System Folder, item by item. I'll tell you which of these things you can safely trash.

Don't have a cow about throwing things away, either. The fewer items you have in your Control Panels and Extensions folders, the quicker your iMac starts up — and the less likely your machine is to crash. Besides, this is not like cleaning your attic, where if you toss that box of your drawings from elementary school, you've wounded your inner child forever. No, *this* stuff you can always get back again if you need it. It's all on the Software Install CD-ROM that came with your iMac.

As a bonus, as you go along, I'll try to point out some handy little treasures you didn't know you had. (Jeez, this is getting to be more like an attic-cleaning with every passing moment.)

The Apple Menu Items folder

Let's start with the stuff in the Apple Menu Items folder, which is, alphabetically speaking, the first thing in your System Folder. You'll recall that anything in this folder also appears in the menu at the left side of your screen.

This is really a two-for-one discussion: Most of the Apple menu items are also desk accessories like the ones you worked with in Chapter 3. So now you'll get to find out what exactly those things in your menu are . . . acquire a deep and abiding appreciation of their importance and value . . . and *then* throw them away.

AppleCD Audio Player — It has Play, Stop, and Rewind controls for playing regular *music* compact discs in your CD-ROM drive; see Chapter 19 for instructions.

Apple System Profiler — A neat little program that gives all kinds of mind-numbing technical details about your iMac. *You'll* probably never use it. But someday, when you're calling Apple in a desperate froth about some problem you're having, they may well ask you to consult the System Profiler to answer a couple of questions.

Automated Tasks — Automated Tasks isn't a program at all. It's merely an alias, dropped by Apple into your menu for convenience. It lists several handy *AppleScripts* — mini-programs, each of which performs one simple timesaving step when opened. For example, Add Alias to Apple Menu puts an alias of a selected icon into your menu. Most of the others, such as Share a Folder and Start File Sharing, have to do with networking.

Calculator and **Note Pad** — You already know about these desk accessories (see Chapter 3). Leave them for now.

Chooser — You *definitely* need this, as you can find out in Chapter 5.

Connect To... — In Mac OS 8.1, this tiny program-ette brings up a simple dialog box into which you can type an Internet or Web address. When you click Connect, your iMac dials and connects to that address, launching your e-mail program or Web browser. (See Chapter 11 for more on Internet connections. This little program is for people who have direct Internet accounts, not America Online.)

Control Panels — This folder is simply a shortcut (an *alias*) to opening your real Control Panels folder. More on control panels later in this chapter.

Desktop Printers — If you own only one printer, throw this away. (See the sidebar "A shortcut for multiple-printer owners" in Chapter 5.)

Favorites — This command gives you quick access to files or folders you use a lot. See "Special folders in Mac OS 8.5 and later," later in this chapter.

Find or **Find File** or **Sherlock** — A turbocharged file-finding feature. Worth its weight in the precious metal of your choice. Just type in what you're looking for, and the iMac finds it . . . *fast*. (See the end of Chapter 4 for a complete demonstration.)

Graphing Calculator — Puts fancy moving 3-D graphs on your screen, so you can show your friends how high-tech and brilliant you've become. And if you're into math, it's actually pretty darned good at graphing little equations like $y = x - 1$.

Internet Access — This set of handy Net-related commands includes:

- ✔ **Browse the Internet** — This command launches your Web browser program, such as Netscape Navigator or Internet Explorer. And it opens to your preferred home page. (You use the Internet control panel to choose both which browser you prefer and which home page you like, as described later in this chapter.)

- ✔ **Connect To** — See "Connect To," earlier in this list.

- ✔ **Disconnect** — Hangs up your modem's phone line after you've been using the Internet. (See Chapter 11.)

- ✔ **Internet Setup Assistant** — Walk through this series of screens while your Internet access company's tech-help agent is on the phone with you, and you'll save yourself a lot of grief in establishing an Internet account for the first time. (See Chapter 11 for details.)

- ✔ **Mail** — This command launches your e-mail program. (Applies to people with direct Internet accounts, not America Online.)

Jigsaw Puzzle — Highly silly desk accessory whose Novelty-Wear-Off Quotient is about five minutes. Upon reaching the sixth minute, trash it.

Key Caps — Another desk accessory. It helps you find out which combinations of keys you're supposed to press when you want to type wacky symbols like ¢ or ¥ or © (see Chapter 6).

Network Browser — For people in an office with multiple Macs networked together. If that means you, use this program as a map of the whole network. If that doesn't mean you, throw this thing out.

Recent Documents, Recent anything — A very handy shortcut! These submenus list the last few documents, applications (programs), and *servers* (other Macs in your office) you've had open, so that you can get to them again conveniently. (If you're not on a network, you can do without Recent Servers. Open your Apple Menu Items control panel and put a zero where it says Servers; the Servers item will disappear from your menu.)

Remote Access Status — This handy Mac OS 8.5 mini-program offers Connect and Disconnect buttons to help you get on and off the Internet (assuming you've signed up for a direct Internet account, as described in Chapter 11). And while you're connected, this window shows how long you've been tying up the phone.

Scrapbook — This desk accessory is worth keeping. Using Copy and Paste, you can put pictures, sounds, movie clips, or blocks of text into it for later use. For example, after you spend three weekends designing an absolutely gorgeous logo for yourself, paste it into the Scrapbook. Thereafter, whenever you need that logo again, open the Scrapbook and copy it, so that it'll be ready to paste into your memo or package design.

SimpleSound — A mini-program that lets you record sounds (using your iMac's built-in microphone). See Chapter 19 for details.

Stickies — How did we *live* before Stickies? Sheer, purest genius. Stickies are electronic Post-It notes. That's all. Just choose New Note from the File menu, jot down what you want, and maybe pick a new pastel hue from the Color menu.

When you try to close Stickies (by choosing Quit from the File menu), you'll be asked nicely if you want the Stickies to reappear each time you turn on the iMac. Say yes, and you'll never forget another dog-grooming appointment.

The Contextual Menu Items folder

You can read about the fascinating *contextual pop-up menu* feature in Chapter 9. For now, know ye that this feature provides shortcut menus when you click things (like icons and windows) while pressing the Control key.

It's technically possible to *add more* commands to these Control-key pop-up menus, and many Web-surfing power users do. If you become one of that special breed, this folder is where you put the additional commands (in the form of special icons).

The Control Strip Modules folder

You can read about the Control Strip in "The Control Panels folder" section to follow. There, you'll learn that the Control Strip is an ever-present floating strip of tiles that offer quick access to iMac settings (such as the speaker volume). This folder is where those tiles are stored.

The Control Panels folder

Control Panels is another folder inside your System Folder. As you can read in Chapter 3, a control panel is a tiny miniprogram that changes some aspect of the iMac's behavior.

Appearance (in Mac OS 8.1) — Offers two satisfying tweaks for the interior designer in you. The Color option lets you change the highlight colors for subtle aspects of your iMac's screen display (scroll bars, "now copying" progress graphs, highlighted text, and so on). The Options option gives you a choice of two typefaces to be used in menus, among other things.

Appearance (in Mac OS 8.5) —*This* beefy Appearance control panel is not to be confused with its spindly predecessor from Mac OS 8. With *this* control panel, you can do far more than meekly change the font used in your menu; now you can change the look and feel of your iMac in much more radical ways. For example:

- **Appearance** — These options let you choose a highlighting-pen color (for use when you drag your mouse across some text) and an accent color (for scroll bars and other tinted on-screen accessories).

- **Fonts** — Click the Fonts tab to view three pop-up menus that let you change the typefaces your iMac uses for menus, labels, and lists.

  Note especially the option called "Smooth all fonts on screen." When you turn it on, the edges of your on-screen type gets softer and smoother (or *antialiased,* as the geeks would say). See the Top 10 list at the end of Chapter 5 for an illustration.

- **Desktop picture** — By clicking the Desktop "tab," you can choose a photo or pattern with which to plaster the backdrop of your screen. (See "Desktop Pictures" later in this chapter.)

✔ **Sounds** — If you click the Sound tab and choose Platinum from the pop-up menu, you get crisp, cheerful little sound effects as you do anything on your iMac, like using scroll bars, menus, icons, the Trash, windows, disks, or almost anything else that requires mouse manipulation. (Health warning: Don't turn on sounds when using your iMac at the public library, at international chess matches, or during microsurgery on a relative.)

✔ **Scroll bars** — If you've forgotten that *scroll bars* are the strips at the bottom and right edges of windows that you use to move around in a window, review Chapter 1. Anyway, the new, steroid-enhanced Appearance control panel offers a fascinating new option (on the Options tab) called Smart Scrolling. It moves both scroll-bar arrows to one end of the scroll bar, as shown here:

That option also makes the *scroll box* (the square handle you drag) larger or smaller to reflect the amount of the document that's visible in the window. That is, if the scroll bar handle is one-third the height of the scroll bar, you're seeing one-third of the document in your document window.

✔ **Themes** — After you've visited all of the various tabs (Appearance, Desktop, Fonts, Sound, and Options) to get the iMac behaving just the way you like it, you can preserve the particular combination of settings you've just established as a *Theme*.

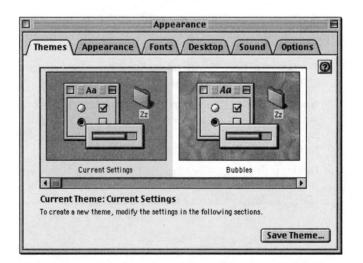

To do so, click the Themes tab, where you'll see a new entry called Current Settings. Click the Save Theme button, give your new "theme" a name, and call it a day. From now on, you can jump to your newly established theme (or any of the predefined ones) by clicking it whenever you feel the need for a change of scene.

Apple Menu Options — This little gizmo provides the submenus in your menu, so that you can (for example) open a specific control panel from the Control Panels command. It also creates, in your menu, folders that track the last bunch of documents and programs you used, which is handy.

AppleTalk — An important item *if* you're on a network. It lets you specify *how* your iMac is connected to other Macs (or laser printers); with Ethernet cables, LocalTalk wires, using the iMac's infrared transmitter, and so on. See Chapter 10 for more on hooking the iMac up to other Macs.

ATM — Adobe Type Manager. A control panel that makes certain fonts look smoother on the screen and in inkjet-printer printouts.

AutoRemounter — Useful only for connecting Macs together — in this case, a PowerBook and an iMac. (It automatically reconnects the two whenever you wake a sleeping PowerBook.) If you have neither PowerBook nor network, send it Trashward.

ColorSync, ColorSync Profile — Software that tries to make colors consistent among scanners, monitors, and color printers. If you don't print in color and don't have a scanner, out this goes.

Control Strip — All this control panel does is hide or show the *Control Strip*. Trouble is, nobody ever bothers to explain the Control Strip to the average iMac fan — but it's a terrific time-saver that's worth meeting.

The Control Strip starts out as a tiny gray tab hugging the edge of your screen, like this:

Click that little tab (and let go) to make the Control Strip stretch out to its full length, like a python sunning itself on the beach. Here's what some of the typical tiles on the Control Strip do (your assortment may be slightly different):

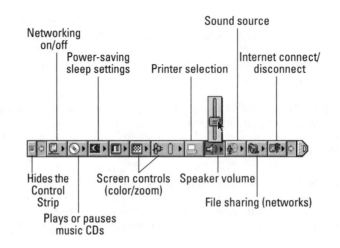

Networking on/off · Power-saving sleep settings · Printer selection · Sound source · Internet connect/disconnect · Hides the Control Strip · Screen controls (color/zoom) · Speaker volume · File sharing (networks) · Plays or pauses music CDs

Each tile, as you can see by the Speaker volume example in the picture, is a little pop-up menu; click a tile to view a menu of choices. You can muddle through life without ever using the Control Strip, of course — most of the tiles' functions are duplicated by the various gizmos in your Control Panels folder. But the Control Strip lets you adjust these settings much more conveniently.

If you click the little end tab, the Strip collapses so that *only* the tab appears, at the very edge of your screen. Another click expands it again. You can also shrink the Control Strip to any length by tugging — *dragging* — its little end tab.

Furthermore, if you press the Option key, you can drag the entire strip *up or down* the side of your screen, or across to the opposite edge. (You can't drag the Strip to the middle of the screen, however; it must hug the right or left side.) The Option key has another handy effect on the Control Strip: If you drag one of the little tiles while pressing Option, you can slide that tile horizontally to a new position.

If there's a tile you find yourself never using, feel free to get rid of it. *If you have Mac OS 8.5 or later:* While pressing the Option key, drag the tile to the Trash. *If you have Mac OS 8.1:* Open your hard drive; open your System Folder; open your Control Strip Modules folder. Trash the icon that corresponds to the one you never use.

Date & Time — Lets you set the iMac's clock. Also controls whether the time appears at the top of your screen. And if you have Mac OS 8.5 or later — and an Internet account — you can even make your iMac set its *own* clock by dialing into some high-tech atomic clock out in cyberspace somewhere. Now *that's* progress.

Desktop Pictures — (Mac OS 8.1) Lets you choose a fancier backdrop pattern for your computer — or even a full-screen picture. (See "Looks are everything" in Chapter 9 for a dramatic illustration.)

Dial Assist — Lets you create and store complicated dialing instructions for making calls with your modem. Unless you work at a company where somebody has told you otherwise, throw this away.

Editor Setup — The command center for OpenDoc, a wizzy new technology that never caught on. Toss this baby, baby.

Energy Saver — Turns the iMac off (or puts it to "sleep") after you haven't used it for, say, half an hour, to save electricity. Pretty useful, really.

Extensions Manager — Here's how it works. As the iMac is starting up, press and hold your space bar. Eventually, you'll be shown a list of almost *everything* listed in this chapter — all the control panels and extensions. By clicking their names, you can decide which of them you'd like to use during the work session that's about to begin. If you're a pack rat, for example, you could simply turn off the ones you don't need instead of throwing them away. *Great* for troubleshooting (see Chapter 16).

FaxStatus — Summons a window that shows the progress of faxes that you're sending or receiving (see Chapter 19 for more on faxing).

File Exchange — This little doodad gives your iMac two magical powers. First, if your iMac has a floppy drive or SuperDisk drive, you can insert a disk from DOS or Windows computers and see its icon appear on the desktop, just as though it's a normal Macintosh disk. (Whether your programs can open the files *on* those disks is a topic for *MORE Macs For Dummies* — but at least you'll be able to see their icons.)

Second, File Exchange performs the highly technical stunt formerly handled by its predecessor, Mac OS Easy Open (described later in this chapter). In other words, File Exchange is occasionally useful.

File Sharing — The central control for *file sharing* (making your iMac's hard-drive contents available to other people on your office's network). If your iMac isn't on an office network, toss this sucker.

File Synchronization — This fascinating doodad is, in effect, a backup program. It's designed to make the contents of one folder on your hard drive up-to-date with another folder (usually on a different disk or another computer on a network).

For example, many people keep all their important work in a Documents folder (see the upcoming sidebar "Secrets of the General Controls"). You could use File Synchronization to back up that Documents folder onto, say, a Zip disk automatically. (See Chapter 18 for more on Zip disks.)

Here's how you set it up: Launch the File Synchronization program. Indicate the two folders you'd like kept up-to-date with each other, by simply dragging them one at a time directly onto the pictures of folders in the File Synchronization program's window, like this:

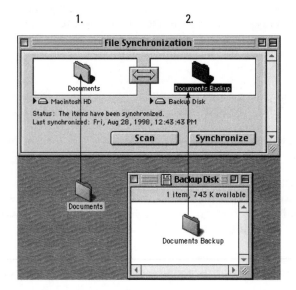

From now on, whenever you open this control panel and click Synchronize, the iMac analyzes each folder and makes them match, copying the most recent files to each, as necessary.

I realize that's a lot of ink to describe one little control panel. But the day your hard drive croaks and only your backup Zip disk saves you from aging 10 years on the spot, you'll thank me.

General Controls — A useful control panel. Sets your cursor-blinking speed, whether you want System Folder Protection turned on (it prevents marauding preteens from dragging anything out of your System Folder), and so on. And have you ever noticed how, after a system crash and you turn the iMac on again, a message scolds you for not having shut down the machine correctly (as though it's *your* fault)? Turn off the "Warn me if computer was shut down improperly" checkbox if you'd prefer the iMac not to rub it in your face.

Infrared — The front panel of your iMac contains a dark red plastic transmitter. It makes possible a glitzy feature: Aim two such transmitters at each other, and you can send files back and forth over an invisible, through-the-air network. This little control panel lets you choose which of two through-the-air languages will be spoken (the unhelpfully named *IRTalk* and *IrDA*). See Chapter 10 for instructions.

Secrets of the General Controls

For many people, the purchase of an iMac is a primal attempt to get their lives, so full of traffic and turbulent relationships and scraps of paper, into some kind of order.

Little do they know what awaits them on the typical iMac: Their important documents get every bit as lost as their paper-based counterparts once did. Even the great Mac gurus of our time have, at one time or another, saved some document — and then found themselves unable to find it again because it got arbitrarily stashed in some hidden folder somewhere.

Enter the Documents folder — one of the features you can turn on in the General Controls panel. See its icon in the picture below? As you create different documents, the iMac housekeeps for you by storing them *all* in this folder automatically. Every time you use a program's Open or Save command, you're automatically shown the Documents folder's contents.

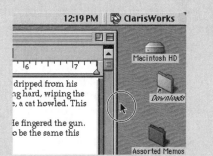

In theory, you'll never lose anything again; everything you do will always be in one place. (That feature makes backing up your work simple, too; you now have only one folder to copy to a different disk.)

The other great feature of General Controls is what I call self-hiding programs. To explain, let me show you what life is like on a regular iMac:

There's actually a significant problem with this setup. A beginner — and we were all beginners once — might, in reaching for the scroll bar, accidentally click outside the word processor window, as shown above. Immediately, the desktop (Finder) jumps to the front, showing files and folders, and the word processor window gets shoved to the back, apparently vanishing, causing (in the beginner) distress, unhappiness, and occasionally hair loss.

Now then, suppose you open General Controls and turn *off* the "Show Desktop when in background" option. When you open a document *now*, the world of the Finder (icons, windows) *disappears,* as shown below. *Now,* if you click outside the word processor window, absolutely nothing happens. In fact, you *can't* return to the desktop without choosing Finder from the Application menu in the upper-right corner of your screen.

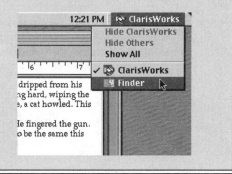

Internet — Shortly after you start hooking up to the Internet (see Chapter 11), you'll discover why only 35 percent of Americans are online: There are too many technical codes to type in when setting up an online account. In *each one* of your Internet programs (your Web browser, your e-mail program, and so on), you have to type your name, address, e-mail address, SMTP codes, social security number, junior-high math teacher's nickname, and so on.

The Internet control panel provides a central place to type in every conceivable shred of Internet-related information — right down to the signature at the bottom of your e-mails —*once*. Thereafter, each of your Internet-related programs can refer to *that* information (instead of making you retype it).

For example, in Netscape Navigator (see Chapter 12), choose Preferences from the Edit menu. Click the Identity icon, and you'll see the "Use Internet Config" check box. (The name of that check box means "Use the info I typed into the Internet control panel," in case you were wondering.) Netscape Navigator then fills in all the necessary blanks for you, based on your Internet control panel information.

Keyboard — Use this control panel to change how a key behaves when you keep it pressed. Does a held-down key start repeating like thisssssssssss? And how fast?

Many first-time iMac users fare better if they turn the repeating-key feature off. That way, if a book happens to lean on the spacebar while you're on the phone for 20 minutes, you won't hang up to find 536 pages of blank space in the letter you were working on.

This control panel also lets you change your keyboard's personality, making it type the correct funny symbols corresponding to Swedish, Italian, Dutch, and any of 18 other languages. People who can fluently speak 21 languages find this a handy feature, although they annoy the heck out of the rest of us.

If you couldn't care less about repeating-key rates or ünûsúål symbøls, throw this one away.

Launcher — What the Launcher *is:* a control panel, just like the others described in this chapter. What it *does* is display a handy, in-your-face window containing jumbo icons for the programs and files you intend to use the most often. For details, see "All about big fat Launcher buttons" in Chapter 4.

Launcher
Applications	Documents	Service & Support
Apple Backup	ClarisWorks	Mouse Practice	SimpleText	Word 5.1

Location Manager — Using this complex control panel, you can change a slew of settings — the time zone, local Internet access phone number, speaker volume, and so on — with a single click of the mouse. (This is all primarily useful for laptop owners. You can probably toss it.)

Mac OS Easy Open — If there's one thing that frustrates novices and old iMac salts alike, it's seeing that infernal "Application not found" message when you double-click an icon. With this control panel installed, when you double-click an icon, you don't get an error message — you get a dialog box that lists the programs you own that *can* open the mystery file.

MacLinkPlus Setup — Designed primarily to open Windows-computer files when you double-click them, translating them into a Macintosh format. If you don't work with files from a DOS computer, out this goes, along with everything else in your System Folder called MacLink.

Map — This control panel is primarily useful for people who do business with different geographical locations. You type a major city's name and click Find, and the Map shows you where that city is. It also tells you how far away it is, and what the time difference is. (Want to see Apple's sense of humor at work? Type *MID* and press Return . . .)

Memory — As the French say, *Ne trashez pas!* You'll need this one. Details on memory, and Memory, in Chapter 15.

Modem — This simple control panel is where you specify the exact brand and model of the modem your iMac has. (**_Hint:_** It should say "iMac Internal 56K.") Pick the wrong one, and your ability to explore the Internet, send faxes, and attain Nirvana will be extremely limited.

Monitors & Sound — Use this control panel to switch between different color settings for your monitor (such as colors, grays, or black-and-white); different *geometries* (if your iMac screen display is shrinking or lopsided); and different *resolutions* (degrees of magnification for the whole screen).

The Alerts portion of this control panel lets you choose which irritating sound effect you want to squawk at you when you make a mistake. And the Sound portion lets you specify what you want the iMac to listen to when recording or playing sounds: a microphone (if you have one), your built-in CD-ROM drive, and so on. (The Sound panel also lets you turn off the 3-D stereo-enhancing feature called SRS, but there's absolutely no reason to do so.)

Mouse — Try this: Move the mouse very slowly across three inches of desk space. The arrow moves three inches. But now *jerk* the mouse across the same three inches. Now the cursor flies across your entire monitor! The Mouse control panel lets you adjust how much of this speed-exaggeration you'll get when you move the mouse. It also lets you decide how fast two clicks must be to count as a double-click.

Numbers — Lets you change the way the iMac punctuates numbers. For example, the French use periods in large numbers instead of commas. You'd say, "Bonjour! You owe moi $1.000.000, Monsieur." If you're satisfied with the comma way of doing things, throw this away.

PC Exchange — Lets you shove Windows-computer disks into your iMac (if you've added an add-on disk drive). If you only work with Macs, and don't anticipate swapping floppy (or Zip) disks with your IBM buddies, send this baby Trashward.

QuickTime Settings — This control panel lets you adjust various settings pertaining to playing music CDs and CD-ROMs. You'll never need any of them except one: If you turn off the AutoPlay CD-ROM option, your iMac is protected against the nasty AutoStart virus (see Chapter 15).

RAM Doubler — A program (didn't come with the iMac; you bought it) that makes your iMac think it has much more memory than it actually does. Details in Chapter 15.

Remote Access — This control panel is where you specify your Internet name, password, and local phone number. No Internet account? Toss it.

Sharing Setup, Users & Groups — More control panels used only for networking. Throw them away unless you want to connect to other Macs over the office network.

Speech or **Speech Setup** — Extremely cool for at least 15 minutes. Lets your iMac read, out loud, what you have typed. Details in Chapter 19.

Speed Doubler — A program purchased by you or somebody you love that speeds up your iMac in a few subtle ways: Empties the Trash faster, makes copies faster, and so on.

Startup Disk — You have one hard drive inside the iMac. Some people purchase another one, or a removable-cartridge thing like a Zip drive, that plugs into the side. Startup Disk lets you choose *which* hard drive's System Folder you want to run the show when you next turn on the computer. If the hard drive in your iMac is your only hard drive, toss Startup Disk.

TCP/IP — If you've signed up for an Internet account (see Chapter 11), this control panel stores the complex numbers that identify the company you've signed up with.

Text — Mr. Pointless. Would let you choose a language software kit other than English for your computer — if you had any installed. You don't. Throw this away.

Web Sharing — This control panel is primarily of interest to networked companies; it lets you make a particular folder on your hard drive available to anyone who dials into your iMac. If you don't have an office guru who explains how to use this, throw it away.

The Extensions folder

An *extension* is a little program that runs automatically when you turn on the iMac. It usually adds some little feature to your iMac that you want available at all times: a screen saver, for example, that automatically blanks your screen after a few minutes of inactivity on your part.

Extensions aren't the only thing in your Extensions folder, however — ooooh, no; that would be far too logical. The Extensions folder also contains something called *shared libraries,* which are little blobs of computer instructions that your various programs call on when necessary. (Any file ending with *Lib* is one of these shared libraries. So don't go to a party and pronounce it "Open Transport Libb." It's "lybe," short for *library.*) Anyway, shared libraries are far less annoying than actual extensions, which make your iMac take longer to start up, use up memory, and contribute to freezes and crashes. Shared libraries don't do any of that.

AOL Link, AOL Scheduler — The Link one is required if you want to use America Online. The Scheduler one isn't as critical; it's useful only if you want your iMac to dial America Online automatically in the middle of the night, unattended.

Appearance Extension — (Mac OS 8.1) Performs the magic dictated by the Appearance control panel, described in the Control Panels section of this chapter. Whatever you do, don't move this extension! Your iMac won't start up without it.

Apple CD-ROM or **Apple CD/DVD Driver, Foreign File Access, anything-Access** — Why does Apple's CD-ROM player need so many little extensions? Heaven knows. All I know is that you need these for playing CD-ROMs on your iMac.

Apple Guide, anything-Guide — Remember, from Chapter 1, the electronic help desk we call the Help menu? These files contain all the Help screens.

Apple Modem Tool, anything-Tool — These are all plug-in items for use with modem software.

AppleScript, Finder Scripting Extension, anything-Script — All components of a very technical feature intended for the kind of person who wouldn't be caught dead reading this book. However, even if you don't use these yourself, some of the iMac's best features depend on these extensions, so leave them in place.

AppleShare, File Sharing Extension, Network Extension, Network — Still more doodads for networking Macs together. If you're not on a network, out they go.

Application Switcher — This extension is responsible for the Amazing Tear-Off Applications Palette of Mac OS 8.5 and later, as described in Chapter 9. It also lets you switch from one open program to the next by pressing ⌘-Tab. Try it — you'll like it!

Clipping Extension — This is the software responsible for Macintosh Drag & Drop, the word processing shortcut described in Chapter 4's "Puff, the Magic Drag-N-Drop" section.

Color Picker — The Color Picker is that dialog box that shows a big color wheel, allowing you to choose a particular color. It appears, for example, when you're in the Edit menu's Preferences command and you click a label color to change it. This extension adds a More Choices button to that dialog box, allowing you to choose some super-techie options. Trash it.

ColorSync — See "ColorSync" in the Control Panels listing.

Contextual Menu Extension — Brings you the magical pop-up menus that appear when you hold down the Control key and click something. See Chapter 9 for the gory details.

Control Strip Extension — Starting in Mac OS 8.5, the Control Strip (described earlier in this chapter) is easy to modify. You can drag new tiles directly onto it (to install them) or Option-drag them to the Trash (to uninstall them). This extension makes it all possible.

Default Calibrator — This extension adjusts your Apple monitor at startup to ensure that it's colorifically perfect. If, by some fluke, you don't work in the professional color printing industry, toss this one.

Desktop Printing anything — For people whose Macs are attached to *multiple* printers (perhaps in a big office, for example). Adds printer icons to your desktop, so that you can decide which one should print your latest masterpiece (see Chapter 5 for details). If you have but one printer, throw *all* of this out and have a happy life.

DNSPlugin — No joke: Apple describes this as an extension that "allows your computer to receive listings of network objects from DNS directory services." Turns out there's no such thing. Throw this away.

DrawSprocketLib — An extension used by certain games, such as Nanosaur (which comes with the iMac).

EM Extension — Another piece of Extensions Manager, described under "The Control Panels folder," earlier in this chapter.

Energy Saver extension — Does the actual starting up and shutting down you've specified in the Energy Saver control panel (see "Energy Saver," earlier in this chapter).

Epson Stylus — The software for an Epson inkjet printer. (If you don't have one, you don't need this software.) (More on printers in Chapter 5.)

Ethernet (built-in) extension — Required to connect to an office network or laser printer via Ethernet (see Chapter 10).

FaxPrint, FAXstf PPC Shared Library, FaxMonitor — Software that lets your iMac send and receive faxes.

File Sync Extension — Required for the File Synchronization control panel, described earlier in this chapter.

Find, FindByContent, FBC Indexing Scheduler — These extensions let you search for words *inside* your files. For details, read the sidebar "Mac OS 8.5 and later: Super-Find!" in Chapter 4.

Folder Actions — For programmers. Out it goes.

iMac ATI driver, ATI-anything — Your iMac comes with fancy accelerated graphics circuitry that lets the computer draw pictures on the screen faster. These files are the required software. Leave 'em be.

iMac Internal Modem Extension — Your iMac's built-in modem requires this software.

Indeo Video, Intel Raw Video — If you use Microsoft Internet Explorer (see Chapter 12), these extensions got dumped into your System Folder. They let your iMac see movies (which, presumably, you find on the Web) that have been prepared in Windows format (AVI).

Internet Access — If you have Mac OS 8.1, you need this shared library to dial into the Internet. Otherwise, not.

Internet Config Extension — This extension goes with the Internet control panel, described earlier in this chapter. (It also goes with the Internet control panel's predecessor, called Internet Config.)

Iomega driver — Lets your iMac work with Zip drives. If you didn't buy one, out this goes.

IrDALib, IrLanScannerPPC, IR-anything — Lets your iMac beam files to other iMacs (or PowerBook laptops) through the air. Details in Chapter 10.

jgdw.ppc — Installed by Microsoft Internet Explorer. I haven't the faintest idea what it does.

Kodak Precision CP-anything — A color-management system a lot like ColorSync, described earlier. Dumped into your System Folder by PageMaker, CorelDraw, Canvas, and other graphics programs.

Location Manager-anything — See "Location Manager," earlier in this chapter.

MacinTalk anything — Lets your iMac *speak*. See Chapter 19.

Microsoft-anything — You're stuck with all of this crud if you hope to make Microsoft programs work.

Modem Scripts — Before you go online (either with America Online or an Internet account), you're supposed to tell the iMac what kind of modem you own. You choose your model from a really long list. For every corresponding modem name, a file sits here in your Modem Scripts folder.

Take a minute right now to *throw away* every modem-model file except the one you actually own: "iMac Internal 56K." You'll save RAM, hard-disk space, and time when you launch your modem programs.

MRJ Libraries — This folder (which stands for Macintosh Runtime for Java) contains the software necessary for your iMac to run Java programs — that is, animated ads and little games that you find on Web pages as you surf the Internet. You be the judge.

OpenDoc Libraries — Throw this out; OpenDoc is dead.

Open TPT anything — This super-techie collection of System Folder lint (known as Open Transport technology) makes your iMac capable of connecting to the Internet, a network, or America Online.

Printer Descriptions — This folder contains one little file for each individual printer model. Open this folder and discard the icons for any printers you don't use.

PrintMonitor — The genie that grants the miracle of *background printing*, described in Chapter 5.

QTVR anything, QuickTime VR — *QuickTime VR* is a special kind of digital photo. If you drag your cursor around in the picture, you change the camera angle, so that you can look all around you. You don't run across VR (virtual-reality) "movies" very often — but when you do, these doodads make them possible.

QuickDraw 3D-anything — QD3D stands for *QuickDraw 3D*. This assortment of a half-dozen extensions lets your iMac show, create, and accelerate 3D graphics. These extensions are required primarily for a few games — such as Nanosaur (see Chapter 6), one of the games you got with your iMac.

QuickTime-anything — You need these little jobbers if you plan to use (or are using) digital movies on the iMac. You know, little flicks that play inside a Triscuit-sized window right on your screen, complete with sound (see Chapter 19). The QuickTime extension (and accompanying files) make those movies possible; many CD-ROM discs require these items.

Serial (Built-in) — Still more Open Transport crud (see "Open TPT anything").

Shared Library anything — You need these to manage your *shared libraries,* described at the beginning of this section.

Shortcuts — Another piece of Macintosh Guide (see "Apple Guide" at the beginning of this extensions listing).

SLPPlugin — Exactly like the delightful DNSPlugin described earlier in this section.

SOMobjects for Mac OS — Yet another shared library, as discussed at the beginning of this section. This one is required to make your *contextual menus* work (see Chapter 9).

Sound Manager — For sound recording and playback. Leave it for now.

Speech Manager, Voices — For speech recognition and text-reading-out-loud, as described in Chapter 19. If you aren't regularly talking or listening to your iMac — besides just arguing with it — out these go.

STF Toolbox, STFInit — More stuff for your built-in fax modem.

System AV — Required by the Monitors & Sound control panel, described earlier in this chapter.

Text Encoding Converter — All computers understand A through Z, but the wackier symbols (such as curly quotes, foreign diacritical markings, and so on) are internally summoned differently on each type of computer. Ever get an e-mail in which all the apostrophes appear as capital U's? Or in which all the quote marks have turned into weird boxes? Now you know the problem.

The Text Encoding Converter is designed to translate other computers' wacky alphabet references into the iMac's system, so that fewer nutty boxes and U's show up in your e-mail.

Time Synchronizer — The Date & Time control panel (in Mac OS 8.5 and later) can set your iMac's clock *automatically* by dialing into the Internet. This extension makes that feature possible.

UDF Volume Access — Lets your iMac talk to *DVD discs* (which are like CDs, but hold 14 times as much). If you remember paying $400 to have a DVD drive added to your iMac, keep this; otherwise not. ("Volume," in this case, doesn't mean "loudness;" it refers to a *disk*.)

XTND Power Enabler — Given unto you by AppleWorks or ClarisWorks (see Chapter 6). It lets that program open (and create) documents from rival word processors.

WorldScript Power Adapter — Makes word processing slightly faster. Leave it.

The Fonts folder

This folder contains your fonts. (Did you guess?) See Chapter 5 for a detailed explanation of all this junk.

The Launcher Items folder

The purpose of this folder is to let you specify what jumbo icons you want to appear in your Launcher window, the iMac's one-click program-launching bay. See "Launcher" earlier in this chapter.

The Preferences folder

The Preferences folder is filled with information, and *none* of it's for you.

Every single file in this folder was put there by *another* piece of software. Let's say you change a setting in your word processor: You always want it to make your typing double-spaced, for example. Well, where do you suppose the computer stores your new setting? It jots it down in a *preferences file*. And this prefs file lives — wild guess — in the Preferences folder.

Prefs files are famous for frustrating beginners. Because they're for use by your programs, and not by you, virtually every one of them gives you a rude error message if you try to double-click it. You simply can't open a Prefs file; only your software can.

You really can only do one good thing with the Preferences files: throw them away. That is, throw away any that belong to programs you no longer use.

Special folders in Mac OS 8.5 and later

In its noble (but hopeless) quest to neaten up your System Folder, Apple continues to introduce new holding-tank folders. In Mac OS 8.5, for example, these additional System Folder folders debuted:

- **The Application Support folder:** If the various Mac software companies wind up complying with Apple's request, they'll dump all their programs' associated crud — dictionary files, file-conversion stuff, and so on — into this folder.

- **ColorSync Profiles:** As you can read earlier in this chapter, ColorSync is a software scheme for ensuring that scanners, screens, and color printers all agree on what, for example, "red" is. This folder contains individual color-description lists for every model of Apple scanner, monitor, and printer. If color consistency is important to you, use the ColorSync control panel to specify which models you own.

- **The Favorites folder:** "Favorites" means "icons I'd like quick access to from now on." To create a Favorite, click it and choose Add to Favorites from the File menu. It instantly appears in your Favorites command (in the menu), as shown here:

1. Choose Add to Favorites . . .

2. . . . and from now on, your favorite icons are available from the Apple menu.

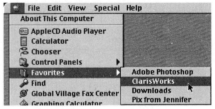

Behind the scenes, the iMac has simply placed an *alias* of that icon into the Favorites folder. (See Chapter 9 for a description of aliases.) In other words, to remove something from the Favorites menu, remove it from this folder.

- **The Help folder:** Apple puts its own help files (which create what you see when you use the Apple Guide feature, for example) into this folder. Other software companies may follow suit.

✔ **The Internet Search Sites folder:** Mac OS 8.5's Find command is
   capable of searching the entire, vast Internet, not just your puny little
   hard drive. The files in this folder each teach the Find command how to
   talk to a different World Wide Web search page. (See Chapter 4 for more
   on using Find, and Chapter 12 for more on Web search pages.)

   ✔ **The Scripts Folder:** A place for programmers to stash their stuff.

Loose in the System Folder

Clipboard — Every time you use the Cut or Copy command in a program,
the iMac, according to what you read earlier, socks the selected material
away on an invisible Clipboard. Well, guess what: it's not actually invisible.
Technically speaking, that info you copied has to be put *somewhere*. This is
where: in the Clipboard file.

Little-known fact: You can double-click the Clipboard file to open a window
that shows the last thing you cut or copied. (Another little-known fact: The
last swallow of a can of soda is 69 percent saliva.)

Extensions (Disabled) — This explanation is tricky and techie, but I'll do my
best. Remember Extensions Manager, described under "The Control Panels
folder" earlier in this chapter? It lets you turn extensions or control panels
on and off. When you click some extension's name to switch it off for the
day, Extensions Manager doesn't *delete* that extension; behind the scenes,
it just *moves* it into this Extensions (Disabled) folder. When the iMac next
starts up, it only "loads" the extensions that are in the actual Extensions
folder.

To turn that particular extension on again, you can, of course, use Extensions Manager again — but you could also, in a pinch, move the file manually back into the regular Extensions folder. (Rival programs, like Conflict
Catcher, work the same way.)

And if you turn off a *control panel,* sure enough, it winds up in a folder called
Control Panels (Disabled).

Finder — This is the most important program on your iMac. Without it, a
System Folder is just a folder, and your iMac won't even turn on. The Finder
file is responsible for creating your basic desktop: the Trash, your disk icon,
windows, and so on.

System — This is *also* the most important file on your iMac. It contains all
kinds of other info necessary for the computer to run: reams and reams of
instructions for the computer's own use. Without a System file, the iMac
won't even turn on, either.

Desktop Printers — The icons for your various printers (*if* you have more than one). See the sidebar called "A shortcut for multiple-printer owners" in Chapter 5.

Scrapbook file, Note Pad file — When you paste something into the Scrapbook or Note Pad desk accessories, behind the scenes, the iMac actually stores it in these files.

Mac OS ROM — Whatever you do, don't fold, move, spindle, or mutilate this one. Throw it away, and you've got yourself a see-through, $1,300 doorstop. (Fortunately, a *clean install,* described in Chapter 16, can bring a thus-crippled iMac back to life.)

Startup Items, Shutdown Items — Fascinating, Captain. Anything you put into the Startup Items folder (a program, a document, a sound, a folder) gets opened with a mysterious automatic double-click whenever you turn on the iMac. If you don't do anything but word process, for example, drag the icon of your word processor into this folder. Thereafter, every time you power up for the day, your word processing program will be on the screen awaiting your brilliance.

The Shutdown Items folder is the same deal, except anything in *here* gets run automatically when you *shut down* the computer. Automatic-backup programs come to mind. A sound that says "Th-th-th-th-th-that's all, folks!" also comes to mind.

Part III
Toward a New, Nerdier You

The 5th Wave   By Rich Tennant

©RICHTENNANT

"Come here, quick! I've got a new iMac trick!"

In this part . . .

There comes a time in everyone's life when just turning the computer on and off no longer brings the surge of excitement it once did. Now it's time to maneuver this baby to the Autobahn, open 'er up, and see what she can do.

That's why the next two chapters move beyond the desperate, what-am-I-doing basics and show you some of the more rarified talents of your machine.

Chapter 9

Putting the Mouse to the Metal

• •

In This Chapter

▶ Forbidden secrets of the Option key

▶ Vandalizing your own iMac, without spray paint or a sledge hammer

▶ Wizzy window stunts of Mac OS 8.5

• •

*T*his chapter is about honing your basic skills. It's about becoming more efficient in the way you work — shortcuts, hidden secrets, and slick tricks to astonish your friends. And it's about turning the basic computer that *millions* of people have into one that's unmistakably yours.

The Efficiency Nut's Guide to the Option Key

Yeah, yeah, everybody knows that you can close a window by clicking its close box. But you didn't fork over good money for this book to learn something that's on page 1 of the iMac manual (if, that is, there *were* an iMac manual).

No, these tips are much choicer. They show you how to unlock the power of that most overlooked of keys, the Option key. It's been placed closer to you than any letter key on the keyboard — and that's no accident.

Closing all windows at once

Suppose you've opened a gaggle of folders and their windows are lying open all over the screen. And suppose that the niggling neatness ethic instilled in you by your mother compels you to clean up a bit.

You could, of course, click the close box of each window, one at a time. But it's far faster to click only *one* window's close box while pressing the Option key. Bam, bam, bam — they all close automatically, one after another.

The silence of the Trash

Let's review: You drag an icon on top of the Trash can and the icon disappears. The Trash can icon overflows. You smile gently at the zaniness of it all. Then you choose Empty Trash from the Special menu, and a little message appears on the screen, saying something like this.

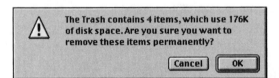

The Trash contains 4 items, which use 176K of disk space. Are you sure you want to remove these items permanently?

Cancel | OK

That's all very well and good, but busy people concerned with increasing their productivity may not always have time for such trivial information. Therefore, if you want to dump the trash, but you *don't* want that message to appear, press Mr. Option Key while you choose Empty Trash. (Option is also the key for emptying the trash when the iMac tells you something is "locked" in the Trash can.)

'Smatterafact, you can shut up the Trash's warning permanently, if you're so inclined. Click the Trash can. From the File menu, choose Get Info. Turn off "Warn before emptying." What an improvement!

Multitasking methods

As you discovered early on, the iMac lets you run more than one program simultaneously. (Remember when you tried some tricks with both the Note Pad and the Calculator open on the screen at once?) You can switch from one program to another by choosing the program's name from the Application menu at the top right of your screen, marked by the icon of whichever program is currently in front.

We haven't yet examined the other commands in this menu, such as Hide Others and Show All. These commands help keep your screen neat and clean. For example, suppose you're trying to use the Calculator, but so many other programs are running that your eyes cross.

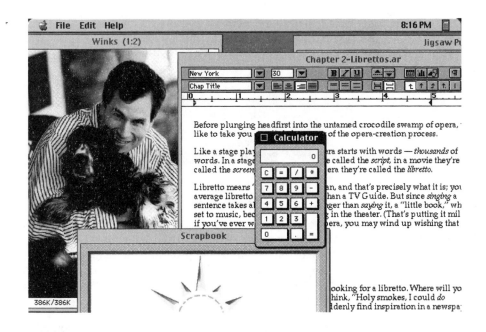

By choosing Hide Others from the Application menu, all windows that belong to other programs disappear, leaving the frontmost window all by itself.

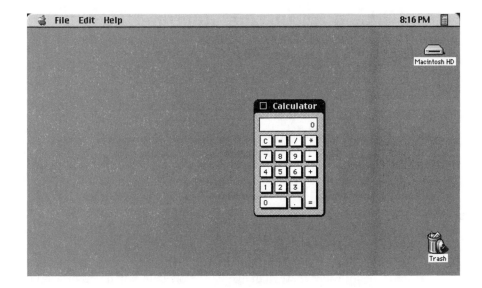

The other programs *are still running,* and they *do* still exist. But their windows are now hidden. You can verify this by checking the Application menu, where you'll see that their icons appear slightly dimmed.

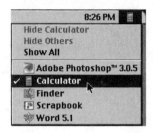

So how does the Option key play into all this? When you switch from one program to another, you can make the program you're *leaving* hide itself automatically. Just press Option while choosing the new program's name (or clicking in its window). That way, you always keep nonessential programs hidden.

And if you've got Mac OS 8.5, you can even press Option as you click different tiles on your *Application Switcher palette* (described at the end of this chapter). Once again, the program you were just *in* gets hidden as you switch to the next program.

Making an instant document copy

In most graphics programs, the Option key has a profound effect on a selected graphic item: It peels off a copy of the selected graphic as you drag the mouse. For example, the left eye (right) is selected and then Option-dragged to the right.

You can accomplish essentially the same thing in the Finder, making duplicates of your files instead of eyeballs. Normally, when you drag an icon from one folder to another *on the same disk,* of course, you simply *move* that icon. But if you press Option while dragging an icon to a new folder (or to the desktop — the gray background), the iMac places a *copy* of the file in the new folder and leaves the original where it was, as shown here.

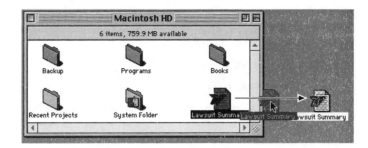

Buried Treasures

Did you enjoy those obscure, Option key tricks? Then you'll really love these equally scintillating techniques, not one of which requires the Option key.

Make an alias of a file

The File menu has a command called Make Alias. Although you might expect this command to generate names like One-Eyed Jake or "Teeth" McGuire, the term *alias* in the Macintosh world represents something slightly different — a duplicate of a file's *icon* (but not a duplicate of the file itself). You can identify the alias icon because its name is in italics, as shown here. (In Mac OS 8.5, a tiny arrow icon appears on the alias, too.)

What's neat about aliases is that, when you double-click an alias icon, the iMac opens the *original* file. If you're a true '90s kinda person, you might think of the alias as a beeper — when you call the *alias*, the *actual* file responds.

So who on earth would need a feature like this? Well, there's more to the story. An alias, for one thing, requires only a tiny amount of disk space (a couple of K) — so it's not the same as making an actual copy of the full-sized, original file. (And you can make as many aliases of a file as you want.) Therefore, making an alias of something you use frequently is an excellent time-saver — it keeps the alias icon readily accessible, even if the real file is buried somewhere four folders deep.

Another very common trick: Place an alias of a program or a document into your ✿ menu, where you don't have to open *any* folders to get at it.

Here's the drill:

1. **Click the real icon once.**
2. **From the File menu, choose Make Alias.**
3. **Open your System Folder.**
4. **Drag the alias into the folder called Apple Menu Items (within the System Folder).**

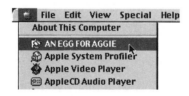

5. **Now look in your menu.**

Sure enough — there's your file! Choose it from the menu to open the original file.

And yet, because you used an alias, the *real* file can be anywhere on your hard disk or on a different disk. You can move the real file from folder to folder or even rename it, and the alias still opens it correctly.

Trash, aliases, and a word of caution

If you trash an alias, you're deleting only the alias. The original file is still on your disk. If you delete the *original* file, however, the alias icons will remain uselessly on your disk, rebels without a cause, babies without a mother, days without sunshine. When you double-click an alias whose original file is gone, you'll just get an error message. (In Mac OS 8.5, the error message offers you the chance to attach this orphaned alias to a *different* "real" file — but the original file is still gone forever.)

Likewise, if you copy your inauguration speech file's *alias* to a floppy disk, thinking that you'll just print it out when you get to Washington, think again. You've just copied the alias, but you *don't* actually have any text. That's all in the original file, still at home on your hard disk.

Have it your way — at Icon King

You don't have to accept those boring old icons for files, programs, and folders. If you want anything done around the iMac, heaven knows, you've got to do it yourself:

1. **Go into AppleWorks/ClarisWorks (the painting window) and make a funny little picture.**

   And I mean *little* — remember, you're drawing a replacement icon for some hapless file. Like this guy here, for example.

2. **Copy your creation to the Clipboard.**

3. **Go to the Finder and click the file whose icon you want to replace (as shown here at left).**

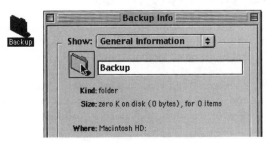

4. **From the File menu, choose Get Info, so that the Get Info box appears (previous picture, right).**

5. **See the folder icon in the upper left? Click that sucker — and then paste away!**

From now on, that little picture is the new icon for the file (or folder or disk). To restore the original icon, repeat the Get Info business, but this time, after you click the icon, press the Delete key.

Just say no

There's a wonderful keyboard shortcut that means *no* in iMac language. It could mean *No, I changed my mind about printing* (or copying or launching a program); *stop right now.* It could mean *No, I didn't mean to bring up this dialog box; make it go away.* Or: *No, I don't want to broadcast my personal diary over worldwide e-mail!* Best of all, it can mean *Stop asking for that CD! I've already taken it out! Be gone!*

And that magic keystroke is ⌘-period (.).

When you begin to print your Transcripts of Congress, 1952–1998, and you discover — after only two pages have printed — that you accidentally spelled it "Transcripts of Congrotesque" on every page, ⌘-period will prevent the remaining 14 million pages from printing. Because the iMac has probably already sent the next couple of pages to the printer, the response won't be immediate — but it will be light-years quicker than waiting for Congress.

Or let's say you double-click an icon by mistake. If you press ⌘-period right away, you can halt the launching and return to the Finder. And if the iMac keeps saying, "Please insert the disk: Purple Puppychow" (or whatever your CD, floppy, or SuperDisk was called), you can tell it to shut up by doing that ⌘-period thing over and over again until the iMac settles down with a whimper. Show it who's boss.

Looks are everything

In the earliest days of computer technology, you could make a few feeble attempts at changing the way your Mac looked. You could, for example, make Teddy Bears your desktop pattern.

But the iMac says, "Teddy Bears? — *Hah!*" Using the Desktop Pictures control panel in Mac OS 8.1 or the Appearance control panel in Mac OS 8.5, you can fill your desktop with not just a repeating pattern, but a *full-screen* picture file!

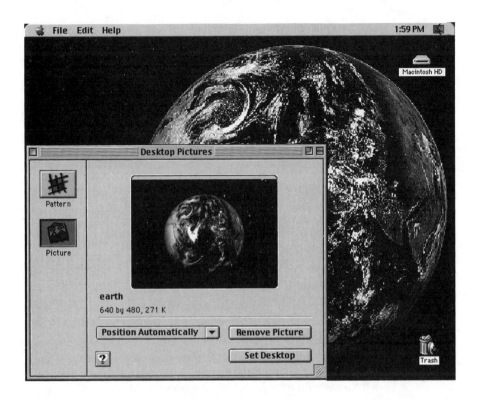

To do so in Mac OS 8.5, open the Appearance control panel, click the Desktop tab, and click the Select Picture button. To do it in Mac OS 8.1, open the Desktop Pictures control panel, click the button that says Picture, and click the Select Picture button.

Either way, you're now asked to locate the graphic file you want to use as a backdrop. As for *getting* such a picture file, well, that's pretty much up to you. But America Online and the Internet are *teeming* with great pictures, from Planet Earth to Bo Derek. It's also easy enough to make your own, using (a) AppleWorks or Photoshop, (b) a digital camera like those described in Chapter 18, or (c) a scanner, also described in Chapter 18.

Handy desktop featurettes

The fun and profit of the Mac operating system goes beyond pure windows and pure looks. A few of the features are actually *useful*. For example:

✔ **Spring-loaded folders:** For years, people wanting to move an icon into a folder that's inside a folder that's inside *another* folder had to cancel all their meetings for the day and lock the door. They'd have to open the first folder into a window; open the folder inside it; drag the icon into place; and then close all the windows they've opened in the process.

On the iMac, however, you can simply drag an icon onto a folder (below, left) — *don't let go!* — and it will open *automatically* into a window (below, right).

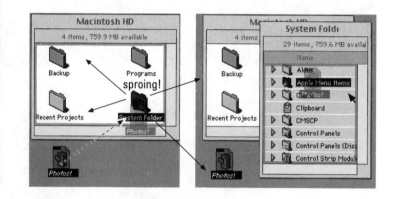

Now you can drag that icon on top of the *next* folder, and it, too, will spring open — *don't let go!* — so that you can drop it on its final, target folder destination.

Now let go. All the windows that opened on your journey snap shut automatically. Using this technique, you can actually place an icon into a folder within a folder within a folder — with a single drag.

✔ **Simple Finder:** This option is for people who sink into trembling hysteria by the presence of too many menus. It gives you (or children or first-timers) a streamlined, simpler Finder with menus greatly shortened to bare technophobe-friendly essentials, like Empty Trash and Shut Down. (No aliases, labels, sleep, or other extraneous commands.)

To try out this Simple Mac view, choose the Preferences command from the Edit menu; in the dialog box that appears, turn on Simple Finder. (Turn it off again the same way.)

Colorizing and Other Acts of Vandalism

The great thing about a Macintosh is that it's not some stamped-out clone made in Korea. It's one of a kind — or it will be after we get through with it. These tips illustrate some of the ways you can make the iMac match your personality, sensibility, or décor.

Color-coding your icons

Here's a pretty neat colorization feature that hardly anyone uses but is still worth knowing about: color-coding. All you do is select an icon or a whole passel of them (below, left), and choose a color from a menu. The color choices are hidden in the File menu, as shown here (below, right).

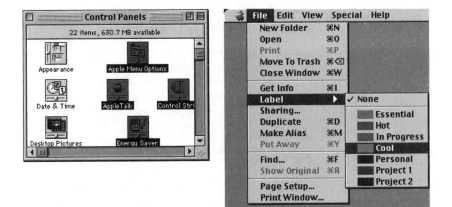

Two questions, then: (1) How do you change the colors and labels into something more useful, and (2) what's the point?

Well, most people never bother with labeling their icons. You could argue, though, that it makes life more convenient since you can use the Find command to search for a file that has a certain label. You might give one label to everything related to, say, a certain book project — *Saddam Hussein: The Sensitive Side* — and then, when it's time to back up your work, use the Find command to round up all files with the Hussein label so you can copy them all at once. (Or, when the project is over, you could happily *delete* them all at once.)

Anyway, if you *do* want to use this feature, you'll probably want to change the labels Apple suggests (Essential, Hot, In Progress, and so on) to something more useful. Here's how: From the Edit menu, choose Preferences. You'll see a list of the label choices, something like this.

To change the wording of a label (remember that you're actually changing the wording of the Label *menu*), just double-click a label and type something new. To change the color, click the color swatch; a dialog box appears where you can select a new color by clicking.

Views and window preferences

One famous aspect of the Mac is the degree to which you can tailor it to your tastes. You can make it look user-chummy and kid-friendly, or you can make it look high-tech and intimidating.

For starters, you can change the typeface used to display the names of your icons. If your vision is going — or you're trying to demonstrate the iMac to a crowd — make the font huge. If you want to make your icons as high as possible per square inch, pick a tiny, compact type style.

The steps differ depending on your iMac's system-software version:

✓ **Mac OS 8.5:** Open your Appearance control panel. Click the Fonts tab.

✓ **Mac OS 8 and 8.1:** From the Edit menu, choose Preferences.

The window that appears is the control freak's best friend. Now you should be looking at font and size controls — something like this.

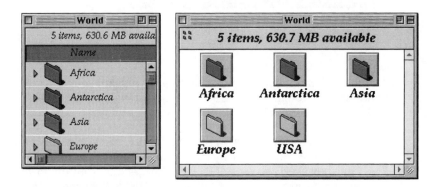

If you've got Mac OS 8.5 or later, you get three pop-up menus, including one that controls the fonts for your menus and your icons.

Go wild with these options. A couple of possibilities are shown here.

You might notice that the "look" in the second example is strikingly idiot-proof: big bold icons. If you could actually click the page of this book, you'd furthermore discover that *one* click on each of these "button" icons opens it, instead of the usual two.

That window got that way only after judicious tweaking — somebody chose the *as Buttons* command from the View menu.

Window-Mania

Your iMac doesn't run Windows; it runs the Mac OS. But that's ironic, because even though the iMac's operating system software isn't *called* Windows, it's really *good* at doing windows. How do we love them? Let us count the ways . . .

Meet Mr. Window

Here's a map of a typical iMac window.

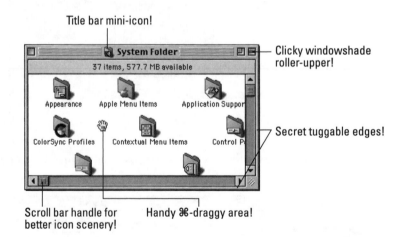

Title bar mini-icon!

Clicky windowshade roller-upper!

Secret tuggable edges!

Scroll bar handle for better icon scenery!

Handy ⌘-draggy area!

Now, since I'm not exactly sure that "Secret tuggable edges" and "Clicky windowshade roller-upper" are the actual official computer terms for these features, let me explain:

- **Secret tuggable edges:** In the olden days, you could move a window around the screen only by clicking its striped *title bar*. In Mac OS 8 and later, however, you can actually hold your mouse button down on the thickened edges of each window — and move the window by dragging.

- **Clicky windowshade roller-upper:** Click this tiny square in the upper right of any window to make the window itself *disappear* — all except the striped title bar. The effect is like the Cheshire cat in *Alice in Wonderland* disappearing completely except for his smile, except that this is actually *useful*. By judiciously clicking the clicky windowshade roller-uppers, you can hide and unhide a bunch of windows with aplomb, easily burrowing your way around without losing sight of the big picture.

✓ **Scroll bar handle for better icon scenery:** You may remember from Chapter 1 that the little square box inside a scroll bar lets you view what's hidden in a window — what's above or below what you're seeing, for example. (Man, I sure *hope* you remember — otherwise, you've been using your iMac all this time without ever writing a memo taller than three inches.)

But on the iMac, if you drag this handle slowly, you actually *see* the icons moving by, so you're much less likely to overshoot.

✓ **Handy ⌘-draggy area:** If you have Mac OS 8.5 or later, you don't need no steenkin' scroll bars. You can move around inside a window just by holding down the ⌘ key while dragging anywhere inside. In other words, you can actually shift your view in a window *diagonally* (instead of having to use one scroll bar at a time).

✓ **Title-bar mini-icon:** While we're talking about new doodads in Mac OS 8.5, check this out: See the tiny folder icon in the title bar (in the previous picture)? It's a *handle.* You can use it to drag the open window to another place, such as your backup disk or (in the case of perfectionist computer-book authors) directly to the trash.

✓ **Rearrangy columns 'n' things:** Another useful Mac OS 8.5 feature: When you're looking at a window in a list view, you can make the columns of information bigger or smaller by dragging the tiny divider lines, indicated by A in this picture.

A   B C

Name	Date Modified	Size	K
▷ 📁 Help	6/3/98	79 MB	fc
▷ 📁 Extensions	Today	70.6 MB	fc
▷ 📁 Preferences	Today	16.2 MB	fc
▷ 📁 Appearance	6/3/98	15.6 MB	fc
📁 System	Yesterday	8.9 MB	s
▷ 📁 Apple Menu Items	6/3/98	8.6 MB	fc

System Folder

35 items, 1.4 GB available

In fact, you can even *rearrange* the columns — putting the Kind column before the Size one, if that suits you — just by dragging the column headings around, such as B in the preceding picture.

Okay, while we're engaged in dead-horse beating, one more thing: You can click the tiny pyramid (marked C) to reverse the sorting order — from Z to A, for example, instead of A to Z.

Now we can all get a good night's sleep.

Poppin' fresh windows

Windows do something else funky, too: They *pop*. If you drag a window to the very bottom of the screen, something bizarre happens.

Drag to the bottom of the screen . . .

. . . and the window turns into a tab.

Sure enough, your little *window* turns into a *tab*. If you click this tab, the window shoots up like a strawberry Pop-Tart; click the tab on top again, and it crumbles back down into its former tab position. The point of this is that you can turn *several* windows that you use a lot into bottom-feeding tabs, like this:

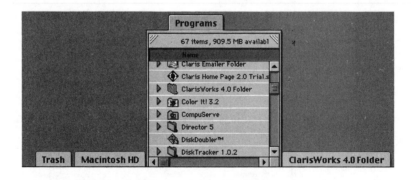

And then you can rapidly switch among them just by clicking tabs. (You don't have to collapse one popped-up windowette before popping up the next — the iMac automatically closes one when you click the next tab.) Try setting up frequently accessed windows this way, such as your Programs, Launcher, and Documents folders.

Oh, by the way: To turn a bottom-hugging tab *back* into a full-fledged window, just tug its tab way high up into the middle of the screen. No problem.

Mac OS 8.5's Program Switcher

After participating in the Information Age for about ten minutes, you notice something funny about software: It gets *replaced* all the time. Suddenly your mailbox is full of come-on postcards urging you to junk the $499 software you bought *last* year and spend $99 to replace it with a bigger, better, upgraded version *this* year.

Buying into these upgrades is optional, of course — even when the software being upgraded is the System Folder, the very software that runs your iMac. But such upgrades to the *operating system* (or OS) are worth paying attention to, because every now and then Apple comes up with something great.

Anyway, the Application Switcher is a feature you have *only* if your iMac has Mac OS 8.5 installed. Mac OS 8.5's upper-right corner is more informative than any other upper-right corner on earth. It shows you the name of the program you're using at the moment — a blessing for the easily confused.

That upper-right corner is still a menu, however, listing all the programs you're running at the moment (the *Application menu,* as it's known). But in Mac OS 8.5 and later, the Application menu has a new talent: If you drag down the Application menu past the bottom, you *tear it off* (below, left).

The menu turns into a small floating rectangle that lists your running programs (above, right); just click a program's name to switch to it.

And if you find this floating palette too wide for your tastes, click carefully just inside the right end of one of its buttons, as shown above — and drag to the left. You've just made the entire palette skinnier.

Isn't technology wonderful?

How to get Mac OS 8.5 for your original iMac

Most of the iMacs sold before November 1998 came with Mac OS 8.1; after that, most iMacs came with Mac OS 8.5 already installed.

If you bought one of the earlier iMacs, you can get a Mac OS 8.5 CD to upgrade your machine for $20 by visiting the World Wide Web page *www.apple.com/macos/up-to-date*; see Chapter 11 for instructions on getting to the Web. (This offer won't be around forever, however.)

Chapter 10

USB, Ethernet, Infrared, and Other Impressive Connections

● ●

In This Chapter

▶ Connecting your iMac to other Macs in the same office

▶ Sending files through the air

▶ Plugging in add-on USB gadgetry

● ●

*T*he iMac doesn't have a floppy drive built-in. But if the object of using floppy disks is to transfer files from your iMac to another computer, the lack of floppy drive is no big deal. In addition to sending stuff by e-mail (see Chapter 14), the iMac can connect to other machines three different ways:

 ✔ By its USB connectors.

 ✔ By an Ethernet network cable.

 ✔ Through its infrared beaming lens.

This chapter shows you how to use those methods.

USB Nimble, USB Quick

The 150 Macintosh models that came before the iMac had all different kinds of connectors: a printer jack, modem port, SCSI connector, ADB port, and so on. You were supposed to know what these jacks were for, what to plug into each one — and *when* to plug things in (that is, only when the computer is turned off). In the place of all those connectors, the iMac offers a new kind of jack called *USB*. (USB stands for Universal Serial Bus, but that won't be on the exam.)

You can react to this news in two ways. Die-hard Mac owners complain that their existing Macintosh gear won't plug into USB jacks without adapters. The rest of us rejoice that, unlike the older-style Macintosh jacks, USB offers a million advantages:

- ✔ You can plug and unplug USB gadgets from your iMac without turning off the computer first. (If you try that on a regular Mac's keyboard or SCSI jacks, you could turn your $3,000 computer into a $3 garage-sale item.)

- ✔ You don't have to know which jack gets which kind of gadget (printers, floppy drives, modems, joysticks, scanners, speakers, digital cameras, keyboards, and mice). On the iMac, they all go into your USB jacks.

- ✔ Many USB gadgets draw power from the iMac itself, sparing you the ugliness and hassle of power cords and plugs for all your external equipment.

- ✔ You can buy adapter boxes that give you more USB jacks. Connect enough of these so-called *USB hubs,* and you can have up to 127 USB gadgets connected to your iMac all at once. (There's no need to fiddle with ID numbers, termination plugs, or cable flakiness, as there is with SCSI. And if you have no clue what those things are, thank your favorite deity — you missed a very unpleasant era.)

For a sampling of USB-ready gadgets, see Appendix D.

Where's the USB?

Your iMac actually has several USB jacks. Two are on the side of the computer, lurking behind the plastic door (the one with the round finger hole). Two more are on your keyboard itself.

Of course, you're supposed to plug the *keyboard* into one of the iMac's USB jacks, and the *mouse* into one end of the keyboard. That leaves two free USB jacks for your choice of other appliances — one on the side of the iMac and the other at the free end of the keyboard.

Installing a new USB doodad

Like most computer add-ons, many USB gadgets come with special software to place on the iMac itself. You'll find this software, if it's necessary, on a CD that came with your USB gadget. Just insert the CD and look for an icon called Installer; double-click the icon and follow whatever instructions appear. After that, your USB gadget should work as advertised.

How to plug your older Macintosh equipment into your iMac

The question always comes up: "I've got a favorite keyboard/mouse/printer/digital camera that's designed for a pre-USB Macintosh. How do I plug it into my iMac?"

Easy: By using USB *adapters,* little connectors that translate between the Macintosh gadgets you already own and the iMac's USB connectors. Appendix D lists a bunch of these.

Some adapters, like the Momentum USB Serial Adapter, are inexpensive and require no special installation — but they don't accommodate *all* gadgets (especially not MIDI and LocalTalk networking, if you know what those are). Others, like the Griffin iPort, require dealer installation — but they offer a true-blue Macintosh serial port that accommodates every kind of older Macintosh add-on, including MIDI, LocalTalk, external modems, and so on. You can also plug non-USB keyboards and mice into your iMac; all you need is a Griffin iMate adapter. You can plug older inkjet printers (like Apple's StyleWriter line) and laser printers into the iMac, too, using a Farallon iPrint adapter (see Appendix D).

Someday, however, no adapters will be necessary; all future Mac models will come with USB jacks, and therefore every kind of add-on gadget alive will eventually be available in a USB-jack version.

Ethernet Made Eathy

When the time comes to transfer stuff to your iMac from another Mac — or vice-versa — you'll be thrilled with the iMac's innate file-transferring talent. *Ethernet,* a special kind of Mac-to-Mac connection, is fast, easy, and fun to pronounce. It lets you copy files between two Macs just by dragging the files' icons, which comes in handy when you want to make backup copies, distribute your work to a co-worker, or copy files to your laptop.

If your iMac is part of a big office network, somebody smart is probably on hand to make your iMac a new, welcome branch on the network tree. I'll leave it to that guru (or this book's companion, *MORE Macs For Dummies*) to walk you through setting up such a network.

However, you, O Individual iMac User, might like to know how to use Ethernet for something simpler — like connecting your iMac to *one* other Mac. Doing so is easy, quick, inexpensive, and requires only one cable (unlike bigger networks, which require the purchase of electronic boxes called *Ethernet hubs*). Here's how you do it.

Step 1: Get the cable

To connect your iMac to one other Mac (or even another iMac), you need a special cable called a *twisted Ethernet,* or *Ethernet crossover,* cable. (You can get such a cable for $10 or less at computer stores like CompUSA or from a mail-order joint such as Global Computer Supplies, at 310-635-8144.) Plug this cable into each computer's Ethernet jack. Your iMac's Ethernet jack is the hole on the side of your machine (behind the plastic pop-open door) that looks like an overweight telephone jack.

Step 2: Set up the software

Next, turn your attention to the software on the Macs involved. The Mac's networking software is amazingly sophisticated. You could spend days setting up passwords, different degrees of access to different folders on each Mac, and so on — and many professionals do.

But if you're the only person who uses your iMac, all that rigmarole is overkill. If you have two Macs — an iMac and a PowerBook laptop, let's say — then you're probably more interested in some fast-and-easy system of transferring files between them.

For clarity, let's pretend that you're seated at a PowerBook and want to bring the *iMac's* icon onto the screen. (You could just as easily reverse the procedure, of course, and access the laptop from the iMac.) Fortunately, you have to go through all of the following steps only *one time*! Thereafter, you'll be able to connect the computers with a quick double-click.

Setting up the iMac

Follow these steps on the iMac:

1. **Open the AppleTalk control panel (from the Control Panels item in your menu), choose Ethernet from the pop-up menu, close the window, and save changes.**

   You may be asked if you want AppleTalk turned on; you do.

2. **Open the File Sharing control panel and, in the dialog box, type your name and a name for the iMac.**

   If you're the only one who uses this iMac, use a short, easy-to-type name for yourself, such as your initials or "me." (Leave the password blank for this security-free scenario.)

3. **Click the upper Start button, close, and save; when you're warned that you haven't specified a password, just click OK and get on with your life.**

Setting up the PowerBook

Your iMac is ready for action. Here's how you bring the iMac's icon onto the PowerBook's screen (follow these steps on the *PowerBook*:)

1. **Open the AppleTalk control panel; make sure Ethernet is selected in the pop-up menu; close and save.**

   Again, let the machine turn on AppleTalk if it proposes doing so.

2. **Open the File Sharing control panel; type the same name or initials that you did in Step 2 of "Setting up the iMac;" close the window, clicking OK if you're warned about the lack of password.**

3. **Open the Chooser and click AppleShare (below, top left).**

4. **On the right, where you see the name of your iMac (as shown below in the top dialog box); double-click its name. A window like the middle one in the following figure appears; click OK in this dialog box and the next.**

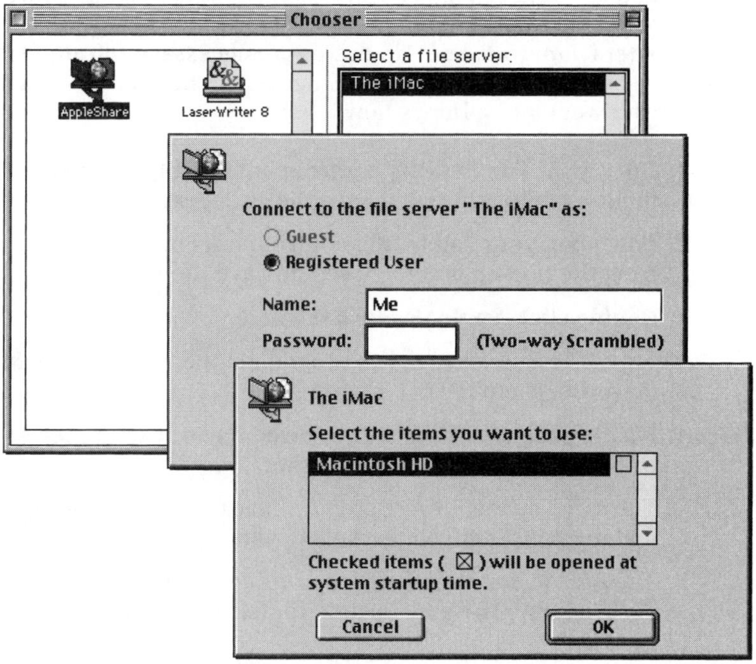

The iMac's hard-drive icon should now appear at the right side of your PowerBook's screen.

You can open the iMac's window and use its contents as usual.

To save time the next time, make an alias of the iMac drive icon, which is now on your PowerBook's screen. (See Chapter 9 for details on making aliases.) The *next* time you want to hook up, you won't have to bother with *any* of the steps you've just read. Instead, just double-click the alias you just made and click OK. The iMac's hard drive icon pops onto your screen.

Oh, and one more thing: If your iMac isn't turned on and connected by the Ethernet cable, your PowerBook will display a mysterious message at startup. Just click OK and ignore it. (Next time the iMac *is* connected and turned on, no message will appear when you turn the PowerBook on.)

Infrared Beaming

Despite the awesome fluidity of the prose you've just read, my little iMac-to-PowerBook example contains one glaring flaw: If you really *have* an iMac and a PowerBook (or two iMacs), you don't need Ethernet, cables, AppleShare, and all that jazz. Both iMacs and PowerBooks are equipped with an *infrared transmitter* — a small, dark red plastic lens that can send files to other such computers *through the air.* No cables are necessary. Infrared transferring of files takes much longer than the Ethernet method does— but you can't beat it for sheer coolness. Here's how it goes:

1. **Open your File Sharing control panel and type a name for yourself in the top blank; close and save the changes.**

2. **Now open your AppleTalk control panel and choose Infrared Port from the pop-up menu; close and save the changes.**

3. **Double-click Apple IR File Exchange.**

   Apple IR File Exchange is a program in the Apple Extras folder on every PowerBook and iMac hard drive.

4. **Position the two Macs within three feet of each other so that their transmitters are facing each other.**

   The icons of any PowerBooks or iMacs in range show up as "drop-box" folder icons, as shown in the following figure.

5. **The person sending the files or folders simply drags icons *from the desktop* onto the appropriate folder, as shown here.**

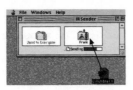

When the progress bar indicates that the job is over, open the Apple IR File Exchange folder on the *other* computer. Inside is a folder called IR Receiver — which contains the stuff that was beamed through empty space!

If you can't seem to beam to a PowerBook, by the way, open the Infrared control panel on the PowerBook. Select IrDA from the pop-up menu. Close and save.

Part IV
The Internet Defangled

The 5th Wave   By Rich Tennant

INTERNET ACCESS
.50¢ - Min.

In this part . . .

The "i" in *iMac* stands for *Internet*.

I know, I know: If you hear *one more person* start droning on about the Internet, the Web, or the Information Superhighway, you'll tie them to a chair to watch 18 hours of the Home Shopping Network.

Actually, though, despite the overwhelming abundance of ridiculous, time-wasting chaff in cyberspace, there's also a lot of useful stuff, plus Dilbert cartoons for free. The next three chapters tell you how to get it.

Chapter 11

Faking Your Way onto America Online and the Internet

*I*f you haven't heard of America Online or the Internet by now, you must've spent the last ten years in some Antarctic ice cave. These days, you can't make a move without seeing an e-mail address on someone's business card, a World Wide Web address (like *www.moneygrub.com*) on a magazine ad, or the glazed raccoon look of the all-night Internetter on a friend's face.

Going online gains you endless acres of features: the ability to send e-mail, instantly and for free, to anyone else who's online; incredible savings when you buy stuff (no middleman!); vast amounts of reading and research material (*Time* magazine, *The New York Times*, and so on, *free*); discussion bulletin boards on 29,000 topics (left-handed banjo-playing nuns, unite!); live, typed "chat rooms" that bring you together with similarly bored people from all over the world; and much more.

Before you begin this adventure, though, a grave warning: Going online is every bit as addictive as heroin, crack, or Presidential sex scandals, but even more dangerous. As you explore this endless, yawning new world, filled with surprises at every turn, you're likely to lose track of things — such as time, sleep, and your family. Take it slow, take it in small chunks, and use these services always in moderation.

Above all, remember that the Internet wasn't designed by Apple. It existed long before the Macintosh. It was invented by a bunch of military scientists in the '60s whose idea of a good conversation was debating things like *TCP/IP*, *FTP*, and *ftp.ucs.ubc.ca*. As a result, going online is all quite a bit more complicated and awkward than everyday iMac activities.

In other words, if you can't figure out what's going on, *it's not your fault.*

First, the Modem

Fortunately, your iMac came with a built-in *modem,* the little electronic box that connects your computer to the phone jack on the wall. Fortunately, it's the fastest one money can buy — a so-called *56K* modem, which you can think of as "56 miles per hour."

Now then: When the iMac makes a call, it dials the phone many times faster than, say, a teenager, but ties up the phone line just as effectively. When your iMac is using the modem, nobody else can use the phone. Therefore, you need to figure out how you're going to plug in your modem:

- ✔ **Share a single line with the modem.** You can visit your local Radio Shack to buy a *splitter,* a little plastic thing that makes your wall phone jack split into two identical phone jacks — one for your phone and the other for your iMac. This arrangement lets you talk on the telephone whenever you aren't using the modem and vice versa.

- ✔ **Install a second phone line.** This is clearly the power user's method: Give the modem a phone line unto itself.

   Pros: (1) Your main family phone number is no longer tied up every time your modem dials up the latest sports scores. (2) You can talk to a human on one line while you're modeming on the other. (3) If you're in an office with one of those PBX or Merlin-type multiline telephone systems, you have to install a new, separate jack for the modem *anyway.*

   Cons: (1) This option is expensive. (2) It involves calling up the phone company, which is about as much fun as eating sand. (3) You run a greater risk of becoming a serious modem nerd.

Either way, plug the computer end of the telephone wire into the iMac's modem jack. (It's behind the right-side plastic door — the jack at the far right.)

America Online or Direct to the Internet?

When it comes to visiting the vast, seething world of cyberspace, you have two on-ramps. You can become an America Online member, or you can sign up for a direct Internet account with a company like EarthLink. The geeks call Internet-access companies (like EarthLink) *ISPs,* short for *Internet Service Providers*.

I find the term Internet Service Provider — let alone *ISP* — overly nerdy, like calling a pilot an "Aerodynamic Services Provider." Unfortunately, you can't crack open a magazine or visit a computer club without hearing people talk

The birth of the Confusion Superhighway

The Internet began as a gigantic communications network for the U.S. military. The idea was to build a vast web of computer connections all over the country so that, if an enemy bomb destroyed one city, the government's electronic messages could still reach their destinations. (Gee, *that's* reassuring. Yeah, okay, New York is in cinders — but hey!, at least the company picnic memo got delivered.) As a result, you might send an e-mail message to your next-door neighbor — but it might reach him only after traveling from your Macintosh to Omaha, bouncing down to Orlando, returning to Toronto, and finally reaching the house next door.

There's no central location for the Internet; it's everywhere and nowhere. Nobody can control it; nobody even knows how many computers are connected to it. It's impossible to measure and impossible to control — which is why American teenagers love it, and governments try to ban it.

Anyway, when the U.S. government threw open the Internet to the public, it triggered an incredible explosion of interest, commerce, and nauseating buzzwords like *information superhighway.* There's a lot of useful stuff out on the Internet — and, as a pure time-killer, there's nothing like it. But there's also a lot of chaff to wade through. Let this chapter and the next be your guides to finding your way.

about ISPs. ("My ISP only charges $18 a month!" "Really? Maybe I'll change ISPs then.") So, with your permission, I'll refer to the companies who rent you time on the Internet as *ISPs,* just like everyone else does.

In this chapter, I'll show you both methods of getting online. Each route has significant pros and cons, however, which you'll find in the following table. Photocopy, distribute to your family members, and discuss over dinner.

America Online	*Internet Service Provider (ISP)*
$22 per month, unlimited access.	$20 per month, unlimited access.
Frequent busy signals between 6 p.m. and midnight.	Busy signals are rare.
Hangs up on you after several minutes of your not doing anything.	Doesn't hang up on you.
Long hold times for help, but fairly Macintosh-savvy agents are available.	Help agents are sometimes clueless about the iMac.
The one program on your hard drive — the America Online program — does everything: e-mail, World Wide Web surfing, chat rooms, and so on.	You need a separate program for each Internet feature: e-mail, Web surfing, and so on.

(continued)

America Online	*Internet Service Provider (ISP)*
Generally safe for kids; no pornography on America Online itself.	Adult supervision required.
Very simple, sometimes frustrating; the geeks look down on people with AOL accounts.	More complex, less limiting; nerds admire you for having a "real" Internet account.

America Online (often called AOL) is an *online service*. That is, its offerings are hand-selected by the company's steering committee and sanitized for your protection. Contrast with the Internet itself, where the offerings constantly change, nobody's in charge, and it's every iMac for itself.

Going onto AOL is like going to a grocery store, where every product is neatly organized, packaged, and labeled. Going onto the Internet, by contrast, is like going to a huge farmer's market that fills a football stadium, filled with whichever vendors happened to show up with their pickup trucks. At the farmer's market, wonderful bargains may await — but it's hard to find anything particular, the turnips may be rancid, and there's no clerk to ask for help.

On the other hand, don't forget that America Online *also* gives you the actual Internet, *in addition* to its own hand-picked goodies. That is, the AOL grocery store has a back door into the farmer's market. But parents, don't freak out: America Online offers extensive, easy-to-use features for blocking the raunchy stuff so that your kids don't see it.

America Online (AOL), the Cyber-Grocery

Your iMac came with the America Online (AOL) folder already on the hard disk (inside the Internet folder). Inside this folder is the America Online *program* whose icon you double-click to get started.

The first time you double-click this icon, you'll be guided through a series of setup steps. You'll be asked:

- ✔ For your name, address, and credit-card number. Remember, though, that you get 100 hours of time online (during the first month) for free. Cancel within the first month, and your card is never charged.

- ✔ To choose a local *access number* from a list (and a backup number). Fortunately, AOL has worked out a clever scheme that lets you, as one of 90 percent of Americans living near metropolitan centers, make a *local* call to America Online. Somehow, this system carries your call all the way to Virginia for free. (That's where the actual gigantic AOL computers live.)

- ✔ To make up a "screen name" and a password.

The *screen name* can be ten letters long, but you can't use punctuation. You can use a variation of your name (A Lincoln, MTMoore, Mr Rourke) or some clever CB radio-type handle (FoxyBabe, Ski Jock, NoLifeGuy). Do understand, however, that America Online has over *12 million* members, and *each* of them (including you) can choose up to five different names, one for each family member. In other words, you can pretty much bet that names like Helen, Hotshot, and Mac Guy were claimed some time in the Mesozoic Era.

If you pick a name that someone has already claimed, the program will make you keep trying until you come up with a name that hasn't been used before.

When all this setup information is complete, your modem begins screaming and making a hideous racket, and you see an AOL logo screen that says things like "Checking Password." Finally, if everything goes well, you're brought to this screen.

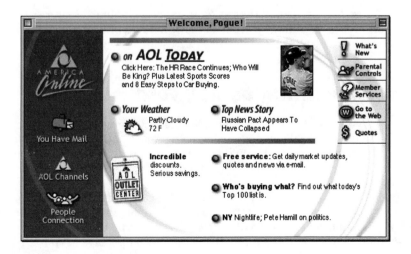

You also get to hear a recording of the famous Mr. Cheerful, the man who says "Welcome!" as though you're *just* the person he's been waiting for all day. If you've got e-mail waiting, he also says "You've got mail!," which he's *really* happy about. (To read the mail, click the "You have mail" icon.)

Exploring by icon

AOL, you'll quickly discover, is a collection of hundreds of individual screens, each of which represents a different service or company. Each day, several of them (one of which is always News) are advertised on the welcome screen. To jump directly to the advertised feature, click the corresponding icon.

On AOL, you don't always have to *double-click* to open icons, as you've learned to do on the iMac in general. Sometimes it's once, sometimes it's twice . . . come to think of it, just double-click all the time. An extra click won't hurt anything.

The broader America Online table of contents, however, appears when you click the AOL Channels button on the opening screen. Each of *these* buttons takes you to yet another screen, where you can visit related services — for example:

 ✔ The *Research & Learn* (called *Reference Desk* in some versions) button lets you consult a dictionary, a national phone book, or a choice of encyclopedias.

 ✔ The *Personal Finance* page is stock-market city: You can check quotes, actually buy and sell, get mutual-fund stats, read tax and investing advice, and so on.

 ✔ Another one of those "You can do *that* online?" features: If you click the *Travel* button, you can actually look up plane fares and even make reservations.

Navigating by keyword

If you poked around enough, clicking icons and opening screen after screen, you'd eventually uncover everything America Online has to offer. In the meantime, however, you'd run up your phone bill, develop mouse elbow, and watch four Presidential administrations pass.

A much faster navigational trick is the *keyword* feature. A keyword is like an elevator button that takes you directly to any of the hundreds of features on AOL, making no stops along the way. Just type the keyword of your choice into the strip at the top of the screen (where it says "Type Keyword/Web address"). When you press Return, you're teleported directly to that service.

Here are a few typical AOL services, along with their keywords. Arm yourself with this list so that you make the most of your free month-long trial.

Keyword	Where It Takes You
Access	A list of local phone numbers for America Online. Use this before a trip to another city.
Banking	Check your accounts, pay bills, and so on (certain banks only).
Beginners	A collection of help topics for Mac newcomers.
Billing	Current billing info, disputes, and so on.
Encyclopedia	Your choice of several different published encyclopedias. You just saved $900!
Help	Assistance about America Online itself.
Homework	A place for students to get live, interactive help with homework and research.
Macgame	Files, messages, and discussions of Mac games.
Star Trek	*Star Trek.*
Stocks	Check the current price of any stock. You can even see your current portfolio value.

And how, you may well ask, do you find out what the keyword *is* for something you're looking for? Easy — just type in keyword: **keyword!** You'll get a screen that offers a complete list of keywords.

How to find your way back to the good stuff

With several hundred places worth visiting on AOL — and several *million* places worth visiting on the Internet — it'd be nice if there were a way to mark your place. Suppose you stumble onto this *great* English Cocker Spaniel Owners' area, for example, but you've already forgotten which buttons you clicked to get there.

Simple solution: When you're looking at a screen (or Web page) you might someday like to return to, choose Add to Favorite Places from the Window menu. Thereafter, whenever you want to revisit one of your thus-marked Favorite Places, choose its name from the Favorite Places icon/menu, like this.

To delete something from this list, choose the very first command (Favorite Places) from the Favorite Places icon/menu. In the resulting window, just click a place's name once and then choose Clear from the Edit menu.

The e-mail connection

One of the best things about AOL is the e-mail — mainly the sheer, ego-boosting joy of *getting* some.

If, in fact, anybody has bothered to write to you (which you'll hear announced by Mr. "You've got mail!"), click the YOU'VE GOT MAIL button on the welcome screen to see your messages.

After you've read the message, you can (a) reply to it (by clicking the Reply button); (b) save it on your hard disk (by choosing Save from the File

┌Use these controls to change the font,
size, color, and style of your typing.

Click here to open your Address Book,
where you can store and retrieve e-mail
addresses you use a lot.

untitled

Send To \ **Attachments**

BarneyT@earthlink.net

Address Book   Detach Files   Attach Files

Send Now

Subject: My 1st E-mail

☐ Request "Return Receipt" from AOL members

Send Later

Palatino ▼   14▼   **B** *I* U   A A

Is this right? Did I do it right? Did I? Huh? Did I?

I can't believe I actually figured out how to do e-mail. This is VERY cool!

Your friend,
Harold

Mail Extras

Click here to send your mail (or press the Enter key).┘

menu); (c) print it (by choosing Print from the File menu); or (d) close its window without saving it. If you do that, the message hangs around in your Old Mail folder for about a week and then disappears forever.

To *send* a message to somebody, click Write on the toolbar. Type your lucky recipient's e-mail address, a subject, and your message in the appropriate blanks. (Don't forget to press the Tab key to move from blank to blank.) When you're done typing, just press Enter (or click the Send Now button).

If you need to look up somebody's screen name, use this keyword: *members*.

The party line

By far the most mind-blowing aspect of AOL is, of course, the *chat rooms*. In a chat room, you'll find up to 23 people chatting away (by typing). The nutty thing is that everybody's talking at once, so the conversation threads overlap, and hilarious results sometimes ensue.

Nonetheless, the chat rooms are an unusual social opportunity: For the first time, you can be the total belle of the ball (or stud of the studio) — the wittiest, charmingest, best-liked person — without so much as combing your hair.

To get to the chat rooms, choose Chat Now from the People menu/icon on your toolbar. If you click the button called "Find a Chat," you'll discover that dozens of parties are transpiring simultaneously, each founded on a different topic. Double-click a room's name to go there.

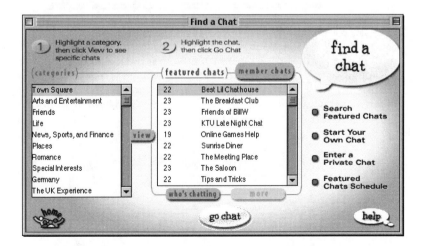

Things to know before entering the Party Zone

If it's your first time in a chat room, you may be nonplused by the gross excesses of punctuation that seem to go on there. Every five minutes, it seems that somebody types {{{{{{{{{ Jennifer!!!}}}}}}}}} or ****BabyBones!****

Actually, there's nothing wrong with these people's keyboards. The braces are the cyberspace equivalent of hugging the enclosed person; the asterisks are kisses. That's how you greet friends who enter the room — online, anyway.

Talking behind their backs

What makes the live chats even more fun is that you can whisper directly into the ear of anybody there — and nobody else can hear you. This kind of behind-the-scenes direct communication is called an Instant Message. To send one, choose Send Instant Message from the Members menu (or press ⌘-I). You get a box like this:

As soon as you type your whispered message and click Send (or press Enter), the window disappears from your screen — and reappears on the recipient's screen! That person can then whisper back to you.

Meanwhile, somebody *else* in the room may have been Instant-Messaging *you*.

If you try to maintain your presence in the main window *and* keep your end of all these whispered conversations in *their* little windows, the hilarity builds. *Nothing* makes a better typist out of you than the AOL chat rooms.

How to find — and get — free software

Of course, for many people, the best part of AOL is the free software. Heck, for many people, that's the *only* part of AOL. Just use keyword: *filesearch;* click Shareware; in the Find What? blank, type the name of the file, or kind of file, you're looking for; and click Search.

In a moment, you're shown a complete listing of all files in the AOL data banks that match your search criteria. Keep in mind that roughly 300,000 files hang out on those computers in Virginia, so choose your search words with care.

If you think a file sounds good, double-click its name to read a description. If it *still* sounds good, click Download Now. Your modem will begin the task of *downloading* (transferring) the picture file to your hard drive. (Make sure that you read the section "When You Can't Open Your Downloaded Goodies," later in this chapter, for a follow-up discussion on downloading stuff.)

Signing Up for an Internet Account (ISP)

If you've decided to sign up for a direct Internet connection (instead of going the AOL route), send a thank-you note to Apple; signing up for such an account on an iMac is as easy as signing up for AOL.

Locate and open the program called Internet Setup Assistant; it's in the Internet folder on your hard drive. The Internet Setup Assistant asks you if you want to set up your iMac for Internet use; yes, you do. Then it asks if you already have an Internet account; no, you don't.

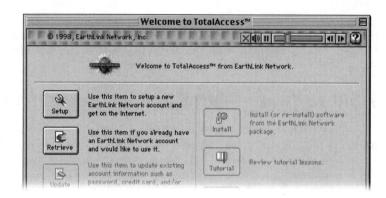

Now the EarthLink Total Access sign-up program takes over, showing you a series of screens, asking for your name, address, credit-card number, and so on. (Start by clicking the Setup button on this screen.)

While this goes on, a *voice* starts explaining what's happening. (Scared the bejeezus out of me the first time I heard it.) Your modem dials an 800 number a couple of times. Along the way, you'll be asked to make up a cybername for yourself (such as *SeinfeldNut83*) and a password that protects your account.

When it's all over, you'll be an official, card-carrying member of the Internet. Now you, too, can have an e-mail address with an @ sign on your business card. Now you, too, can banter at cocktail parties about the ghastly new color scheme on the Microsoft Web site. Now you, too, can slowly drift away from family, job, and reality as you recede into cyberhermitdom.

What's on the Internet

In the following pages, you'll read about the various things that you can do on the Internet. The most useful of these features are called *e-mail*, *newsgroups*, and the *World Wide Web*. As you read, keep in mind that all these features are available to you regardless of whether you have an AOL account or a real Internet (ISP) account.

E-mail

If you have America Online, see "The e-mail connection" earlier in this chapter. If you've signed up for an ISP like EarthLink instead, see Chapter 14. Either way, get psyched for a feature that'll change your life; as a technology, e-mail ranks right up there with cable TV, frequent-flyer miles, and microwave popcorn.

Newsgroups

The next important Internet feature is called *newsgroups*. Don't be fooled: They have nothing to do with news, and they're not groups. That's the Internet for ya.

Instead, newsgroups are electronic bulletin boards. I post a message; anyone else on the Internet can read it and post a response for all to see. Then somebody else responds to *that* message, and so on.

The little > symbols mean that this portion of the message is being quoted from a previous message, so everyone will know what this guy is responding to.

```
┌──────────────────── Madonna????? ─────────────────────┐
│ Message 1 of 1 Subject 76 of 325                       │
│ ┌──────────────────────────────────────────┐          │
│ │ Subject: Madonna                          │          │
│ │ From: kcmoer@aol.com                      │          │
│ │ Date: 11 May 1997 20:17:47 GMT            │          │
│ │ Message-ID: <19970512001700.UAA06944@ladder02.news.aol.com> │
│ │ >I truly believe that Madonna is a new art form unto herself, │
│ │ >that she has reinvented the musical form as we know it, │
│ │ >that neither music nor film will ever be the same. │
│ │                                           │          │
│ │ Well, that's just the kind of pathetic balderdash we might expect from a │  Send New
│ │ brainless moron like you. Why is it that nobody under the age of 30 has │  Message
│ │ the least idea of what good art is anymore? I think you Madonna fans │
│ │ should go stick your heads into the microwave and hit Defrost. │
│ │                                           │          │
│ │      Brian                                │          │
│ │      "We are the knights who say NI!"     │          │
│ └──────────────────────────────────────────┘      ?   │
│      <-- Previous    More     Next -->                 │
│   Mark Unread    Reply to Group    E-mail to Author    │
└────────────────────────────────────────────────────────┘
```

It's typical for Internet weenies to sign their names with some kind of whimsical quotation. Don't ask me why; personally, it drives me crazy.

By the way: You might notice, in the previous illustration, that the writer is somewhat nastier online than he might have been in your living room. That's an interesting Internet lesson — people tend to be ruder than they would in person. There are two reasons: First, you're anonymous — nobody can see you, so it doesn't seem to matter as much if you're a jerk. Second, millions of messages appear here every day; some people think they need to be extra-dramatic just to be noticed.

There are about 29,000 different newsgroups, ongoing discussions on every topic — chemists who like bowling, left-handed oboists, Mickey Mouse fans who live in Bali — anything. Here's how you reach these discussion areas:

✔ **On America Online:** Use keyword *newsgroups*. If you then click Read My Newsgroups, you see a starter list of topics; just keep double-clicking topics that interest you until you're reading the actual messages. (To add newsgroup topics to your starter list, use the Search All Newsgroups button.)

  After you've read a message, you can either respond to it (click the Send New Message button) or just keep reading (click the Next→ button).

✔ **With an ISP:** Use Outlook Express, which came with your iMac. (It's the same program you use to read e-mail, as described in Chapter 14.)

  Once you're online and running Outlook Express, click the Microsoft News Server icon on the screen. You'll be shown a new window containing dozens of newsgroups that all pertain to Microsoft software.

  Now, I'll be the first to admit that reading about Microsoft products all day is not what you'd call, er, realizing the full potential of the Internet. Therefore, if you think you're up for the full list of 29,000 discussion topics, try this:

  From Outlook Express's Edit menu, choose Preferences, click the News icon, click New Server, type *Newsgroup List* (or something similar to that), click OK, tab to the Server Address blank, and type out the your ISP's *news server address*. (For EarthLink, it's *news.earthlink.net*. If you have another ISP, call it up and ask what the news-server address is.) Click the Make Default button and then click OK.

  From now on, whenever you feel like reading several million bulletin-board notes, launch Outlook Express. You'll see an icon called *Newsgroup List* (or whatever you called it) at the left side of the screen; double-click it. Finally, from the View menu, choose Get Complete Newsgroup List. Wait five minutes for the full list of thousands to arrive on your screen — and then, at last, you can begin reading the messages on the world's largest bulletin board. Just double-click a topic name; choose Refresh Message List from the View menu; and then double-click a message name to read it. (Click the Reply icon at the top of the window if you'd like to respond to something somebody has written. But be nice.)

  I realize that this process involves 500 steps, but as I said, nobody ever called the Internet easy.

How to use the Internet as a giant backup disk

As described in Chapter 4, *backing up* means making a safety copy of your work. Some iMac fans buy disk drives for this purpose (see Chapter 18). Others send files to themselves as e-mail attachments (see Chapter 14). But one of the most convenient ways to back up your iMac is to use an Internet-based service like BackJack.com or iMacBackup.com.

Here's how these services work. Using your Web browser (see the next chapter), visit the service's Web page (*www.backjack.com* or *imacbackup.com,* respectively). Download the free software. Along the way, you'll be asked for your name and credit-card information.

Once you run this downloaded software from your hard drive, you'll be asked to make up a password. You can then set the software up to run, all by itself, at whatever times you specify (such as the middle of the night). You also tell it which folders on your hard drive you'd like backed up. (If you need help running the setup program, call BackJack at 888-421-0220.)

Then every night, at the appointed time, the BackJack software automatically dials the Internet and sends copies of your important files to the backup company's computers. Your stuff is encrypted (scrambled) before it's sent, so nobody — not even the backup-company's people — can see it. Only you (with your password) can ever see what's in those files.

Using this kind of system, you're always backed up without even having to think about it; if anything gets accidentally thrown away, or if your hard drive dies, you can retrieve a copy from the Internet at any hour of the day or night. An Internet backup system is nice, too, because it's off-site; even if your office is hit by fire, burglar, or plague of locusts, your backup copies are safely somewhere else.

On the other hand, Internet backup services are expensive ($17.50 per month for BackJack, for example). The coupon in the back of this book should help a little; it saves you $30 on getting started with BackJack.

The World Wide Web

Except for e-mail, by far the most popular and useful Internet feature is the World Wide Web. In fact, it gets a chapter all to itself (the next chapter). For now, all you need to know is this:

✔ **On America Online:** A Web browser is built right into your AOL software. In many cases, you wind up on the Web just by innocently clicking some button within AOL — that's how tightly the Web is integrated with America Online these days.

✔ **With an ISP account:** You have your choice of two free Web-browsers: Netscape Navigator and Microsoft Internet Explorer, both described in the next chapter.

How to Hang Up

When you're finished with an AOL session, hanging up is no big deal; just choose Quit from the File menu, making your phone line available once again to the other members of your family.

Getting off the Internet if you have a direct Internet account (ISP), however, is trickier. Allow me to propose an analogy: Imagine that you call another branch of your family tree on New Year's Day. You yourself place the call, but then you hand the phone off to various other family members. "And now here's little Timmy! Timmy, talk to Grandma. . . ."

Using the Internet works the same way. Your iMac places the call. But aside from tying up the phone line, your iMac doesn't actually *do* anything until you now launch one of the programs you read about in this chapter: an e-mail program or a Web browser, for example. Each of these Internet programs is like one of your family members, chatting with the Big Internet Grandma for a few minutes apiece.

The point here: When you quit your e-mail or Web program, *the phone line is still tied up,* just as though Timmy, when finished talking to Grandma, put the phone on the couch and wandered out to play. When you're finished Internetting, therefore, end the phone call by doing one of the following:

- ✔ From your menu, choose Control Panels and open the one called Remote Access. Click the Disconnect button.

- ✔ Wait. After about 15 minutes of your not doing anything online (or whatever time you've specified in the Remote Access control panel), your iMac hangs up automatically.

- ✔ If you have Mac OS 8.5 or later, choose Remote Access Status from your menu and click Disconnect.

- ✔ Or — here's another Mac OS 8.5-or-later feature — choose Disconnect from the Remote Access tile on your *Control Strip* (see Chapter 8), like this:

When You Can't Open Your Downloaded Goodies

It's easy to download software — either from AOL or the Internet. Maybe you find something on a Web page worth downloading (see the next chapter). Maybe somebody sends you a family picture as a file that's attached to an e-mail. Unfortunately, the first word out of the beginning downloader's mouth, on examining the freshly downloaded loot, is generally this:

"Wha — ?"

First of all, people often can't *find* whatever-it-was that they downloaded. (*Hint:* Downloaded stuff usually winds up in a folder called Downloads, inside the folder of the Internet program you were using — inside the America Online folder, the Outlook Express folder, and so on.)

Second of all, the first thing many people read when they double-click a file they've just downloaded is this: "The application is busy or missing."

And *that's* because of *compression*. As you sit there waiting for your Santa Claus graphic to arrive on your iMac, you're tying up the phone line and drumming your fingers. Therefore, almost everything on America Online (or the Internet or *anywhere* in cyberspace, for that matter) arrives in a compact, encoded format that takes less time to transfer.

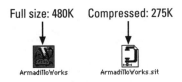

Full size: 480K   Compressed: 275K

ArmadilloWorks   ArmadilloWorks.sit

Which is terrific, except for one thing: How are *you* supposed to expand your downloaded file back into usable form?

Any file whose format is indicated by the suffix *.sit* has been "stuffed" using a program called StuffIt. As an added convenience, the America Online software unstuffs these files *automatically* when you log off the service.

But what if (a) you're getting your goodies straight from the Internet, or (b) the letters at the end of your precious loot's name *aren't* .sit?

The solution to all of these problems is the set-it-and-forget-it answer to the downloader's prayers: StuffIt Expander. It's free, thank heaven, and already on board your iMac. (Open your hard drive; open the Internet folder; open the Utilities folder; open the Aladdin folder; open the StuffIt Expander folder. There it is: the StuffIt Expander program.)

This little program gracefully re-expands just about any geeky Internet file you drop on it, from *.sit* to *.cpt* and *.hqx*. While you're at it, you may as well install its companion program, too, called, awkwardly enough, DropStuff with Expander Enhancer — it's a little steroid pill that lets StuffIt Expander *also* open *.gz, .z, .ARC, .ZIP,* and *.uu* files, too. (This doodad, too, is in the Aladdin folder; it's hidden in the icon called DropStuff with EE Installer.)

After you've got this thing safely installed on your hard drive, here's the handy two-step scheme for expanding something you downloaded from cyberspace.

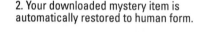

1. Drag the downloaded mystery item on top of the StuffIt Expander icon.

2. Your downloaded mystery item is automatically restored to human form.

Top Ten Best/Worst Aspects of the Net

No question: The Internet is changing everything. If you're not on it now, you probably will be within a few years. Here's what to look forward to:

1. Best: Everyone is anonymous, so everyone is equal. It doesn't matter what you look, sound, or smell like — you're judged purely by your words.

2. Worst: Everyone is anonymous, so everyone is equal. You can pretend to be someone you're not — or a *gender* you're not — for the purposes of misleading other Internet surfers.

3. Best: the cost — $20 a month for unlimited access.

4. Worst: the cost — $20 a month is a lot, especially when you consider the required equipment.

5. Best: The Internet connects you to everyone. You're only an e-mail or a Web page away from anyone else on the planet.

6. Worst: The Internet *disconnects* you from everyone. You become a hermit holed up in your room, as family, friends, and relationships pack up and leave.

7. Best: The Internet is drawing people away from TV. Statistics show that as more people discover the Web, they spend less time in front of the boob tube.

8. Worst: The Internet is drawing people away from TV. The TV industry is going crazy wondering what to do.

9. Best: The Internet is complete freedom of speech for everyone. No government agency looks over your shoulder; the Net is completely unsupervised and uncontrolled.

10. Worst: The Internet is complete freedom of speech for everyone. Including pornographers, neo-Nazi groups, and others you may not want your 10-year-old getting chummy with.

Chapter 12
The Weird Wild Web

*T*he most popular part of the Internet is the World Wide Web — you can't help hearing about this thing. Fourth graders run around urging school-mates to "check out their Web pages." Web "addresses" show up every-where — on business cards, in newspaper ads, on TV. (Have you noticed *www.sony.com* or *www.spam.com* flashing by at the end of movie ads and car commercials? Those are Web addresses.)

The Web has become incredibly popular for one simple reason: It *isn't* geeky and user-hostile, like the rest of the Internet. It looks friendly and familiar to actual humans. When you connect to the Web, you don't encounter streams of computer codes. Instead, information is displayed attractively, with nice typesetting, color pictures, and interactive buttons.

Internet Made Idiotproof: Link-Clicking

Navigating the Web requires little more than clicking buttons and those underlined blue phrases, which you can sort of see in the following figure.

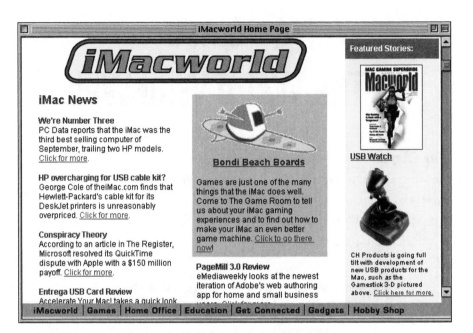

When you click an underlined phrase, called a *link,* you're automatically transported from one "page" (screen) to another, without having to type in the usual bunch of Internet codes. One page may be a glorified advertisement; another may contain critical information about a bill in Congress; another might have been created by a nine-year-old in Dallas, to document what her dog had for lunch.

Unfortunately, all of this amazing online multimedia stuff stresses your modem nearly to the breaking point. Even with your iMac's 56 Kbps modem, the fastest standard modem there is, you still wait five or ten seconds for *each* Web page to float onto your screen.

Getting to the Web via America Online

To get to the Web once your online with America Online, choose "Go to the Web" from the Internet icon, as shown here.

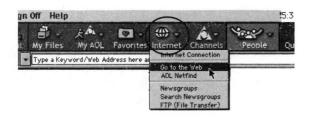

If you've been given a particular Web address to visit (such as *www. hamsters.com*), you can also treat it as a keyword. (See Chapter 11 for instructions on using keywords.) That is, type in that Web address into the Keyword box (or the strip at the top of the AOL 4.0 screen); it'll automatically open up a Web window and take you to the appropriate page.

Getting to the Web via an ISP

If you've signed up for a direct Internet account (such as EarthLink, as described in Chapter 11) instead of America Online, you'll be using a special program for browsing the Web — called, with astounding originality, a *Web browser*.

Most people use either the Netscape Navigator or Microsoft Internet Explorer browser. Both are free; both are on your iMac's hard drive (in the Internet folder).

How do you choose which browser to use? In a nutshell, Navigator is faster, but doesn't have many features. Explorer is slower, but has a lot of nice features (such as the capability to turn off blinking animations on Web pages, which otherwise drive you quietly mad).

To go a-browsing, launch your Web browser. If you have, in fact, signed up for an Internet account (see Chapter 11), the iMac dials the phone automatically, hisses and shrieks, and finally shows you a Web page.

Where to Go, What to Do on the Web

Once you're staring at your first Web page — whether via America Online or an Internet access company — getting around is easy. (The picture below shows Netscape Navigator, but you'll find the same basic elements in Internet Explorer, too.) Just *look* at all the fun things to see and do on the Web!

A. Click the Back button to revisit the page you were just on — or the Forward button to return to the page you were on *before* you clicked the Back button. (Does that make sense?)

B. Type a new Web page address into the thin horizontal strip at the top of the browser window and press Return to go to the site. A Web address, just so you know, is known by the geeks as a *URL* — pronounced "U. R. L."

And where do you find good Web addresses? From friends, from articles, on television, and so on. Look for *http://* or *www* at the beginning of the address — a guaranteed sign that the address points to a Web page.

C. Enjoy the little animated meteor shower in the upper-right-corner logo. It means "Wait a sec, I'm not done painting this Web page picture for you. As long as I'm animating, you'll just have to wait."

D. Clicking a picture or a button often takes you to a new Web page.

E. Clicking blue underlined phrases (called *links*) *always* takes you to a different Web page. (As a handy bonus, these links change to some other color when you see them next. That's to remind you that you've been that way before.)

F. Click in a Search blank and type what you're looking for. (Click the Search button when you're finished typing.) Similar blanks appear when, for example, you're asked to fill out a survey, type in your mailing address, and so on.

G. When you see a picture you'd like to keep, point to it, hold down the mouse button, and watch for a pop-up menu to appear at your cursor tip. From this pop-up menu, choose "Save this Image As" (in Navigator) or "Download Image to Disk" (in Explorer). After you click the Save button, the result is a new icon on your hard drive — a graphics file containing the picture you saved.

H. Use the scroll bar to move up and down the page — or to save mousing, just press the spacebar each time you want to see more.

Ways to search for a particular topic

Suppose you're looking at the Kickboxing Haiku Web page. But now you want to check the weather in Detroit. Because the World Wide Web is indeed a big interconnected web, you could theoretically work your way from one Web page to another to another, clicking just the right blue underlined links, until you finally arrived at the Detroit Weather page.

Unfortunately, there are about 200 million Web pages. By the time you actually arrived at the Detroit Weather page, the weather would certainly have changed (not to mention Detroit). Clearly, you need to be able to *look something up* — to jump directly to another Web page whose address you don't currently know.

For this purpose, the denizens of the Web have seen fit to create a few very special Web pages — whose sole function is to search all the *other* Web pages. If you're on the Web, and don't know where to look for, say, information about Venezuelan Beaver Cheese, you can use the Find commands at any of the following sites:

- *www.yahoo.com*
- *www.altavista.com*
- *www.infoseek.com*
- *www.hotbot.com*

All of these search pages work alike. Here, for example, is what it would look like if you used the search page called Yahoo! (the first address listed above) to find information about Venezuelan Beaver Cheese.

After clicking the Search button, you'd be shown a brand-new Web page listing *hits* — that is, Web pages containing the words "Venezuelan," "Beaver," or "Cheese."

YAHOO! SEARCH

Found 108650 matches containing **venezuelan beaver cheese**. Displaying matches 1-20.

- **Cheese** collector's checklist - **Cheese** collector's checklist. Red Leicester. Boursin. Tilsit. Bresse-Bleue. Caerphilly. Perle de Champagne. Bel Paese. Camembert. Red Windsor. Camembert...
  --http://www.cs.und.nodak.edu/~dahl/montypython/cheese.htm
- **Venezuelan** Criminal Justice Links - **Venezuelan** Criminal Justice Related Sites. There are currently no Internet resources in Venezuela devoted to criminal justice. What follows, instead, is a.
  --http://www.ojp.usdoj.gov/ORIC/ven.html
- AP Labs' **Venezuelan** Rep - **Venezuelan** Representative. Corporation: von Suckow Gavea Representaciones Av El Empalme Ed. Fedecamaras Piso 4 Officina CH4 El Bosque, Caracas Venezuela...
  --http://sd.aplabs.com/APLabs/corporate/international/Venezuela.html
- **VENEZUELAN** FILM VIDEO COLLECTION - Reviews of the Titles held in the **Venezuelan** Video Collection (Part II) GOLPES A MI PUERTA (1993) Dirección: Alejandro Saderman. Con...
  --http://www.charityconnect.com/webpages/Venezuela/video2.htm

See how useful a search page is? This handy Yahoo! thing narrowed down our search to a mere *108,650 Web pages!* You're as good as home!

Not. You can see here, in a nutshell, the problem with the Web: There's so much darned stuff out there, you spend an *awful* lot of your time trying to find exactly what you want. In this case, we probably should have clicked the little Help button on the main Yahoo! screen. It would have told us that to find a page containing the three words "Venezuelan Beaver Cheese" *together*, as a phrase, we should have put quote marks around them. That would have ruled out all the "hits" containing sentences like, "The beaver population has been halved by pollution. In this photo, Venezuelan cleanup engineer José Sanchez says 'Cheese!' for the camera."

Who ever said these things were user-friendly?

Useful Web pages: The tip of the iceberg

But there's more to the Web than getting meaningful work done (as millions of American office workers can attest). Here are some good starting places for your leisure hours. Technically, each of their addresses begins with *http://*, but you and I can both leave that off. Your Web browser will supply those letters automatically when you're finished typing.

(*Disclaimer:* Web pages come and go like New York City restaurants. I guarantee only that these pages existed the day I typed them up.)

- *mistral.culture.fr/louvre* — The Louvre museum home page, where you can actually view and read about hundreds of paintings hanging there.

- *amazon.com* — An enormous online bookstore, with three million books available, all at a 20 percent discount (or better). Reviews, sample chapters, the works. Don't freak out about typing in your credit-card number online; you're far more likely to be ripped off by handing your Visa card to the gas-station attendant or restaurant waiter.

- *www.dilbert.com* — Today's Dilbert cartoon. And a month of past issues.

- *www.shopper.com* — Here, you can comparison shop among hundreds of computer-stuff mail-order catalogs instantaneously — with the results listed in price order.

- *pathfinder.com* — The electronic editions of popular magazines like *People*, *Time*, *Money*, *Fortune*, and more. Lots of graphics — nice, if you're willing to wait for the pictures to arrive.

- *www.____.com* — Fill in the blank with your favorite major company: Honda. Sony. ABC. Apple. CBS. Disney. NY Times. Macworld. McDonald's. Try it — you'll like it.

- *www.davidpogue.com* — The charming, attractive, and highly entertaining Web page of your eminently modest author.

Navigator vs. Explorer: The Tip-O-Rama

Unless you're an America Online subscriber, you spend much of your Internetting time using the Netscape Navigator or Microsoft Internet Explorer browser.

Their makers, Netscape and Microsoft, are bigger rivals than Rocky Balboa and Apollo Creed (or whatever his opponent's name was). Each company has vowed to keep beating up the other until it crawls out of the ring with puffy black eyes screaming, "ADRIANNN!"

Anyway: Unlike your America Online-subscriber comrades, you, O Internet subscriber, swallowed hard and opted for a hard-core, bona fide *ISP account,* as described in Chapter 11. One of the perks of doing so is a raft of cool features in your Web browser. Here, for example, are some time-savers and little-known features that work in both major browsers.

Type almost nothing

As you may have read earlier in this chapter, most Web addresses take the form *http://www.Spam.com,* where *Spam* is the name of the company or place. Thank goodness, you don't have to type all that! Whenever the desired address takes that form, you can type (into that top strip where the address goes) *just the name of the company* — such as Apple, Microsoft, IBM, Snapple, Mentos, Pepsi, McDonalds, Spam, and so on. The browser fills in all the *http:// . . . com* junk for you automatically.

Go get the plug-in

Web browsers can show you text and pictures. But every now and then, you'll stumble onto some page where a *sound* or a *movie* is the main attraction. Unfortunately, Navigator and Explorer don't know how to play these multimedia morsels — but they know somebody who does!

What I'm driving at is *plug-ins* — small add-on programs that, after installed in the Plug-Ins folder on your hard drive, teach Navigator or Explorer how to play those extra goodies like sounds and movies. Plug-ins are free; you just must know where to go to get them on the Web. Lucky you: I'm about to tell you.

Go to the Web address *www.plugins.com* or, if you feel like typing today, *http://home.netscape.com/plugins/index.html.* There you'll find all the little plug-ins looking for a home on your iMac.

I'm not saying you can't live a long, healthy, fulfilling life without any of this stuff. I'm just pointing them out in case you try to visit some Web page and get nothing but an error message saying something like, "Sorry, you can't visit this page until you spend all afternoon downloading and installing Such-N-Such plug-in."

Where's home for you?

Every time you sign onto the Web, your browser starts by showing you the same darned starting page — let me guess: the browser company's page. Yeah, that's *realllll* interesting. Wouldn't it be great if you could change the startup page?

You can! From the Edit menu, choose Preferences. Click the icon at the left side of the screen that says Navigator (in Navigator) or Home/Search (in Internet Explorer), as shown here.

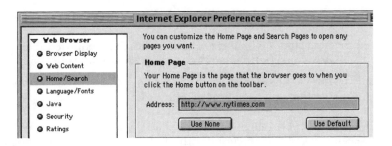

Now just change the Web address in the Home blank to a more desirable starting point. For example, you might prefer *www.apple.com,* which is all about Apple . . . or *www.macintouch.com,* which is daily news about the Mac . . . or even your own home page, if you've made one.

Faster — please, make it faster!

If the slug-like speed of the Web is making you sob quietly into your late-night coffee, despair no more. You can quadruple the speed of your Web surfing activities — by *turning off the pictures.*

Yes, I realize that graphics are what make the Web look so compelling. But all those pictures are 90 percent of what takes Web pages so darned long to arrive on the screen! You owe it to yourself to try, just for a session or two, turning graphics *off*. You still get fully laid-out Web pages; you still see all the text and headlines. But wherever a picture would normally be — wherever you would have had to wait for eight seconds — you'll see an empty rectangle containing a generic "graphic goes here" logo. Here, for example, is the Macworld magazine page (*www.Macworld.com*, of course) with all its graphics gone.

If you like the sound of this arrangement, here's how to make it so:

- ✔ **Netscape Navigator:** From the Edit menu, choose Preferences. Click the Advanced button and then turn off Automatically Load Images.
- ✔ **Internet Explorer:** From the Edit menu, choose Preferences. Click Web Content and then turn off Show Pictures.

The speed you gain is incredible. And if you wind up on a Web page that seems naked and shivering without its pictures, you can choose to summon them all — just on this one page — by choosing Load Images or View Images from your browser's View menu.

Bookmark it

When you find a Web page you might like to visit again, you're not condemned to writing the address on the edges of your monitor, like some kind of geeky bathroom graffiti. Instead, just choose Add Bookmark from the Bookmarks menu (in Navigator) or Add to Favorites from the Favorites menu (in Internet Explorer).

```
Bookmarks
Add Bookmark                                          ⌘D

Honda
Welcome to McDonald's
AltaVista Technology, Inc.
World Wide Web Browsers
MacInTouch Home Page
Pogue's Pages (David Pogue, computer-book author)
Welcome to Pizza Hut!
Smartcode Software
Welcome to the Freshest World of Mentos!
Welcome to Snapple
```

You're rewarded by the plain-English appearance of that page's name in the Bookmarks (or Favorites) menu! Thereafter, the *next* time you want to visit that page, you're spared having to remember *http://www.madmansdream.com* or whatever; you can just choose the page's name from your menu.

To get *rid* of something in your Bookmarks menu, choose Bookmarks from the Window menu (or choose Open Favorites from your Favorites menu). Click the page's name and then press the Delete key.

Chapter 14

E-mail for He-males and Females

● ●

● ●

*I*f you have any intention of getting the most from your expensive high-tech appliance, you *gotta* get into e-mail. E-mail has all the advantages of the telephone (instantaneous, personal) with none of the disadvantages (interrupts dinner, wakes you up). It also has all the advantages of postal mail (cheap, written, preservable) with none of *its* drawbacks (slow speed, hassle to reply, paper cuts).

Chapter 11 covers the glorious world of e-mail on America Online. If you're on the Internet courtesy of an Internet access company (an ISP) like EarthLink, however, read on.

Getting into E-Mail

To read and write electronic mail, you need an e-mail *program*. Microsoft Outlook Express, for example, is sitting right there on your iMac's hard drive (in the Internet folder). There's also a Mail function that's built right into the Internet Explorer Web browser program (see Chapter 12), but Outlook Express is a much superior e-mail program. It's the one that opens when, for example, you double-click the Mail icon that's sitting out on your desktop when you first turn on the iMac.

The grisliest part of joining the e-mail revolution is setting up your account for the first time. Fortunately, the Internet Setup Assistant (described in Chapter 11) does all of that setup for you. You're all ready to go a-mailing. (If you *didn't* use the Setup Assistant before trying to use Outlook Express, the program asks you to fill in a bunch of evil-looking blanks. Don't say I didn't warn you. Call up your Internet company and ask for help filling them in — or just run the Internet Setup Assistant.)

Sending e-mail

To write an e-mail, choose New Message from the Outlook Express File menu. An empty e-mail message appears, filled with blanks to fill out. (The To, Subject, and message areas are the only mandatory ones.) Here's what your finished message might look like.

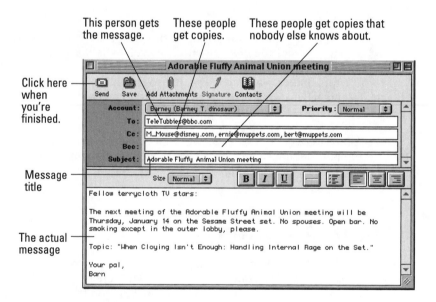

This person gets the message.

These people get copies.

These people get copies that nobody else knows about.

Click here when you're finished.

Message title

The actual message

As you'll quickly discover, e-mail addresses can't include any spaces, always have an @ symbol in them, and must be typed *exactly* right, even if they look like *cc293fil@univ_amx.intermp.com*. Capitals don't matter.

When you're finished writing, click the Send button at the top of the message window. If everything's set up right, your modem now dials and sends that e-message.

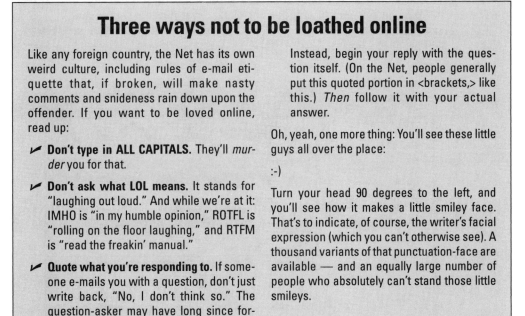

Three ways not to be loathed online

Like any foreign country, the Net has its own weird culture, including rules of e-mail etiquette that, if broken, will make nasty comments and snideness rain down upon the offender. If you want to be loved online, read up:

✔ **Don't type in ALL CAPITALS.** They'll *murder* you for that.

✔ **Don't ask what LOL means.** It stands for "laughing out loud." And while we're at it: IMHO is "in my humble opinion," ROTFL is "rolling on the floor laughing," and RTFM is "read the freakin' manual."

✔ **Quote what you're responding to.** If someone e-mails you with a question, don't just write back, "No, I don't think so." The question-asker may have long since forgotten his/her own query!

Instead, begin your reply with the question itself. (On the Net, people generally put this quoted portion in <brackets,> like this.) *Then* follow it with your actual answer.

Oh, yeah, one more thing: You'll see these little guys all over the place:

:-)

Turn your head 90 degrees to the left, and you'll see how it makes a little smiley face. That's to indicate, of course, the writer's facial expression (which you can't otherwise see). A thousand variants of that punctuation-face are available — and an equally large number of people who absolutely can't stand those little smileys.

Sending mail in batches

When you click Send, your iMac sends the single message you've just composed. In many cases, though, it's much nicer to be able to write *several* messages at a time — and send them all in a batch when you're good and ready.

To bring about that happy situation, choose Preferences from the File menu. Click the General icon, turn off the check box called Send Message Immediately, and click OK. From now on, as you write (or reply to e-mail) messages, they pile up in your Out Box. (Click the Out Box icon to see them.) When you're good and ready, click the Send & Receive icon (on the Outlook Express toolbar). Your modem dials and sends all of the mail at once — and *gets* all waiting mail from the Internet at the same time.

Getting your mail

If the messages you send out to your friends are witty and charming enough, you may actually get a few responses.

To check your e-mail, click the Send & Receive icon (on the Outlook Express toolbar). In a spasm of hideous shrieking, your modem then dials cyberspace's home number and fetches any waiting mail. You'll see it in a list, as shown here.

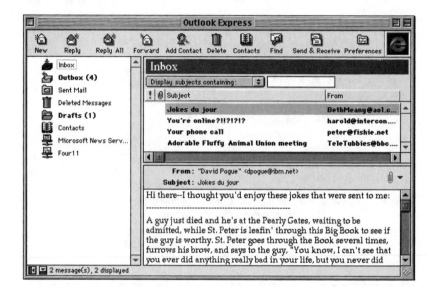

To read one of your messages, just click its name. A window opens, where you can read and enjoy your incoming memo.

Processing a message you've read

When you're finished reading an e-mail, you have four choices:

- ✔ **Write a reply.** To do so, click the Reply button on the toolbar. Now you're back into I'm-Writing-An-E-mail-Message mode, as described in "Sending e-mail," a couple of pages back. (Your e-mail software thoughtfully pretypes the e-mail address of the person you're answering — along with the date, time, and subject of the message. If I had a machine that did *that* for my U.S. mail, I'd be a much better paper correspondent.)

  If you drag your mouse through some pertinent portion of the original message before clicking the Reply button, your e-mail program pre-pastes that passage into the reply window, like this.

Hello there! I have a Macintosh 6100CD with 16 megs of
RAM and a floppy drive and a keyboard and a mouse and a
screen and a printer. It's cased in beige plastic, roughly
rectangular, with an Apple logo on the front and a power
cord on the back. Anyway, my question is this:

How do I insert a CD?

Re: basic Mac question

ments Signature Contacts Check Names

avid Pogue)
on@ranco.com

Label side up, hole in the middle. Hope this helps!

--David

>From: HSmitherson@ranco.com
>To: David Pogue
>Subject: basic Mac question

>Anyway, my question is this:
>
>How do I insert a CD?

This common Internet technique helps your correspondent grasp what
the heck you're talking about, especially since some time may have
passed since he or she wrote the original note. As in the illustration,
when the original e-mail contains a lot of irrelevant background material, this kind of bracketing helps both of you focus on the actual point
(if any).

✔ **Trash it.** Click the Delete icon on the toolbar, which sends the message
to the great cyber-shredder in the sky.

✔ **Print it.** From the File menu, choose Print.

✔ **Save it for later.** To do so, close the message window. If you want, you
can file the message away by dragging its name into one of the folders
at the left side of the screen.

By the way: You can, and should, create your own specially named
folders. Do that by choosing New Folder from the File menu.

Attaching Files to E-Mail

Fortunately, there's more to e-mail than just sending typed messages back
and forth. You can also send files from your hard drive — in the form of
attachments to your e-mail messages.

Companies use this method to exchange design sketches, movie clips, and
spreadsheets. Authors turn in chapters (written in Microsoft Word or
AppleWorks) to publishers this way. And families send baby pictures this
way, to the eternal boredom of most recipients.

Sending a file

To pull this off, start by writing a normal e-mail message, making sure that you include a phrase like: "By the way, I've attached an AppleWorks file. It's a drawing little Cindy did of a tobacco-company executive in a paroxysm of self-loathing and doubt."

Then locate the icon of the file you want to send. (This may involve opening some folders and rearranging some windows on your screen.) You need to adjust the windows on your screen so that you can see *both* your e-mail message *and* the icon of the file you want to send, like this.

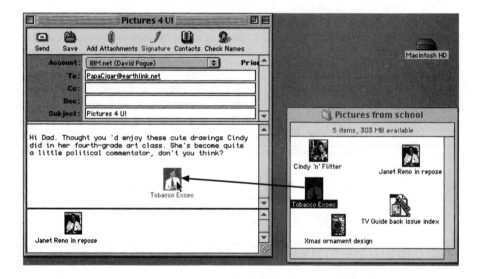

Drag the icons straight into the e-mail window. As in the preceding figure, the icons show up at the bottom of the window to indicate that your dragging was successful.

That's it! When you send the message, the attached iMac files go along for the ride.

Getting a file

You may *receive* files as part of an e-mail message, too. The telltale signs that you've received some picture or other file is (a) a special paper-clip icon and (b) a normal-looking Macintosh file icon beneath the message, like this.

Just double-click the file icon to open it. If it doesn't open, see the section "When You Can't Open Your Downloaded Goodies," in Chapter 11.

The Anti-Spam Handbook

No doubt about it: Unsolicited junk e-mail, better known as *spam*, is the ugly underbelly of e-mail paradise. You'll know it if you've got it — wave after wave of daily messages like "MAKE EZ MONEY AT HOME CARVING TOOTH-PICKS!" and "SEXXXY APPLIANCE REPAIRMEN WAITING FOR YOUR CALL!"

If the names and addresses of the lowlife scum that sends out these billions of junk e-mails were ever published, the problem would take care of itself — the Internet population would drive over to the spammers' homes and rip apart each cell of their miserable little bodies.

But that's the thing — spammers hide. Their e-mail doesn't include a phone number or postal address; you're generally expected to visit a Web site or respond by e-mail. Meanwhile, our e-mail boxes fill up with useless crud that makes it harder to find the *real* messages among them.

Whatever you do, *never reply* to a piece of spam e-mail — even if the message says that you can get *off* the e-mail list by doing so! Ironically, your response to the e-mail will simply flag your e-mail address as a live, working account manned by somebody who takes the time to *read* the stuff. Your name will become much more valuable to junk e-mailers, and you'll find yourself on the receiving end of a new wave of spam.

You may have wondered: How did you wind up on these junk lists to begin with? Answer: They get your e-mail address from *you*. Every time you post a message on an online bulletin board, chat in a chat room, or even put your e-mail address up on your Web page, you've just made yourself vulnerable to the spammers' software robots. These little programs scour America Online, newsgroups, and the Web, looking for e-mail addresses to collect.

"But if I can never post messages online," I can hear you protesting, "I'm losing half the advantages of being online!"

Not necessarily. Consider setting up a second mailbox — that is, a second e-mail address for your same America Online or Internet account. (That's easy to do on AOL; go to keyword *names* to set up a new one. If you have an Internet account, call your ISP's help line to arrange an additional mailbox.)

Thereafter, the game is easy to play: Use *one* e-mail address for public postings, chats, and so on. Use your second, private one *for e-mail only*. Spam robots can't read private e-mail, so your secret e-mail address will remain virginal and spam-free.

Part V
Troubleshooting Made Tolerable

The 5th Wave   By Rich Tennant

"Brad! That's not your modem we're hearing! It's Buddy!! He's out of his cage and in the iMac!!"

In this part . . .

Now it's time to take the bull by the horns, the sword by the hilt, the fish by the gills, and really take off. I bestow unto you the Mother of All Troubleshooting Guides, and then you'll find out where to go from there, with your trusty iMac ever by your side.

Chapter 15

When Bad Things Happen to Good iMacs

• •

In This Chapter

▶ The top ten problems that beginners encounter and how to solve them

▶ The next ten after that

▶ The next ten after that

• •

Introduction to Computer Hell

As a new computer owner, you probably aren't cheered up very much by the fact that this troubleshooting guide is the fattest part of the book.

But let's face it: Computers are appliances. As such, they have minds of their own. And like other expensive appliances (cars, homes, pacemakers), they tend to get cranky at the worst possible times.

Now, when that happens, most beginners immediately suspect the circuitry. I understand the instinct. I mean, when VCRs, lawnmowers, or electric razors go on the fritz, you're right — you need a repair shop. But a computer's different; it has *software*. When your iMac starts behaving oddly, it's probably a software problem, not a mechanical one. That means that you can fix it yourself, for free. Almost always.

This chapter and the next show the steps you can take to restore your iMac's software to health. (By the way: Another excellent, if terse, source of troubleshooting information is the Emergency Handbook that came with your iMac.)

About the cookbook

It turns out that about 90 percent of the things that go wrong with your iMac can be solved using the same handful of troubleshooting steps. To save you reading and me writing, I've consolidated them all into Chapter 16. As you read through this chapter's symptom-by-symptom listings, I'll refer you to one or another of those steps.

The iMac Freezes or Crashes

Two scary conditions are enough to make even pro iMac jockeys swallow hard. The first of these conditions, a *System crash,* occurs when the following message appears on the screen.

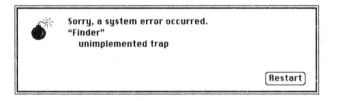

```
Sorry, a system error occurred.
"Finder"
      unimplemented trap

                              [ Restart ]
```

Your current work session is over, amigo; you need to restart the computer. (Safest way to restart is to use "The Restart Hole," as described in the next chapter.) Anything that you've typed or drawn since the last time you saved your work is gone.

A System *freeze* is different — and, as horrific computer nightmares go, it's preferable. You get no message on the screen; instead, the mouse cursor freezes in place. You can't move the cursor, and nothing that you type changes anything. The iMac, as far as you can tell, has silicon lockjaw.

Escaping a System freeze right now

First resort: Try the amazing "Force Quit" keystroke. (See the section "The Amazing 'Force Quit' Keystroke," in the next chapter.) That should get you out of the locked program, at least.

Last resort: If the Magical Force-Quit Keystroke doesn't work — and sometimes it doesn't — you have to restart the iMac. This time, see "The Restart Hole," in the next chapter.

Escaping repeated System freezes

Ninety percent of the time, freezes and crashes are related either to memory or to *extension conflicts*.

First resort: Increase the amount of memory allotted to the program that you were using, as described in the section "Giving More Memory to a Program," in the next chapter. Give the program 10 percent more, for example.

Second resort: Something, or *several* somethings, are clashing in your System Folder. See "Solving an Extension Conflict" in the next chapter. If you're in a hurry to get your work done and can't take the time, just restart your iMac while pressing the Shift key. That turns *all* extensions off. For this work session, of course, you won't be able to use your CD-ROM drive, send faxes, use America Online or the Internet, or use Microsoft programs, but at least you can get into your iMac and do basic stuff without the hassle of system crashes.

Third resort: Maybe one of your programs is either (a) buggy or (b) out-of-date. You can't do anything but contact the software company and hope for the best.

Last resort: If the crashes still haven't stopped, something in your System Folder may be gummed up. You're in for a 20-minute, but *very* effective, ritual known as a *clean reinstall* of your System Folder. For instructions, see the section "Performing a Clean System Reinstall," in the next chapter.

Mac OS 8.5 and the Amazing Self-Repairing iMac

A system crash on an iMac running Mac OS 8.5 or later (see Chapter 1) is just as emotionally wounding as it is on any computer. Yet the feeling doesn't last, thanks to what comes next. As soon as your computer starts up again after the crash, it gets to work *repairing itself.*

You'll see a big dialog box on the screen and a progress bar showing how long the self-surgery will take. In brief, your iMac is checking out its own hard drive to make sure nothing was damaged during the system crash. If it finds anything wrong, the iMac fixes it automatically.

Since this is all taking place immediately following the crash, newborn problems get nipped in the bud, before they can grow up to be big, strong, meat-eating problems.

You *can* turn off this feature, if you like; open your General Controls control panel (see Chapter 8) and click to turn off the check box called "Warn me if computer was shut down improperly."

But *why* would you want to do that?

Problems in One Program

If your troubles seem to be confined to just one application, your trouble-shooting task is much easier.

First resort: Give the program more memory, as described the section "Giving More Memory to a Program," in Chapter 16.

Second resort: First, some technical background: Whenever you launch a modern software program, it generally consults the *preferences file* in your Preferences folder. This preference file is where the program stores its little notes to itself about the way you like things set up: where you keep your toolbars on the screen (if it's Microsoft Word), what your favorite Web sites are (if it's Netscape Navigator or Internet Explorer), whether your prefer list views or icon views (if it's the Finder), and so on. If that file is damaged, so is your work session.

Now, what do we do when our government's malfunctioning? We throw out the components that aren't working and elect new ones. That's exactly the idea here: Open your System Folder, open your Preferences folder, and trash the program's preferences file. The very next time you launch that program, it will automatically create a *new* preferences file. Best of all — and here's where my political analogy breaks down — your new preference file is guaranteed to be uncorrupted.

This trick is especially useful in that most frequently used program of all, the Finder. The Finder Prefs file stores all kinds of settings important to your iMac work environment: the font and icon-layout settings used for Finder windows; window settings; whether or not the "Are you sure?" message appears when you empty the Trash; and so on.

Therefore, if you start noticing weird goings-on with your icons, windows, or Trash, try discarding the Finder Preferences file. Restart the iMac to generate a fresh, clean copy.

Last resort: If all else fails, try reinstalling the program in question — an updated version, if possible.

It's also conceivable that one of your extensions or control panels is causing trouble for this program. See "Solving an Extension Conflict" in the next chapter.

Error Messages

Let's start the troubleshooting session in earnest with a few good old American error messages. Yes, kids, these are the '90s equivalent of "DOES NOT COMPUTE." These are messages, appearing in an *alert box* like the fictional one shown here, that indicate that something's wrong.

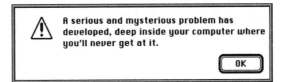

> ⚠ A serious and mysterious problem has developed, deep inside your computer where you'll never get at it.
>
> [OK]

"Application not found"

First resort: Not everything on the iMac is meant to be a plaything for you; the iMac reserves a few files for its own use. Certain items, especially in your System Folder, give you the "Application not found" message if double-clicked because they're there for your iMac's use, not for yours — such as icons in the Preferences folder, for example, or various other support-file icons for non-Apple stuff.

Second resort: In Chapter 3, you can read about programs and the documents that they produce (like parents and children). Sometimes, the "Application not found" message means that you're trying to open a document (child), but the iMac can't find its parent (the program used to create it).

So if you double-click an AppleWorks document, but the AppleWorks program itself isn't on your hard disk, the iMac shrugs and asks, in effect, "Yo — how am I s'posed to open this?" To remedy the situation, reinstall the missing program on the hard disk.

More often, though, you're double-clicking something you downloaded from the Internet or America Online — something created by *someone else,* using a program you don't have. For example, let's say I send you a word processor file, but you don't have the same word processor program I do.

To read such files, launch *your* word processor *first* and then choose the Open command from the File menu (next figure, left).

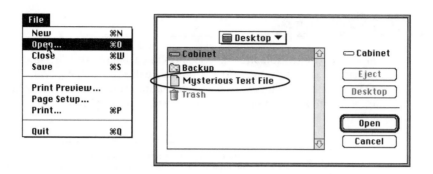

The usual list box appears, and you'll see the text file listed there (above, right). Double-click to open it.

The same applies to generic *graphics* documents. These files, in technical-sounding formats like PICT, JPEG, and GIF, can be opened by almost any program. (America Online or Netscape Navigator, for example, can open all three.) Yet if you try to *double-click* a generic graphics file, you'll be told, "Application not found." (That's because graphics files can be opened by *so many* different programs that the iMac doesn't know which one you want to use.) Again, the solution is to launch your graphics program *first* (America Online or Netscape Navigator or ClarisWorks or Photoshop, for example) and *then* open the file via the Open command.

Third resort: Are you, by chance, trying to open a file that you received via America Online e-mail — from somebody *not* on America Online? In that case, you may be out of luck. AOL has this unfortunate habit of garbling e-mail attachments that originate from the Internet itself. (See Chapter 14 for more on e-mail, and the end of Chapter 11 for more on opening downloaded goodies.)

Last resort: Sometimes you get the "Application not found" message even if you're sure that the document's parent program *is* on the disk. (You double-click an AppleWorks document, for example, and you're told that the application — AppleWorks — can't be found, even though it's *sitting right there* on the disk in plain sight!)

In a situation like this, the iMac's genealogical gnomes have become confused: The computer has lost track of which program is associated with which kinds of documents. In the words of Mac gurus everywhere, "You gotta rebuild the desktop." For instructions, see the "Rebuilding the Desktop File" in the next chapter.

The only virus worth worrying about

There are plenty of reasons to be glad you use a Macintosh. Consider computer viruses (software written by some sociopath to gum up the works of any computer it encounters): while 10,000 different computer viruses attack Windows-compatible computers, until 1998, there was not a *single virus* that could destroy Macintosh files.

Nowadays, there is one Mac virus — called AutoStart. If your iMac "catches" this virus, you'll notice three odd symptoms: first, the iMac restarts itself just after you insert a disk of some kind. (That's your iMac coming down with the virus.) Second, your hard drive starts thrashing and making noise about every half hour. Third, some of the files on your hard drive may become corrupted and un-openable.

Fortunately, it's easy to protect your iMac against this virus: From the menu, choose Control Panels and open the control panel called QuickTime Settings. Turn off the CD-ROM Auto-Play option. That's it — you're protected. (It's perfectly okay to leave "Enable *Audio CD* AutoPlay" turned on. That option makes music CDs start playing when you insert them into your iMac, and it's completely safe.)

The AutoStart virus is also very easy to eliminate once you've caught it. Visit *www.macvirus.com* on the Web (see Chapter 12). There you'll find free programs like WormScanner, which wipe out the virus instantly.

"You are running low on memory"

Believe it or not, this message appears even on iMacs with *boatloads* of memory. It doesn't mean that your *iMac* is running low on memory; it means that your *program* is gasping for air, even though the computer itself has gallons and gallons of memory just sitting around.

Each program, when it comes from the factory, has been given a memory *limit*. It's not allowed to use more memory than its limit, even if there's lots available on the iMac.

Fortunately, you can *change* this limit; if a program you use often is acting flaky, crashing, or giving "running low on memory" messages, you should raise the program's memory limit. Complete instructions are under "Giving More Memory to a Program," in the next chapter.

"Application has unexpectedly quit"

Your program has probably run out of memory. Again, see the section in the next chapter called "Giving More Memory to a Program."

"Can't empty trash" or "Can't be deleted"

First resort: A locked file or folder is probably in the Trash can. Press Option while choosing Empty Trash from the Special menu to override its stubbornness and delete the locked item.

Second resort: Maybe the iMac has become confused about the trashability of some file or folder in the Trash. Restart the iMac and try again.

Last resort: About once in every iMac user's life, the iMac gets *so* confused that it simply will not delete a folder in the Trash, even if you've tried all the logical things. Your System Folder is simply having a psychotic break.

Here's a sneaky trick to get around its obstinacy:

1. **Drag the undeletable folder to the desktop.**

   Let's say the folder's called Rescued Items.

2. **Change the recalcitrant folder's name to the name of another folder on your disk.**

   If you have a Downloads folder, for example, change the name of Rescued Items to Downloads.

3. **Open the original Downloads folder and drag everything inside it into the newly named Downloads folder on your desktop.**

4. **Trash the *original* Downloads folder and move the new Downloads folder from your desktop to the location of the *former* Downloads folder.**

You should now be able to empty the Trash, having successfully outfoxed the iMac at its own game. After all, you're now trashing a perfectly ordinary folder.

"DNS Entry not found" or "Error 404"

You get these messages when using your Web browser (see Chapter 12). It means that the Web page you're trying to visit doesn't exist. Usually this means you've made a typo as you typed the Web address (sometimes called a *URL*), or the page's address has changed and you don't know it, or the computer the Web page is on has been taken off the Internet (for maintenance, for example).

Numbered error messages

This may strike you as hard to believe, but the numbers in some error messages (Type 11, Type 3, Error 49, and so on) are *no help at all*. They're valuable only to programmers — and even then, not very. A few examples:

Error code	Message	Meaning
−1	qErr	Queue element not found during deletion.
−2	vTypErr	Invalid queue element.
−3	corErr	Core routine number out of range.
−4	unimpErr	Unimplemented core routine.

As an Apple programmer once explained it, it's like finding a car smashed into a tree with its tires still spinning. All you can say for sure is that something went wrong. But you have no idea what *led up* to the crash. Maybe the guy was drunk, or distracted, or asleep. You'll never know.

Same thing with your iMac. The machine knows that *something* happened, but it's way too late to tell you what. Restart it and get back to business.

Out of Memory

As a service to you, the Tremulous Novice, I've gone this entire book without even a word about memory management, which is a whole new ball of wax. I hoped that you'd never need to think about it. Memory becomes an issue only when you get the message "There is not enough memory to open Word" (or whatever program you're trying to open), and that's why you're reading about memory in a troubleshooting chapter.

Your iMac has a fixed amount of memory. Think of the iMac as a station wagon. You can pack it with camping gear, or you can pack it with your kid's birthday-party friends — but probably not with both. Even if you manage to cram in the kids *and* the gear, if you *then* try to cram in the dog, somebody in the family is going to say, "There is not enough room to take Bowser."

That's what the "not enough memory" message is trying to tell you.

Each program that you open consumes a chunk of the iMac's limited memory. You're entitled to run as many programs as you want simultaneously — the Note Pad, the Calculator, your word processor, and so on — *provided* that they all fit into the amount of memory your iMac has. If you try to open one too many programs, you'll get that message about the dog. (*You* know what I mean.)

Before we begin, remember that there are two different kinds of memory shortages. First, there's the "You are running low on memory" type, which indicates that a *program* doesn't have enough memory; see "Giving More Memory to a Program" in the next chapter.

Second, there's the "Not enough memory to *open* this program" problem, which means that your *iMac's* memory is all used up. The following discussion applies to this second scenario.

First resort: Quit programs

If you're told that you're out of memory, the easiest way out of the situation is to *quit* one of the programs you're already running. (You quit a program by choosing Quit from the File menu.) So if you're running Word and you try to open AppleWorks, and you're told that there's not enough unused (free) memory, you'll just have to quit Word first.

Often, you may have programs running and not even know it. Remember that just because a program has no *windows* open doesn't mean it isn't *running.* When you're done working on something, did you just *close the window,* or did you actually *choose Quit* from the File menu? If you didn't actually Quit, then the program is still running and still using up memory.

To get rid of that program, choose its name from the Application menu (in the very upper-right corner of the screen). Then choose Quit from the File menu.

Second resort: Defragment your RAM

Imagine an obnoxious driver who parks on the divider line, thus occupying two parking spaces. Half a parking space is wasted on either side. Those two wasted gaps, when added up, equal one whole parking space — but that's of no help when you want to park your *whole* car.

In the same way, your iMac's memory can get broken up into pieces as you launch and quit various programs during the day. Suppose your System Folder is using 12, then there's an empty block of 4, then America Online is using 8, then there's an empty block of 4, and so on. You might try to launch, say, AppleWorks — but even though your calculations show that you *should* have enough memory to do so, you get the "out of memory" message. Your iMac, it turns out, doesn't have enough *continuous,* unbroken memory to run that latest program.

The solution to this problem (which is called, geekily enough, *memory fragmentation*) is to *quit* all your programs, and *then* launch all the programs that are supposed to fit in your iMac's memory. This time, you won't leave holes in your memory setup, and you'll be able to use all the memory you deserve. (Restarting the iMac achieves the same purpose.)

Third resort: Get RAM Doubler

Here's a fascinating possibility for the RAM-shy iMac fan: Buy a $60 program called *RAM Doubler*.

RAM Doubler uses several potent, deeply technical tricks to make your iMac *behave* as though it has twice or three times as much memory as it really does. The only fundamental understanding of RAM Doubler that you need is this: It lets you run *more small programs at the same time*. It doesn't let you run one *big* program that requires more real memory than you have.

So Billy Bob, who has a 32-meg iMac and who wants to run AppleWorks, Quicken, Photo Soap, and America Online at the same time, is made in the shade. He no longer has to quit one of those programs just to free enough memory to launch another. RAM Doubler lets him keep all of those programs going.

Jenny Sue, however, wants very much to run MindReader Pro, which requires 36 megs of RAM, on her 32-meg iMac. She's out of luck. RAM Doubler's double-memory tactics don't let you run any *big* programs that you couldn't run before.

Fourth resort: Use virtual memory

As with RAM Doubler, virtual memory (a free, built-in feature) lets you run programs whose combined memory requirements add up to much more than your iMac should be able to handle.

Although you may not have realized it, the virtual memory feature has been turned on since the day you bought your iMac. In times of memory shortage, however, here's how to crank its level higher, thus letting you run even more programs simultaneously:

1. **From the menu, choose Control Panels; in the resulting window, double-click Memory.**

   The Memory control panel appears, like this.

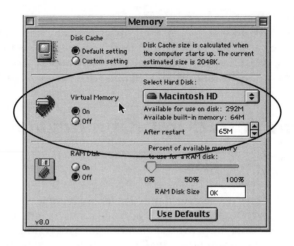

2. **Make sure the Virtual Memory switch is On.**

   On an iMac, virtual memory should *always* be on, at least a little bit (see Step 3). The technical details would curl your nose hairs, but let's just say that having virtual memory turned on makes these models run faster and use memory more efficiently.

   (*Geek disclaimer:* The only time virtual memory should be off is if you've bought RAM Doubler, described in the previous section. It replaces virtual memory.)

3. **Using the little up- and-down-arrow buttons next to the words "After restart," specify how much total memory you'd like to wind up with.**

   Virtual memory works by using a chunk of your *hard disk* to simulate additional RAM.

   For some mysterious technical reason, however, you can't just use the Memory control panel to dial in the amount of *additional* memory you'd like. The iMac must reserve hard-disk space equal to *all* the memory, real and "virtual." (That's why you won't be allowed to turn on virtual memory if your hard drive is full.)

   Now, the iMac should, at the very least, have virtual memory set *1MB* higher than its actual installed RAM. If your iMac has 32 megs of RAM (consult this book's Cheat Sheet), virtual memory should be set to at least 33MB.

   It's safe to crank your total memory, using the virtual memory controls, up to *double* your real memory. But be careful: the higher you set this number, the slower your iMac may run. If you have 32MB of RAM, your total memory (including virtual) shouldn't exceed 64MB; things will get so slow as to be unworkable.

4. **When you're done with your virtual-memory setup, restart the iMac.**

Last resort: Buy more

After a certain point, knocking yourself out to solve out-of-memory problems reaches a point of diminishing returns. You get so worn out from workarounds that they're not worth doing.

At that point (or much sooner), just spring for the $50 or $75 and *buy more memory*. You can get it from any mail-order company (see Appendix B). When you call, tell them that you have an iMac; they'll tell you what kind of memory chips you need and in what quantities they're available.

If you've got a knowledgeable buddy looking over your shoulder, you can install the new memory chips yourself. (For instructions, double-click the Mac OS Info Center icon on your desktop; click Tell Me About My Computer; and then click Installing Additional Memory.) Otherwise, get an Apple dealer to do it for you.

Having lots of memory to kick around in is a joy. Your iMac runs faster, has fewer crashes and glitches, and acts like a new machine. It's a situation that I heartily recommend.

Startup Problems

Problems that you encounter when you turn on the iMac are especially disheartening when you're a new Mac user. It does wonders for your self-esteem to think that you can't even turn the thing *on* without problems.

No chime, no picture

First resort: Chances are very, very, very good that your iMac simply isn't getting electricity. It's probably not plugged in. Or it's plugged into a power strip whose On/Off switch is currently set to Off.

Second resort: You're supposed to turn the machine on by pressing the round key at the upper-right of your keyboard. Maybe the keyboard isn't plugged in. Try the identical power button on the front of the iMac.

Last resort: If those steps don't solve the problem, your iMac is as dead as Elvis. Get it in for repair. But that's virtually never the actual problem.

Picture, no ding

Every iMac makes a sound when you turn it on. The speaker-volume slider (in the Monitors & Sound control panel) controls the sound of the startup chime.

First resort: Open the Monitors & Sound control panel and make sure that the volume slider isn't all the way down. Make sure the Mute check box isn't turned on.

Last resort: When headphones are plugged into the iMac, no sound can come out of the iMac speakers. Unplug the headphones, in that case.

A question mark blinks on the screen

The blinking question mark, superimposed on a System Folder icon, is the iMac's international symbol for "I've looked everywhere, and I can't find a System Folder."

The blinking question mark means that your hard drive's not working right — or that it's working fine, but your System Folder got screwed up somehow. In either case, here's what to do:

First resort: After ten seconds of panic, turn the iMac off and try starting again or just restart it. (See "The Restart Hole" in the next chapter.)

Second resort: Find the Software Install CD that came with your iMac. Put it in the CD drive. Restart the iMac (see "The Restart Hole" in the next chapter) while pressing the letter C key until the smiling Mac appears.

Once you're running, find the program called Disk First Aid. Run it and use the Repair button. Most of the time, Disk First Aid can repair your hard drive.

Third resort: If the hard-drive icon still doesn't appear, perhaps the System Folder is calling in sick. Reinstall the System Folder from your Software Install CD, as described in the section "Performing a Clean System Reinstall," in Chapter 16.

Fourth resort: Try *zapping the PRAM* (pronounced PEA-ram). See the section "Zapping the PRAM" in Chapter 16.

Last resort: If nothing has worked and you still can't make your hard-drive icon appear on the screen, your hard drive is sick. Call your local dealer or Mac guru, and do *not* freak out — chances are very good that all your files are still intact. (Just because the platters aren't spinning doesn't mean that they've been wiped out, just as your Walkman tapes don't get erased when the Walkman runs out of batteries.)

In fact, if you've purchased an add-on disk drive (see Chapter 18), you may be able to rescue the data from your disk yourself. Buy a disk-recovery program, such as Norton Utilities or TechTool Pro. That'll let you grab anything useful off the disk and may even help heal what's wrong with it.

The power button on the keyboard doesn't work

If pressing the power button at the upper-right corner of the iMac keyboard doesn't turn on the machine — but the identical power button on the *front* of the iMac *does* turn it on — then you may be witnessing a peculiarity of the iMac keyboard. This keyboard does not, in fact, turn on the iMac unless it's plugged directly into the side of the iMac — not when it's plugged into a *USB hub* (see Chapter 10).

Either turn on your iMac by pressing the front-panel power button, or plug your keyboard directly into the iMac.

Some crazy program launches itself every time you start up

In the words of programmers everywhere, "It's a feature, not a bug."

Inside the System Folder, there's a folder called Startup Items. Look inside it. Somebody put a program or document in there.

Anything in the Startup Items folder automatically opens when you turn on the iMac. This feature is supposed to be a time-saver for people who work on the same documents every day. Open the Startup Items folder and remove whatever's bothering you.

Printing Problems

If you're like most people, you own a second computer without even knowing it: your printer. Yes, like a computer, today's printers have their own memory, microchips — and problems.

"Printer could not be opened" or "Printer could not be found"

First resort: These messages appear if you try to print something without turning on the printer first (or letting it warm up fully). Turn it on, wait a whole minute, and then try again.

Second resort: Of course, it may be that you haven't performed the critical step of selecting the printer's icon in the Chooser desk accessory. See Chapter 5 for step-by-step instructions. (If you're using an adapter, such as a Farallon iPrint, to make an older, non-USB printer work with your iMac, double-check the setup steps provided in Chapter 5.)

Third resort: Maybe a cable came loose. Track the cable from your iMac's USB port all the way to the printer. If you're using an Ethernet network (you know who you are), try reseating, or even replacing, the cable.

Last resort: If you're using a laser printer, you are, believe it or not, on a network, no matter how small. A network works only if AppleTalk is *active* (check the Chooser, in your menu) and if the correct *kind* of network (such as LocalTalk or Ethernet) is selected; visit the control panel called AppleTalk and confirm the setting.

Inkjet printers: Blank pages come out

It's your cartridge.

First resort: If you haven't used the printer in a while, try your printer's "clean nozzle" command. (You'll need to consult the manual to find out exactly how you invoke it.)

Second resort: If you bought an Epson color inkjet printer when the iMac first came out in the summer of 1998, you've just discovered the software glitch that frustrated thousands. It's easy to fix: Get onto the World Wide Web (see Chapter 12) and go to the Web address *www.apple.com/support/imac*. There you'll find an Updates command that lists, among other things, something called the iMac Update 1.0. It fixes all kinds of problems with add-on USB gadgets; follow the installation instructions included with this software. (If you bought your iMac after November 1998, you don't need this update.)

After installing the iMac Update, direct your Web browser to *www.epson.com/support/pdcip_m.html*. Here you'll find yet another item to download: a new *printer driver* (that is, printer software) for every iMac-compatible Epson printer model. Download the one that matches your model.

Last resort: Your cartridge is probably empty. Replace it.

Finder Foul-ups

The Finder, you'll recall, is your home base. It's the desktop. It's the Trash can and icons and all that stuff. It's where you manage your files, rename them, copy them — and sometimes have problems with them.

You can't rename a file

The file is probably locked. Click it, choose Get Info from the File menu, and deselect the Locked check box. Or maybe the file is on a locked *disk*, such as a CD-ROM disc. You *can't* rename anything on a locked disk.

You can't rename or eject a disk

Well, you can't rename a CD, ever. A CD is permanently locked.

But suppose you've equipped your iMac with one of the add-on disk drives (such as a floppy-disk drive or SuperDisk) described in Chapter 18. I'm gonna take a wild shot at this one. I'll bet you've got File Sharing turned on (in the File Sharing control panel). Right?

It's true: If you're using this feature (known as *file sharing*), you're not allowed to change your hard drive's name. You'd wreak havoc with the other people on the network, who are trying to keep straight who you are.

If you really want to bother, open your File Sharing control panel and turn *off* File Sharing. Now you can rename your disk. (You're often not allowed to eject CDs or Zip disks when File Sharing is on, either.)

All your icons show up blank

If you get zapped by the "generic icons" problem, where every document looks like a boring blank sheet of paper, your invisible Desktop file has become corrupted. See "Rebuilding the Desktop File" in the next chapter.

It's January 1, 1904

Ever wonder how your iMac always manages to know what time it is — even when it's been *unplugged?*

Turns out the iMac has a battery — a built-in, five- to seven-year battery that maintains the clock even when the computer is off. When this battery dies, your iMac's clock resets itself to January 1, 1904 (or January 1, 1956)! All your new or modified files get stamped with that date, too. And no matter how many times you reset your clock, it stubbornly jumps back to that date in antiquity.

Because this book was published the same year that the iMac was invented, the dead-battery problem is pretty unlikely to strike you, the new iMac owner, for quite a while. Therefore, if your iMac's clock keeps setting itself to 1904 or 1956, you must be reading this chapter several years *after* the iMac's debut. In that case, I have three questions. First: Just how old *is* your copy of this book, anyway? Second: Aren't you glad that Macs are exempt from the "Year 2000 Glitch"? Third: Who won the World Series in 2003?

I'd love to tell you which Eveready battery to pick up at your local drugstore, but no such luck. Your iMac's internal battery must generally be replaced by an Apple technician, usually at a cost of about $25.

Disk Disasters (Floppies, CDs, and Co.)

Disks are cheap and handy and make excellent coasters. But when they start giving you attitude, read on. (Some of these problems, of course, arise only if you've bought an add-on disk drive — for floppies or Zip disks, for example — for your iMac.)

Your CD vibrates scarily

A CD-ROM disc in the iMac can spin so fast that, believe it or not, it can occasionally start spinning lopsidedly — like an out-of-balance washing-machine load — from the infinitesimal weight of unevenly applied *paint on the CD label*.

Actually, this noisy syndrome is nothing to worry about. If it bugs you, though, visit the World Wide Web, as described in Chapter 12. Go to *www.apple.com/support/imac*. There you'll find an Updates command that lists something called the iMac CD-ROM Update. Download and install it by following the included instructions; it should help the loud, vibrating CD-ROM syndrome.

You can't install a new program from your SuperDisk

If you've equipped your iMac with a SuperDisk drive (as described in Chapter 18), you may run into this peculiar problem. Although most software these days comes on a CD, a few older programs still come on a stack of floppy disks. During the installation of such programs, a normal Macintosh floppy-disk drive automatically spits out Disk 1 when it's time for you to insert Disk 2 — but not the SuperDisk. The *screen* says "Please insert Disk 2," but Disk 1 remains happily nestled in your SuperDisk drive. Weird, huh?

How's this for a low-tech solution? Unplug and then replug your SuperDisk drive's USB connector from the side of the iMac. Disk 1 pops right out. Repeat as necessary with the additional floppies.

Everything's Slow

If the iMac has begun acting slower since you've owned it, something may indeed be wrong.

First resort: After several months of using a iMac, it actually *does* slow down. The problem is a bloated Desktop file; the solution is described in the section "Rebuilding the Desktop File" in Chapter 16.

Last resort: If your hard drive is rather full, perhaps it needs to be *defragmented*. See "Defragmenting Your Hard Drive" in the next chapter.

Hardware Headaches

These glitches aren't as common as software problems, but they're just as frustrating.

Your mouse is jerky or sticky

Like children, mops, and mimes, a mouse does its work by rolling around on the ground. It's bound to get dirty.

To clean it, turn it upside down in your hand. Very firmly rotate the round collar counterclockwise so that you can remove the cute little two-colored ball. Dump the ball into your hand, wash it off under the faucet, and let it air-dry completely.

In the meantime, go to work inside the socket where the ball usually is. With tweezers or something, pull out any obvious dust bunnies and hairballs. The main thing, though, is those little rollers inside the cavity: You'll probably see stripes of accumulated gunk around them. With patience, a scissors blade (or a wad of sticky-side-out Scotch tape), and a good light, lift off that stuff, preferably making an effort not to let it fall inside the cavity. Keep turning the mouse right side up and tapping it on the table to dislodge stuff.

When you put everything back together, both you and your mouse will be much happier.

Double-clicking doesn't work

You're probably double-clicking too slowly, or you're moving the mouse a little bit during the double-click process.

Your monitor's too small

"Your monitor's too small" could mean almost anything. Maybe you're happy with *how much* screen area you have, but you wish you could enlarge it, decreasing the band of empty black space around the screen. Maybe you're having trouble reading text on the screen, and wish you could magnify the whole thing. Or maybe you actually wish you had a larger screen — both magnified *and* more screen area.

First resort: Open your Monitors & Sound control panel. Click Monitors. You can adjust *how much area* the screen shows you by clicking one of the Resolution settings (such as "800 x 600" or "1,024 x 768"). Click lower numbers to make everything on the iMac screen bigger (but therefore showing less of a page when you're word processing). Click higher numbers to make everything on the screen smaller (but thereby getting the bigger picture of your work).

Second resort: Open the Monitors & Sound control panel. Click the Geometry button, as shown here:

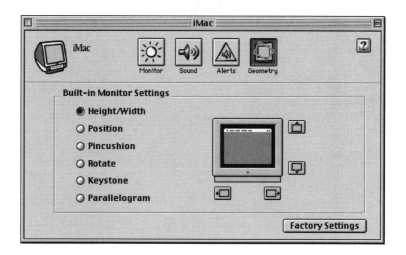

 Click the Height/Width button. Now, by clicking the tiny adjustment buttons on the right side of the window, you can gradually enlarge the entire picture until it fills the plastic border of your screen. (Actually, you can even blow it up *bigger* than that, chopping off the edges of the picture, if you're in one of those moods.) This process doesn't affect how much area you can see; it just enlarges what you're already seeing.

Last resort: If you buy and install an iPort adapter (see Appendix D), you can actually attach a second monitor — as large as you like — to your iMac. This is an expensive project, of course, but the result is spectacular: Your new screen acts as an extension of the built-in one. This arrangement is ideal for keeping a graphics program's *tools* on one screen and the artwork on another, or for comparing two Web pages side-by-side, or for feeling like you're an evil computer genius lording over your array of towering machinery.

Chapter 16

The Problem-Solving Cookbook

*I*f you've read the previous chapter, you've now heard about everything that can possibly go wrong, and you're thoroughly depressed.

Here, then, is the literary equivalent of therapy: a chapter containing everything you can possibly do to *fix* the problem. Remember, you'll almost never find out what caused the problem to begin with; just be happy that the following techniques are almost magical in their ability to *cure* things.

Rebuilding the Desktop File

The desktop is a very important file on your disk. How come you've never seen it? Because the Desktop file is *invisible.* (Yes, iMac icons can be invisible. Remember that fact if you ever get involved in antiterrorist espionage activity.) The file is something that the iMac maintains for its own use.

The iMac stores two kinds of information in the Desktop file: the actual *pictures* used as icons for all your files; and information about the parent-child (program-document) *relationships* that you're having trouble with.

If the Desktop file becomes confused, two symptoms will let you know: the "generic icon" problem, where all your icons show up blank white, and the "Application not found" message that appears when you try to double-click something.

Another desktop-related problem: over time, this invisible file gets bigger and bigger. Remember, it's having to store the pictures of every little icon that crosses your iMac's path. And just because you throw some icon away after using it doesn't mean that its image gets cleared from the Desktop file — it doesn't. And the bigger your Desktop file gets, the slower your iMac becomes in its efforts to open windows, display icons, and start up in the morning.

Resetting your Desktop file, therefore, has two delightful benefits. First, it cures the generic-icon syndrome and the "Application not found" problem (because it re-learns the relationships between files and their pictures). Second, it makes your iMac faster (because it purges all the unnecessary leftover icon images from its invisible database).

Here's how you do it:

1. **Turn the computer on.**

2. **As it starts gearing up, press and hold the Option and ⌘ keys.**

   Don't let go. Keep them down until the iMac explicitly asks you whether you want to "rebuild the desktop." Click OK.

After that's done, your document double-clicking will work, your icons will return, and your iMac, having been cleansed of all obsolete icons, will run faster and more smoothly.

Zapping the PRAM

The PRAM ("PEA-ram") is a tiny piece of special memory that's kept alive by your iMac's built-in battery. The PRAM stores the settings you make in your control panels, such as the sound volume, mouse speed, memory, network, and screen settings.

Rarely, rarely (but still sometimes), this tiny bit of memory gets corrupted somehow. Typical symptoms: Your control panels don't retain their settings; you can't print; or you have strange networking problems.

To reset the PRAM, turn off the iMac. When you turn it on again, hold down the ⌘, Option, letter P, and letter R keys until you hear the second or third startup chord. Release the keys.

Afterward, you may have to reset your iMac's mouse-tracking speed, desktop pattern, speaker volume level, clock, network connections, and so on. Still, it's but the work of a moment to reset them using your control panels.

The Amazing "Force Quit" Keystroke

Here's the amazing keystroke for escaping a frozen program: ⌘-Option-Esc. (This is about the only time that you'll ever use the Esc key.)

You get a dialog box that says, "Force [this program] to quit?" and warns you that any work you've done since the last time you used the Save command will be gone forever. Click Force Quit, and — when this trick works — you exit the program you were working in.

So what's the big whoop? Well, if you had several programs running, this technique dumps only the *one* that you were working in — the one that crashed. You now have a chance to enter each of the *other* programs that are still running and save your work (if you haven't done so). Then, to be on the safe side, restart the iMac.

The Restart Hole

To restart your iMac when it's frozen or crashed, press the power button on the front of the iMac. Hold it in for six seconds, or untill the machine restarts.

If that doesn't either (a) restart the computer or (b) display a message that *offers* to do so, then you're probably (a) using one of the early iMac models or (b) experiencing a particularly nasty system crash. In either case, open the plastic door on the right side of the iMac. Locate the tiny hole between the phone jack and the USB connectors (as shown in Appendix A) — and push a straightened paper clip into it until the computer restarts.

And if *that* doesn't work, unplug the iMac from the wall. Plug it back in and turn the machine on. (*That* always works.)

Solving an Extension Conflict

Okay, here it is — the long-awaited extension-conflict discussion.

See, each *extension* (a self-loading background program, such as a screen saver, that you install in your System Folder) was written by a programmer who had no clue what *other* extensions you'd be using. As a result, two extensions may fight, resulting in that polite disclaimer "Sorry, a System error has occurred."

These things are easy to fix, once you know the secret. Shut off your iMac, and then turn it on again. But as the iMac is starting up, *hold down the Shift key* and keep it down until (1) you see the message "Extensions off" or (2) you arrive at the desktop, whichever you notice first.

Your iMac probably won't give you any more trouble — but now, of course, you're running without *any* of your cute little extension programs. No CD-ROMs, no fax software, no Internet access, and so on.

If the point of this exercise is to pinpoint *which* extensions aren't getting along, you have two choices. One is free but takes a lot of time. The other way costs $60 but works automatically.

🖝 *The hard way:* Turn off the iMac and then turn it on again. While the iMac is starting up, press and hold the space bar down. Eventually, you'll be shown a complete list of your extensions, like this:

The point here is that you can *turn off* selected extensions and control panels just by clicking their names. (The little X means *on.*)

Special bonus feature! In the previous picture, see the tiny triangle where it says Show Item Information? Click that to see a top-secret panel that tells you *exactly* what each extension is for. Click an extension's name in the list, and you'll be shown a little caption for it, such as "Warranty Minder Pro: This extension keeps track of how long it's been since you bought your iMac, and it makes sure nothing goes wrong until after the warranty period is over."

But I digress. Using your Extensions Manager list, turn off a few of your extensions and control panels. Then restart the computer (click the Restart button at the bottom of the window).

If the iMac doesn't exhibit whatever unpleasant behavior you've been having, you can pretty much bet that one of the extensions you turned off was the guilty party. If the iMac *does* crash or act balky again, repeat the whole process, but this time turn some more extensions off.

Through trial and error, you eventually should be able to figure out which pair of extensions doesn't get along. Sometimes, just renaming one so that it alphabetically precedes its enemy is enough to solve the problem.

✔ **The easy way:** Buy a program called Conflict Catcher. This program does many useful things for managing your extensions, but its main virtue is catching conflicts. It can figure out, all by itself, which extension (or extensions) caused your iMac's problems. All you have to do is sit there, restarting the iMac over and over, each time telling Conflict Catcher whether or not the problem has been solved yet. By the time the process is over, the program will emblazon the name of the errant extensions on your screen; you then can dismember, disembowel, or trash them as you see fit.

(Yes, yes, okay, I wrote the manual for Conflict Catcher, but that's not why I'm mentioning it. Here's how I can prove my objectivity: I'll leak to you the fact that you can get a *free,* seven-day demo version from America Online or on the Internet at *www.casadyg.com.* It lasts just long enough for you to figure out which extensions were driving you crazy.)

Giving More Memory to a Program

When you turn on your iMac, several megabytes of its available RAM (memory) get used up by your System Folder's contents — your operating system. Then, every time you launch a program, a little bit of the leftover free RAM gets used up.

Here's how to find out where your memory is going at any particular moment:

Go to the Finder. From the menu, choose About This Computer. This helpful dialog box appears, showing several important numbers about your use of memory:

This is how much real memory your Mac has, not counting "fake" memory contributed by RAM Doubler or virtual memory.

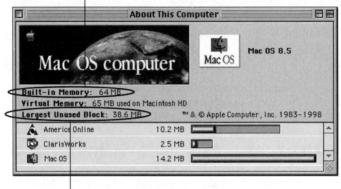

This is the largest chunk of memory you have left, into which you can open more programs. (There may be smaller chunks available, too.)

In the bottom part of the box, you can see what's already taking up memory and how *much* memory each program is taking up (see those bars?).

You may find it useful, however, to *change* the amount of memory that each of your programs uses. If you're experiencing a lot of System crashes, for example, the program may need a bigger memory allotment. If memory is at a premium, you may occasionally be able to give a program *less* memory, freeing some for other purposes.

Here's how:

1. ***Quit* the program whose memory appetite you want to change and then click its icon.**

   This step frequently confuses beginners; for help in quitting a program, see in Chapter 15. And don't be fooled into clicking the *folder* a program's in, either — open the folder and click the *program icon itself.*

2. **From the File menu, choose Get Info.**

   A dialog box appears; if you're using Mac OS 8.5, choose Memory from the Show: pop-up menu.

   In any case, you should now see a window like this:

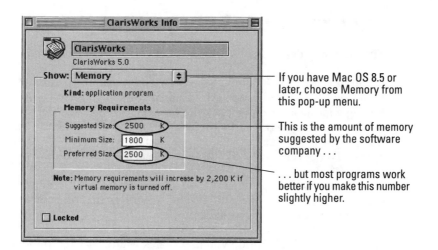

If you have Mac OS 8.5 or later, choose Memory from this pop-up menu.

This is the amount of memory suggested by the software company . . .

. . . but most programs work better if you make this number slightly higher.

3. **Change the number in the Preferred size box.**

This number is the amount of memory that the program will actually consume when you run it. If your aim is to make this program stabler or faster, try increasing this number by, for example, 10 percent.

Unless System crashes make your life more interesting, don't set the Preferred size much *below* the Suggested size, though.

Performing a "Clean System Reinstall"

This procedure is just a wee bit technical. But it's *amazing* how many problems it solves. Font problems, crash problems, freeze problems, glitch problems, weird things you can't even describe very well — all of them go away when you do a *clean install.*

As the gears of your System Folder grind away day after day, little corruptions and rough edges can develop. The following procedure replaces your old, possibly corroded System Folder with a brand-spanking-new one. It's nearly *guaranteed* to wipe out any erratic, bizarre crashes or freezes that you've been having; after all, it restores the iMac to the exact condition it was in the day it left the factory.

This process requires the Software Install CD that came with your iMac.

Step one: Install the fresh software

This first step depends on which system version you have (see Chapter 1).

If you have Mac OS 8.5: Insert the Software Install CD (if your iMac came with Mac OS 8.5) or the Mac OS 8.5 CD (if you bought Mac OS 8.5 *after* buying your iMac). Double-click the Mac OS Install icon. After you've clicked the Start button on the Software Installations screen, click the Options button on the regular Installer screen. You'll be offered a "Create additional System Folder (clean install)" option — that's the one you want.

If you have Mac OS 8.1: Insert the Software Install CD. Double-click the Mac OS Install icon. Click Continue. On the Select Destination Screen, click the Perform Clean Installation check box.

Regardless of which option you used, click whatever OK, Continue, or Install buttons you're offered, until the installation process is complete.

Step two: Restore your personal belongings

The result of all these shenanigans is a virgin, clean System Folder, free of any corruptions. Your iMac will run smoothly, fast, and trouble-free — I guarantee it.

Unfortunately, all your customized fonts, control panels, preferences, and menu items are stranded back in your *old* System Folder!

Ideally, you should install each of these items from their original, store-bought disks. If that's too much hassle, set up your old System Folder and your new System Folder side-by-side in tall, skinny, list-view windows. Now copy anything that's not in your *new* System Folder, item by item, from your old System Folder to your new System Folder. (Key folders to compare with their newer counterparts: the Preferences; Extensions; Control Panels; Apple Menu Items; and Fonts folders.) Do so with care, however, so that you don't simply reinstate whatever problems you were having.

(P.S. — If you bought Conflict Catcher, as described earlier in this chapter, you don't have to do this comparison manually. Use its Clean-Install System Merge command to compare your old and new System Folders automatically — and, at your option, to copy any of your personal belongings into the new System Folder.)

Other ways to restore your iMac

In addition to the CD called Software Install (described in the previous steps), your iMac also came with a CD called Software *Restore*. This second CD is useful in more dramatic circumstances, such as your deciding to erase your iMac's hard drive and start over (which might be useful if you plan to sell the iMac or when the FBI bursts through your door).

To use this CD, try this. While the iMac is on, press the CD-ROM tray's eject button. Carefully put in the Software Restore CD and close the tray. Now restart the iMac while pressing the letter C key continuously. Release the C key only after you see the message "Welcome to Macintosh" on the screen.

When you now double-click the Apple Software Restore icon (in this Software Restore CD's main window), you'll see two alarming options. The first, Restore in Place, gives you fresh, clean copies of everything that came with your iMac — including the System Folder and all the free programs — without touching any of the stuff *you've* added, such as your hard-won AppleWorks documents, e-mail, and so on. Do a "Restore in Place" to leave *your* stuff alone, while restoring fresh copies of all the original iMac freebies.

The second option, "Erase 'Macintosh HD' before restoring," is much more extreme. It *wipes out* everything you've ever created on your iMac, erasing the hard drive completely and restoring the iMac (and its pre-installed software) to the way it was the day you opened its box. Use only under dire circumstances.

Defragmenting Your Hard Drive

Your hard drive, if you'll indulge me, is like a closet maintained by a guy who's always in a hurry. When guests are coming over, he cleans up the living room by throwing everything into the closet, not particularly neatly. Every now and then, when he gets time, he unpacks the closet and repacks it neatly, putting everything in a tidy, organized place.

The hard drive, too, is in a hurry. When you ask it to save a file, it doesn't wait around: It shoves that file wherever it can find space. Sometimes, that even means sticking the file in *two* places, splitting it as necessary. Over time, more and more files are stored on your hard disk in pieces. It's no big deal: When you need that file again, the hard drive remembers where all the pieces are and is perfectly able to bring the file back to the screen.

But all this hunting for pieces slows the drive down, especially when your drive gets 80 percent full and stays that way for awhile. And like our busy closet keeper, you'll find it very satisfying, every six months or so, to reorganize the files on your disk so that they're each in one piece, neatly placed end to end on the hard-drive surface.

You can *defragment* your drive (which is the term for it) in two ways. First, you can copy everything onto other disks (such as SuperDisks or Zip disks, if you've bought one of those add-on drives), erase the hard drive, and copy the files back onto it. Second, you can buy a program just for defragmenting your drive. These programs are called things like Norton Utilities and DiskExpress. (Back up your work before using these programs, however; if you're into living dangerously, go skydiving.)

Chapter 17

Beyond Point-and-Click: Where to Go from Here

*Y*ou own the world's most forgiving, self-explanatory computer. But things will go wrong. And not even this astoundingly complete book can anticipate the problems you may encounter while running BeeKeeper Pro or No Namo Scanner Doodad Plus.

Where to Turn in Times of Trouble

When things go wrong, the world is crawling with help possibilities. For example, during the first three months you've owned your iMac, you can call Apple's delightful toll-free hotline at 800-500-7078 and ask your questions of the gurus there.

Beyond those 90 days, Apple charges you for your use of their experts (unless the computer actually turns out to need fixing, in which case the fee is waived). The number for this service is 888-275-8258 (toll-free again), and you can choose to have your wallet milked in any of the following quantities: One call for $35; three for $70; 15 for $340. (They're not quite that stingy, by the way — if it takes several calls to resolve your problem, that's still considered one call.)

The bottom line: Try to have all your problems in the first 90 days.

If spending moolah isn't your way of problem solving, consider these all-expenses-paid avenues:

- ✔ **www.apple.com/support/imac:** Part of Apple's Web site (which you can visit if you have an America Online or Internet account — see Chapter 11). You can get software updates, ask questions in electronic bulletin-board discussion areas, and access the Technical Information Library — a searchable electronic encyclopedia of all things Macintosh. All kinds of common iMac questions and answers are listed there for your perusal pleasure.

- ✔ **AppleFax:** Call 800-505-0171 by telephone, listen to the instructions, punch in your own fax number when you're asked for it, put in a fresh roll of fax paper, and stand back. They'll fax you a list of pretyped answers to common questions.

- ✔ **800-SOS-APPL:** This phone number brings you to a voicemail labyrinth that would freak out Theseus. Dig deep enough into the maze and you can find automated, prerecorded tips, tricks, and troubleshooting techniques.

- ✔ **No Wonder Web page:** Visit this page for free, 24-hour, personal computer help at *www.nowonder.com.*

- ✔ **MacFixIt Web page:** You get hundreds of discussions of little tweaky specific iMac problems at *www.macfixit.pair.com.*

Otherwise, your next resort should be a local user group, if you're lucky enough to live in a pseudometropolitan area. A user group, of course, doesn't exist to answer *your* personal questions; you still have to do some phoning and hobnobbing and research. But a user group *is* a source of sources. You can call up and find out who will know the answer to your question. (To find the nearest user group, call 800-538-9696.)

The other great source of help is an electronic meeting place like America Online, where you may get your question answered instantly — and if not, you can post your question on a bulletin board for somebody to answer overnight. Try keyword **MOS**, for example. (See Chapter 11 for details on keywords.) If you're Internet savvy, you can visit a *newsgroup* called *comp.sys.mac* for similar assistance. (See Chapter 11 for information on newsgroups.)

As for your continuing education — after you spend a month's salary on a computer, I'll bet you can afford $20 more for a subscription to *Macworld, MacAddict,* or *MacHome Journal* magazine. Agreed, huge chunks of these rags may go right over your head. But in every single issue, you'll find at least one really useful item. You can learn all kinds of things just by reading the ads. And if you're not in touch with the computer nerd world at least by that tenuous thread — via magazine — then you might miss stuff like free offers, recall notices, warnings, and other consumer-oriented jazz.

Buy a book — clothe an author

The publisher of this book has decided that, by gum, there's a market for this stuff, so he persuaded me to write two more — the David Pogue Macintosh Library. Without even thinking about it, I've wound up writing an entire course in Macintosh.

First, there's *MORE Macs For Dummies,* which . . .

✔ Goes into greater detail about what to do on the Internet, including making your own Web page.

✔ Describes and rates the top-200 most-advertised Mac/iMac programs.

✔ Reveals a bunch more of those cool hidden Option-key stunts.

✔ Helps you fake your way through Photoshop, Illustrator, Freehand, QuickTime, and other programs.

And then, when you *really* become an expert, you'll be ready for *Macworld Mac Secrets,* which has 1,300 pages, comes with a CD-ROM filled with cool programs, and requires a forklift to move.

Save Changes Before Closing?

If you do decide to pursue this Macintosh thing, I've listed major magazines, Web sites, and mail-order businesses in Appendix B.

But wait a minute — the point of this book wasn't to convert you into a full-time iMac rabbit. It was to get you off the ground. To give you just enough background so you'll know why the computer's beeping at you. To show you the basics and help you figure out what the beanie heads are talking about.

Don't let them intimidate you. So *what* if you don't know the lingo or have the circuitry memorized? If you can turn the thing on, get something written up and printed, and get out in time to enjoy the sunshine, you qualify as a real iMac user.

Any dummy knows that.

Part VI
The Part of Tens

The 5th Wave   By Rich Tennant

Honey- is one of your AOL chat room friends an elephant herder from India?

In this part . . .

Here's what we ...*For Dummies* book authors often refer to as "great stuff that didn't quite fit the outline" — a list of top ten lists, for your infotainment pleasure.

Chapter 18

Ten More Gadgets to Buy and Plug In

$\bullet$ $\bullet$

*I*n this chapter, you'll find out about several impressive and high-tech gadgets you can spend money on — yes, it's Credit Card Workout #4. These devices give the iMac eyes and ears, turn it into a national network, and turn it into an orchestra. You're not obligated to purchase any of them, of course. But knowing about some of the amazing things your computer can do will help you understand why the iMac is such a big deal.

A Scanner

If the point of a printer is to take something on the screen and reproduce it on *paper,* a scanner, then, is the opposite — its function is to scan an image on paper and throw it up on the iMac *screen.* After the image has been scanned and converted into bits and bytes that the iMac understands (meaning that it's been *digitized*), you can manipulate the image any way that you want. Erase unwanted parts, make the background darker, give Uncle Ed a mustache, shorten your brother's neck — whatever. The more dignified use for a scanner is grabbing real-world images that you then paste into your own documents, particularly in the realm of page layout and graphic design. Got a potato-industry newsletter to crank out? Scan in a photo of some fine-lookin' spuds, and you've got yourself a graphic for page one.

So how much is all this gonna cost you? A middle-of-the-line color scanner, such as the Umax Astra pictured on the following page, costs around $130 — including software that can do a decent job of converting scanned articles into typed-out, editable word processor documents. (When shopping, be sure to request an iMac-compatible scanner — one with a USB connector, such as a Umax Astra 1220U or Agfa SnapScan 1212u.)

A Digital Camera

Ordinarily, the concept of paying $500 for a camera that lacks any way to insert film would seem spectacularly brain-dead. Yet that's exactly the point of *digital cameras,* like those from Kodak, Casio, Olympus, Sony, and others. They store between 10 and 150 photos without film — actually, in *RAM,* now that you know what that is — and when you get home, you can dump the images into your iMac (after connecting a cable), thereby freeing your camera's RAM for another round of happy-go-lucky shooting.

For people who need instant, no-cost developing (doctors, people needing pictures for World Wide Web pages, real-estate hounds, fraternity party animals, and so on), these cameras are a godsend. As a matter of fact, just to prove the point, I took most of the photos in Chapter 19 using a little Olympus jobber. The results aren't pro quality — you'll have to pay $5,000 or more for digital cameras that take magazine-quality photos — but they're great for, say, illustrating computer books.

Incidentally: Some digital cameras, such as the Kodak DC220 and DC260, have USB connectors (which is what you need to hook into your iMac). Others require a serial-to-USB adapter, such as those listed in Appendix D.

A Better Mouse

The iMac's mouse is much more amazing than most mice. For example, it's see-through — and the little rubber ball inside is two-toned so that you can see it rolling as it moves.

Unfortunately, the iMac's mouse is also a royal pain. Unlike every other mouse in the world, it's perfectly round, so you can't tell by touch whether you've got it pointed straight, and it doesn't fit your hand as well.

If you're fine with the iMac mouse, great. Otherwise, getting a replacement is extremely easy and inexpensive. The iMac mice sold by Macally, Belkin, or iMaccessories, for example, are translucent, just like the iMac's original mouse — but they are oval-shaped like most mice, and they are therefore more comfortable and easier to position without looking.

Surprisingly enough, you can even get USB mice that are generally sold for *non*-Macintosh computers and plug them right into the iMac (or the iMac's keyboard). These mice have multiple buttons, instead of the iMac's one, but never mind — all three buttons do the same thing.

A Joystick

The iMac, with its high-speed G3 chip inside and superb graphics, makes a great game-playing machine (especially if you bought your iMac after November 1998, with OS 8.5 pre-installed; these models come with faster 3-D graphics circuitry). But how can you get the feeling of soaring over the fields of France in a fighter plane using a *mouse* to control the action? You can't. You need a joystick. It works just like a real airplane joystick, controlling your movement in flight simulation, driving simulators, shoot-'em-ups, and other games. They cost between $20 and $50, and they're listed in Appendix D.

Speakers or Headphones

Oh, yes indeedy: The iMac is more than hi-tech — it's hi-*fi*, capable of churning out gorgeous stereo sound. When you listen to the iMac's tinny two-inch built-in speakers, though, there's very little chance you'll mistake your living room for Carnegie Hall.

But if you get a pair of miniature speakers designed for the purpose, you're in for a tintinnabulating treat. If you play iMac games, particularly CD-ROM discs, you won't believe what you've been missing; the sounds are suddenly much richer and deeper.

If you don't do much more with sound than listen to your iMac's startup chord, don't bother buying external speakers. And if you *do* want speakers, not just any old speakers will work. They must be *self-powered,* and they must be *shielded;* the magnets inside normal stereo speakers are enough to distort the image on your monitor like the Sunday comics on Silly Putty. In other words, buy speakers designed for the purpose; Apple, Yamaha, Sony, and many other companies make lines of iMac-ready speakers.

You may also have noticed, by the way, that the iMac's front panel offers *two* headphone jacks — ideal for music listening with a loved one or battle games with a not-so-loved one. If add-on speakers are too involved for your taste, you'll get the same extremely rich sound by popping a pair of Walkman headphones into one of these front-panel jacks. (When you do so, the iMac's built-in speakers automatically shut up.)

Music and MIDI

MIDI, pronounced like the short skirt, stands for Musical Instrument Digital Interface. What it *means* is "hookup to a synthesizer." What it *does* is let your iMac record and play back your musical performances using a synthesizer attached to it. When you record, the iMac makes a metronome sound — a steady click track — and you play to the beat. Then, when you play back the music, your keyboard plays *exactly* what you recorded, complete with feeling, expression, and fudged notes; you'd think that Elvis's ghost was playing the instrument, except that the keys don't move up and down. Then you can edit your fudged mistakes and wind up sounding like [insert your favorite musician here].

All you need is a little box that connects your iMac to the synthesizer. (If it doesn't have a USB connector — be sure to ask! — you'll need, as usual, a *serial-to-USB* adapter, such as those described in Appendix D.) It's called a MIDI interface (about $50). You also need a program that can record and play back the music, called a *sequencing program.* Some easy-to-use and inexpensive ones are MusicShop and Freestyle. And, of course, you need to get your hands on a synthesizer. Or, for making sheet music, investigate Encore, Overture, or Finale (in increasing degrees of completeness and complexity). Check out a music store and get jammin'.

A Trackball

People who don't like computer mice often take great delight in replacing their iMac mouse with a trackball. A trackball looks like an eight ball set into a six-inch square base; you move the pointer on the screen by rolling the ball in place with your fingers. (See Appendix D for some USB-compatible trackball possibilities.)

Zip, SuperDisk, SparQ, & Co.

As I'm sure you're aware by now, the iMac comes without a floppy-disk drive. In truth, that's no big deal; floppies are embarrassingly old, slow, and low-capacity.

On the other hand, many people need *some* kind of disk to store stuff on; backing up your work on the Internet (see Chapter 11) or onto another Mac on the network (see Chapter 10) isn't for everybody.

So what are you supposed to do? Go back to writing on Post-it notes? Well, you could always buy an add-on disk drive for your iMac — one that plugs into the iMac's USB jacks. Your choices are

✔ **A floppy drive:** For $80 or less, you can equip your iMac with the missing limb it's always dreamed of: a true-blue, bona fide floppy disk. Newer Technologies, for example, makes one.

✔ **A SuperDisk drive:** Spend a little more; get a little more. The $140, translucent, iMac-colored SuperDrive accepts *both* floppy disks *and* SuperDisks, which look, smell, and act exactly like floppies — except that they hold about 83 times as much. Additional SuperDisk disks cost about $10 each, and they hold 120 megabytes each. A handy double-duty solution, though slow.

✔ **A Zip drive:** Here's yet another add-on disk-drive attachment. This one comes in translucent blue. It accepts Zip disks, which look like floppy disks that have been hitting the Ben & Jerry's a bit too often. Each holds 100MB and costs about $15; the Zip drive, the player, costs $140. These Zip disks, like SuperDisks, are convenient, sturdy, and easy to work with; the advantage here is that hundreds of thousands of people already own Zip drives. You can carry your project around on a Zip disk in your pocket, for example, confident that your friendly neighborhood Kinko's, corporate office, or print shop is likely to have a Zip drive that can accept it (the disk, not your pocket).

✔ **A Sparq drive:** If you're into digital movies, enormous graphics, or encyclopedia-writing, you're probably muttering: "120 megabytes?! I spit on your steenking 120 megabytes!" You're probably longing for something that holds *much* more. The solution, in your case, is a Sparq drive (made by SyQuest at *www.syquest.com*). Like the other disk systems described here, this $250, translucent red doodad accepts removable disks — but these babies hold much more, about a gigabyte (1,000 megs) each. (The disks are priced higher, too, around $50 per.)

For details, see Appendix D.

A QuickCam

The QuickCam (see Appendix D) is a golf-ball-sized movie camera. It plugs into your iMac's USB jack and lets you make smallish — but genuine — digital movies, recording whatever you point it at. There's no less expensive way to try your hand at filmmaking.

A Surge Suppresser

This thing looks like an ordinary multiple-outlet extension cord from the hardware store, but it's supposed to have an additional benefit — circuitry that can absorb an electrical voltage surge and thus protect your iMac from such electrical anomalies.

No, a surge suppresser won't protect your computer from acts of God; a direct lightning hit to your house, not to mention floods and plagues, can still give your iMac a bad hair day. (And if you live in an area where the power goes out occasionally, an *uninterruptible power supply* is the better, although more expensive, gizmo to buy.) On the other hand, a surge suppresser is a handy place to lend a little bit of protection to everything plugged into it at once.

Chapter 19

Ten Cool Things You Didn't Know Your iMac Could Do

· ·

*I*t's fast, it's hip, and it complements any décor. But the iMac does more — much more. Try *these* some lazy Saturday afternoon.

Play Music CDs

Yup, it's true. Pop your favorite music CD — Carly Simon, 10,000 Maniacs, Smashing Pumpkins, the soundtrack to *Lethal Weapon XIV* — into the iMac's CD-ROM drive. Some iMacs are set up to begin playing such music CDs automatically; others you have to command to begin playing.

Either way, if you'd like to control your music CDs the way you would on a $300 CD player, use the "front panel" in your menu called AppleCD Audio Player. It should look familiar.

Hunt around long enough, and you'll figure out how to make your CD play, stop, skip randomly among the songs, play louder or softer, and so on.

In fact, if you click the tiny down-pointing triangle (below the NORMAL button), you'll expand the panel so that you can view the names of the individual songs on the CD. Unfortunately, they start out being called "Track 1," "Track 2," and so on — it's up to you to click such names and type the correct song titles. (Press Return after each title to move down to the next blank or Shift-Return to move upward. While you're at it, click the words *Audio CD*, just above the track list, and type the name of the disc, too.) After you do all this, the Player will automatically remember the album and song titles the next time you insert the disc.

But here's the best part: Click the PROG button. Now you can drag any title on the left side to any slot on the right side. (Drag it back to the left if you change your mind.) You also can drag titles up or down on the right side. What's great about this feature is that you can drag your favorite songs into the "playlist" on the right side *more than once* — and leave the annoying songs out of the playlist completely.

Talk

It's been said that we spend the first year of a child's life trying to get it to talk, and the next 18 years trying to get it to shut up. Well, with the iMac, getting it to talk is fantastically easy.

Lots of programs are capable of talking. Word 98, AppleWorks, America Online, and WordPerfect are some examples. But the program that requires by far the least manual-reading (when it comes to talking) is the delightful, bargain-basement word processor known as *SimpleText*.

Find one of your copies of SimpleText (use your Find command). Launch it and then type up something you've always wanted to have said to you, such as, "You are *such* a god! Holy smokes — *everything* you do turns out fantastically! I'd give anything to be more like you."

Then move that mouse on up to your Sound menu and choose Speak All. Aren't computers great?

Now: For added hilarity, go back to the Sound menu. There you'll find a Voices command that lists as many as 18 different voices to choose from. They're great: male, female, kids, deep voices, shaky voices, whispered voices. You'll spend hours, I predict, making up funny sentences for each character voice to say.

Of course, Apple didn't create a talking iMac just for you to fool around making up silly sentences. This technology has some actual, useful uses. For example, there's no better way to proofread something important than to listen to it being read to you.

Sing

Although it's a little humbling that your iMac may be more talented than you are, it does indeed sing. It has a somewhat limited repertoire — in fact, it knows only four songs — but it can use any lyrics you want, and it never even stops to take a breath.

To make your iMac sing, you simply need to get it talking, as described in the preceding section. Then choose one of these voices from the Voices menu:

- ✔ **Pipe Organ:** Sings to the tune of the Alfred Hitchcock theme.
- ✔ **Good News:** Sings to the tune of "Pomp & Circumstance," otherwise known as the graduation march.
- ✔ **Bad News:** Sings to the tune of the funeral march.
- ✔ **Cellos:** Sings to the tune of "In the Hall of the Mountain King," from *Peer Gynt,* by Edvard Grieg. Such culture!

Hint: Punctuation marks make the iMac start over from the beginning of the melody. Sample lyrics for the Good News graduation-march melody, for example, should look like this:

You just won the jackpot good luck and God bless

Too bad you owe half to good old IRS!

Play Movies

Your iMac is quite handy with movies. It can make them, record them, and show them.

The cornerstone to all this is a technology bundle called *QuickTime,* which takes the form of some files that are probably sitting in your System Folder at this very moment (in your Extensions folder).

Getting movies to play on your screen is simple: Just double-click a movie file's icon to open it. It'll probably launch good old SimpleText and appear as a smallish rectangle, as shown here.

Click here to start   Drag this doodad to   Click to move one "frame"
or stop playback   jump around in the   of the movie forward or
                         movie   backward

To play the flick, click the little "play" triangle to make it play back. You'll quickly discover a few disappointing facts about digital movies: They often play back kind of jerkily; they're small (playing in a small window); and they're generally short. That's because QuickTime movie files take up obscene amounts of hard drive space for each minute of footage.

The bigger challenge, therefore, is simply *getting* a movie you want to watch. Several sources spring to mind: You can download movies from the Internet or America Online (see Chapter 11), although these enormous files take enormous amounts of time to transfer to you by modem.

You can also make your *own* movies, as long as you've equipped your iMac with the appropriate circuitry; read on.

Make Movies

"Say *what*?" you're saying. "This crazy author is suggesting I plug my camcorder into my computer? What's next — plugging my microwave into the vacuum?"

It's true. The hottest use of a Macintosh is as a movie-making machine. You can actually plug a little golf-ball-sized doodad called a QuickCam into your iMac — and capture digital videos onto the iMac with color and sound. Then you can edit them, play them backward, edit out the embarrassing parts, or whatever. (See Chapter 18 for more information on the QuickCam and see *MORE Macs For Dummies* for a chapter on editing your movies.)

Send Faxes

Because your iMac has a built-in fax modem, you're in for a delicious treat. Faxes sent by an iMac come out looking twice as crisp and clean when they're received by a real fax machine. And sending faxes couldn't be more convenient for you — no printout to throw away, no paper involved at all. Your iMac sends the thing directly to another fax machine's brain. (The iMac can *receive* faxes, too, if you've given it its own personal phone line.)

Here's what you do. Begin by typing (or opening) whatever it is you want to fax. Usually, this means a letter you've written in your word processor. Make sure it's in front of you on the screen.

Now take a look at your File menu and notice where it says Print. Got it?

Okay, let go of the mouse now. With one hand, press and hold down the *Option and ⌘ keys* on your keyboard. With the other, go back up to the File menu and look at the word Print. If all went well, that word Print has now changed to *Fax!*

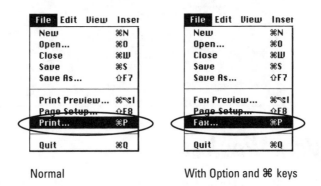

Normal   With Option and ⌘ keys

If you choose the Fax command, you'll be shown a window like this.

From the Fax Numbers pop-up menu, choose Temporary Address to specify your lucky recipient's fax number. When you're finished, you'll see that person's name on the right side of the window; click Send to send the fax.

If, by the way, you plan to send faxes to the same person more than once in your lifetime — a distinct possibility — you may wonder how to avoid having to use the Temporary Address feature every time you fax.

Easy. Find the program called Fax Browser on your hard drive (in a folder called FAXstf). Launch it. From the Window menu, choose Fax Numbers; in the next window, click the New Contact button and then type your correspondent's name, fax number, and other info (pressing Tab to jump from blank to blank). Repeat until you've input all your fax numbers.

From now on, whenever you send a fax, specifying the recipient is as easy as dragging the recipient's name from the left-side list to the right-side list, like this.

Fit in Your Pocket

It happens to the best of us: You've truly integrated your iMac into your life. It's got your calendar, your phone numbers, your to-do list — everything you need. And now you need to leave the house. What's an iMac fan to do?

Your options are:

✔ Stuff your iMac into your pocket before each trip. Shred your clothes and look like an imbecile as you walk into business meetings with unsightly bulges.

✔ Get a PalmPilot.

The PalmPilot is one of those amazing $300 handheld computers, about the size of an audio cassette. It comes with a little stand that plugs into your computer and sucks out a copy all your critical information: your calendar, phone book, to-do list, memos, and even e-mail. You can't run iMac *programs* on this thing, but you *can* keep your life's critical information with you without buying a second computer or new wardrobe.

The really great part is that, when you return home from your trip, you plug the PalmPilot back into your iMac — and any changes you made while on the road are automatically sent *back* to the calendar and address book on the iMac.

Using a PalmPilot with your iMac requires several purchases. First, get the $15 Mac Pac, which contains a cable adapter for the little stand (to make it fit a standard Mac). Second, you need some way to plug that cable adapter into your iMac — namely, one of the *serial-to-USB adapters* described in Appendix D. (Or just wait until 3Com, the PalmPilot company, gets around to making a USB stand — or a way to connect the PalmPilot to your iMac via infrared transmitter. Both are in the works as of this writing.)

Record Sounds

The iMac has a microphone built right into the front. It's not exactly the same one Madonna licks in her videos, but it's good enough for what we're about to do. And that is to change the little beep/ding sound the iMac makes (when you make a mistake) into some other sound, like "Oops!" or a game-show buzzer or a burp or something.

How to record a sound

Here's how it works:

1. **From the menu, choose SimpleSound.**

   You get something like this.

Alert Sounds

Quack
Simple Beep
Single Click
Sosumi
Whit
Wild Eep

Add...   Remove

2. Click the Add button.

Now you see this.

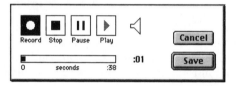

Record Stop Pause Play   :01

0   seconds   :38   Cancel   Save

3. To record, just click Record and speak into the microphone.

Be ready to click Stop when you're done, or else you'll accidentally include a bunch of silence and fumbling at the end of your sound.

You can play back your new sound in a plethora of ways. You could, mnemonically enough, click the Play button. Then again, you could click Save and give the sound a title so that you'll be able to preserve it for your grandchildren. When you return to the list of sounds in the Sound control panel, click your new sound's name to play it. If you leave it selected in the list, though, you've just selected it to be your new error beep.

A sound-playing fact for the detail-obsessed

Here's a way to play a sound that doesn't even involve opening a control panel: If you're a double-clicking kinda person, open your System Folder and then double-click the System *file*. It opens into a window showing all your fonts and all your sounds. Just double-click any sound's icon to hear it played.

How to adjust your iMac's speaker volume

While we're on the subject of sound, now would be as good a time as any to show you how to adjust your iMac's sound volume.

The easy way, of course, is to use the Control Strip, described and illustrated in Chapter 8.

The macho way (*translation:* long way) is to choose Control Panels from your menu. Open the one called Monitors & Sound. You'll see the master volume sliders for all the various sound-makers attached to your iMac.

This is also, by the way, where to tell the iMac *what* it should be recording: the sounds from your microphone, for example, or the sounds from a music CD you've put into your CD drive. Use the Sound Input pop-up menu to switch between them.

Run Windows Programs

It's true: Never again must you feel game-deprived. The iMac can run almost any Windows program alive. All you need is a program like SoftWindows or Virtual PC. No, your Windows programs won't run quite as fast as they would on the fastest actual Windows *computers* — but you, O lucky iMac owner, will find it fast enough.

Print Photos

Armed with a digital camera (see Chapter 18) and a color printer (see Chapter 5), there's no reason for you to spend money and time waiting for your photographs to get developed. Now you can spend money and time printing them from your iMac, instead.

The bad news: The glossy photo paper costs $1 per letter-sized sheet. You can't make enlargements — if you try to enlarge your digital photos, they start to look grainy. The digital camera (but not the printer) is expensive.

The good news: The printing is fairly fast. It looks amazing, especially on the $1-a-sheet glossy paper. And you can edit your photos before you print them, correcting the color tint, adding or removing bushes, adding or removing unwanted family members.

Chapter 20

Ten Things that Look Like the iMac

● ●

*L*et's face it: One of the iMac's chief virtues is its looks. Compute, schmompute — most people just want to get their *hands* on this thing. Stand beside passersby in a computer store, and you'll inevitably hear comparisons with the following items:

- ✔ A Volkswagen Beetle
- ✔ George Jetson's TV
- ✔ A beach ball
- ✔ A dollop of Gillette Shaving Gel (Extra Sensitive)
- ✔ An alien's egg
- ✔ The helmet end of a 1950s salon hair dryer
- ✔ Marge Simpson's hair after a shower
- ✔ A blue bar of Neutrogena soap
- ✔ A piece of furniture in Pee-Wee's Playhouse
- ✔ A spearmint jelly bean left on the dashboard in the sun too long

Part VII

Appendixes

In this part . . .

Here they are: The appendixes you've been waiting for. How to set up an iMac; what stuff to buy for it, and where to get it; and how to translate what the geeky magazines say when they talk about it.

Appendix A
How to Set Up an iMac

‧ ‧

Setting up the iMac should take less than five minutes; all you have to do is plug in a few cables. (See Chapter 5 for instructions on plugging in your printer.)

I Took Off the Shrink Wrap! Now What?

When it comes to setting up your iMac, a few pointers:

- ✔ When you lift the computer, use the handle on top, sure — but support the bottom front edge with your other hand. (The handle-like thing on the *bottom* isn't actually a handle, and it won't support the weight of the iMac. So don't carry it upside down.)

- ✔ Figure out where you're going to put the thing. Unless you're into pain, don't put it on a desk where the keyboard will be higher than your elbows.

- ✔ Decide whether or not it's worth flipping out the "foot" bar at the bottom of the iMac's front edge. Try the viewing angle with and without the foot.

Once you've nestled the iMac into its new home, here's how to set up the rest of it:

1. **Plug the mouse into one end of the keyboard.**

   It makes no difference which side — if you're left-handed, you'd presumably plug the mouse into the left end of the keyboard.

2. **Plug the keyboard into one of the two small rectangular *USB jacks* on the right side of the iMac, as shown here:**

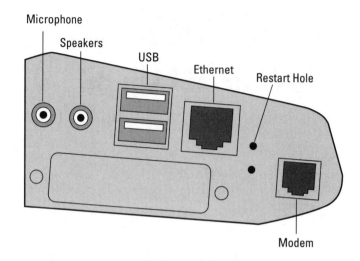

These jacks, like all the iMac jacks, are hidden behind the plastic door on the right side of the machine. Open this door by sticking your finger into the big hole and pulling; the door opens downward.

3. **Plug the iMac's power cord into the wall.**

4. **If you plan to sign up for the Internet or America Online, plug the included piece of telephone wire into the modem jack on the side of the iMac, as shown in the preceding diagram.**

The other end of the phone wire goes into a telephone jack in the wall, as described in Chapter 11.

Switching the iMac on

Quick! Flip to Chapter 1!

The shocking truth about the iMac's side panel

All of the iMac's jacks are neatly concealed behind the panel door on the right side of the machine.

Surprisingly enough, however, the *cables* aren't supposed to snake out through the big round hole in the middle of the door; instead, they're supposed to emerge through the two gaps at the *bottom* of this side-panel door, on either side of the hinge. (The big round hole in the middle is for your finger, so that you can pull the door open.)

On the other hand, hundreds of thousands of people mistakenly trail their cables through the round finger hole, and nobody's yet been arrested.

What you've got here

You'll hear all kinds of numbers and specifications tossed around when you go computer shopping. But the only four that matter are (1) how big its hard drive is, (2) how much memory it has, (3) what processor chip is inside, and (4) how fast it runs. I thought you might be interested in knowing how your iMac rates.

Hard-disk space. The first number that matters is the size of the hard disk inside the iMac. The size is measured in *gigabytes*. (If you're at a cocktail party, you can say *gigs* for short.)

The stuff that you'll be creating — letters, manuscripts, whatever — is pretty small. This entire book would take up about *2* megabytes of the 4,000 available on your hard disk. (There are 1,000 megabytes in 1 gigabyte.) But if you plan to work with graphics or digital movies, your hard drive could actually fill up over time.

The iMac's hard drive is 4 gigs; most computer hard drives are between 2 and 8 gigs these days.

Memory. As described in Chapter $1\frac{1}{2}$, *memory* is where your work resides while you're actually working on it (as opposed to the hard drive, where your work hangs out when the computer is off). But memory is much more expensive than disk space, so you get a lot less of it; the iMac comes with 32 megs of memory. The

more memory you have, the more you can do with your computer simultaneously (type in one window, surf the Web in another, and so on).

Newspaper ads often give you both critical numbers (memory and disk space) separated by a slash. You may read, for example, "iMac 32/4G." In your newfound savvy, you know that this model has 32 megs of memory and a 4 gig hard drive for permanent storage.

Processor chip model. The third important number is the name of the primary processor chip. The heart of an iMac is the famous *PowerPC G3* chip.

Processor chip speed. A chip's speed is something like blood pressure; it's how fast the data moves through the machine's circuits. The range of speeds, measured (get this) in *megahertz,* is 8 (on the original 1984 iMac) to 366 or more (the latest Power Macs). Your iMac runs at 233 MHz.

(*Caution:* You can't compare megahertz ratings among different chips or different kinds of computers. For example, you might think that a 233 MHz iMac would be just as fast as a 233 MHz "Intel inside" clone. Nope! The iMac would be much faster.)

How Big Is Your Monitor?

The iMac's screen is adjustable. You can zoom in or out, magnifying or shrinking everything on the screen. Of course, when you're zoomed out, everything's smaller — but you can see a larger area. For example, you can zoom out the 17-inch screen and see two entire pages side by side.

To do so, use the Control Strip, which is described in Chapter 8. It's the little tab peeking out the left side of your screen, as shown here (top):

To magnify or shrink your screen, find the tile that looks like a checkerboard (the lower image above); click the mouse on it and hold; and choose one of the different screen sizes from the pop-up menu. As you go through life with your awesome new iMac, keep this fact in mind — and feel free to adjust the monitor setting depending on the kind of work you're doing.

A bit about color bits

Your iMac can show three degrees of color richness. That is, you can switch your screen from showing a total of 256 different colors (which makes photos look kind of blotchy), thousands of colors (which makes photos look great), or *millions* of colors (which makes photos look unbelievable, but makes your screen slightly slower to repaint itself).

To switch among these different settings, use your Control Strip, as shown in the previous illustration. This time, however, click the tile that looks like a rainbow. You'll be offered several choices — "256 Colors," "Thousands of Colors," and so on. Use "Thousands" or higher when you're editing photos or movies. (The original iMac's circuitry can't manage the "Millions" setting when you've selected the 1024 x 768 magnification mode, as described two paragraphs ago. The revised iMac, released in November 1998, can.)

Aren't you glad you asked?

The Resource Resource

Magazines

MacHome Journal
(For beginners, students, at-home Mac users)
415-957-1911
www.machome.com

Macworld
(News, reviews, analysis; more advanced)
800-288-6848
303-447-9330
www.macworld.com

MacAddict
(Fun, irreverent, lots of games and gadgets; every issue comes with a CD-ROM filled with goodies)
800-666-6889
415-468-2500
www.macaddict.com

User Groups

Apple User-Group Info Line
800-538-9696 ext. 500
Call to get the number of the nearest Mac club.

Deep-Discount Mail-Order Joints

Contact these outfits when you're interested in buying any of the programs or add-ons described in this book.

MacConnection
www.macconnection.com
800-800-4444

MacWarehouse
800-255-6227

Mac Zone
www.maczone.com
800-248-0800

Cyberian Outpost
www.outpost.com
(800) 856-9800
(860) 927-2050

Great iMac Web Pages

MacSurfer
www.macsurfer.com
A daily roundup of articles about the Mac from newspapers and magazines around the country. Click a listing to read that article.

iMacintouch
www.imacintouch.com

TheiMac.com
www.theimac.com

iMacworld.com
www.imacworld.com

iMacCentral
www.imaccentral.com
News, updates, tricks, and product announcements — all about the iMac.

EvangeList
www.evangelist.macaddict.com
Facts, surveys, articles, and success stories to give you ammunition when Windows bigots put down the Macintosh.

SiteLink

www.sitelink.net
A Web page that links to other Web pages about the Mac (and the iMac). You'll be on the Web until you're 90.

MacOS Rumors

www.macosrumors.com
The *National Enquirer* of the Macintosh world — wild, juicy, sometimes erroneous rumors about Apple's secret plans for the future.

Appendix C

The Techno-Babble Translation Guide

● ●

active window — The window in front. Usually, only one window can be *active;* you can recognize it by the stripes across the title bar, like this:

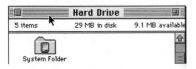

alert box — A message that appears on the screen; the iMac's attempt to maintain an open and communicative relationship with you. Unfortunately, as in most relationships, the iMac tends to communicate only when something is wrong. An alert box is marked either with the International Exclamation Point or a warning hand, like this:

> 🖐 **The resale value of your computer system has just sunk to 25% of what you paid for it.**
>
> [OK]

alias — A duplicate of a file's icon (not of the file itself). Serves as a double-clickable *pointer,* or reference, to the original file, folder, or disk. Indicated by an italicized icon name.

Apple menu — The menu at the far left end of your menu bar, marked by the symbol — a piece of multi-color fruit. In the menu, you'll find a list of your desk accessories (miniprograms, such as the Calculator), as well as any files, folders, documents, control panels, and even disks (or their aliases) that you care to see there.

AppleShare — The icon you click in the Chooser desk accessory when you want to connect to another computer on the network. Also the general name for the Mac OS networking technology.

AppleTalk — The language that your iMac speaks to other Macs (and laser printers). For example, to print on a laser printer, you must make sure that AppleTalk is active (in the Chooser).

application — Nerd word for *program.*

Application menu — The rightmost menu in the menu bar, marked by an icon. This menu lists whichever programs you have open and displays a check mark next to the frontmost program. (Got Mac OS 8.5 or later? Then see "The Program Switcher" at the end of Chapter 9.)

ATM — Short for *Adobe Type Manager,* a piece of software that makes certain fonts look really great on the screen (and in nonlaser printouts).

back up — To make a copy of a file for use in case some horrible freak accident befalls your original copy (such as your throwing it out).

background printing — A feature that returns control of the iMac to you immediately after you use the Print command; the iMac will print your document, taking its own sweet time, always giving priority to what you're doing on the screen. The alternative, known as *background printing is off,* takes less time to print but takes over the iMac, preventing you from working and displaying a "now printing" message until the printing is over.

Balloon Help — See the little Help menu? Choose Show Balloons from it; then point to various elements of your little iMac-screen world. Cartoon balloons pop out to identify what you're pointing at.

baud rate — The speed of a modem (see *modem*).

beta test — Means *test,* but adding a Greek word makes it sound more important. When a program is still so buggy and new that a company doesn't dare sell it, the company gives it away (to people who are called *beta testers*) in hopes of being told what the bugs are.

bitmap — A particular arrangement of colored dots on your screen. To your eye, a particular bitmap may look like the letter *A* (bitmapped text) or a coffee mug (a bitmapped graphic); to the computer, it's just a bunch of dots whose exact positions it has to memorize.

boot — (v.) To start the computer.

bps — Bits per second. The technically proper way to measure the speed of a *modem* (instead of *baud,* which everybody still says out of force of habit).

bug — A programming error in a piece of software, caused by a programmer too wired on Jolt and pizza, that makes the program do odd or tragic things when you're working to beat a deadline.

button — You'll have to deal with two kinds of buttons: the big one on the mouse, and the many oval or round ones on the screen that offer you options.

byte — A piece of computer information made up of bits. Now *that* made everything clear, didn't it?

cache — A trick, involving a special piece of memory, that makes an iMac faster. You can adjust the everyday cache in the Memory control panel; the iMac also has a cache *chip,* which uses high-speed memory to pull off the same speed enhancement.

Caps Lock — A key on your keyboard that makes every letter you type come out as a capital; it doesn't affect numbers. Press it to get the capitals; press it again to return to normal.

CD-ROM — A computer compact disc. CD-ROMs can show pictures, play music or voices, display short animations and movies, and display reams and reams of text. (A typical CD holds 600 megs of information; compared with the 4,000-meg hard disk that comes in an iMac.)

character — (1) A single typed letter, number, space, or symbol. (2) The scoundrel who got you into this Macintosh habit.

Chooser — A desk accessory, therefore listed in the menu, that lets you specify what kind of printer you have. Failure to use this thing when you set up your iMac is the #1 reason why beginners can't print.

click — The cornerstone of the Macintosh religion: to point the cursor at an on-screen object and then press and release the mouse button.

clip art — Instead of possessing actual artistic ability, graphic designers can buy (or otherwise acquire) collections of ready-made graphics called *clip art* — cutesy little snowmen, city skylines, Santa Clauses, whatever — that they can use to dress up their newsletters, party invitations, and threatening legal notices. (ClarisWorks/AppleWorks comes with a lot of clip art.)

Clipboard — The invisible holding area where the iMac stashes any text or graphics when you use the Copy or Cut command.

clock rate — The speed of your computer's main processor chip, measured in *megahertz.* The 1998 iMac's clock rate is 233 MHz.

close box — The little square in the upper-left corner of a window (as opposed to the little square who sold you the iMac), which, when clicked, closes the window.

Close box

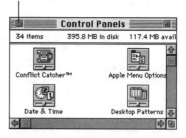

Command key — The one on your keyboard, right next to the space bar, that has a ⌘ (Command) symbol on it. When you press this key, the letter keys on your keyboard perform commands instead of typing letters — for example, ⌘-P = Print, ⌘-S = Save, ⌘-Q = Quit, and ⌘-Z = Undo. (Well, they can't *all* be mnemonic.)

Control key — A keyboard key (sometimes labeled *ctrl*) that makes secret menus pop out of windows and icons you click.

control panel — A window full of settings that pertain to some aspect of the iMac's operation. There's a control panel for the mouse, another for the keyboard, another for the monitor, and so on. To view the selection of control panels, choose (what else?) Control Panels from the menu.

CPU — What it *stands for* is *central processing unit.* What it *means* is either (a) a computer's main chip, such as the iMac's G3 chip, or (b) the actual computer — the box that contains the real brains. As distinguished from things like the monitor, the printer, and the keyboard. (On the iMac, the screen and CPU are integrated.)

crash — A very ugly moment when the iMac abruptly malfunctions, usually with scary-looking sounds and visuals. Requires restarting.

CRT — The screen. If you must know, it stands for *cathode ray tube.*

cursor — The pointer on the screen that moves when you move the mouse across the desk.

data — Isn't he that white-makeup guy on *Star Trek: The Next Generation*?

database — An electronic card catalog — for example, a mailing list — that can be sorted very quickly or searched for a specific name.

default — (1) The factory settings. For example, the *default* setting for your typing in a word processor is single-spaced, one-inch margins. (2) De blame for hooking you on de iMac hobby.

defragment — To restore, in one continuous chunk, something that's all broken up and scrambled. Usually refers to the information in memory or on a hard disk, but can also be applied to hamburger meat.

Delete key — In the typewriter days, this key was named Backspace.

deselect — To *un*highlight some selected text or graphic. (You usually do it by clicking someplace else.)

desktop — (1) The top of your desk, where the iMac sits, as in "I don't want a laptop; I want a desktop computer." (2) The home-base environment, where you see the Trash can, icons, and all that stuff. Also known as the Finder. (3) The actual (color-patterned) background of that home-base view. You can drag an icon out of its window and onto this table-cloth, and announce to your coworker that you've just placed an icon on the desktop.

desktop file — A file the iMac maintains for its own use, in which it stores information such as what your icons should look like and which kinds of documents can be opened by which programs. This file is invisible, but when it becomes damaged or bloated and starts causing problems, it's not quite invisible enough for most people.

desktop publishing — The act of cranking out nice-looking printouts from your iMac instead of paying to have the work typeset.

dialog box — The message box that the iMac puts on the screen when it needs more informa-tion from you (for example, the one that appears when you print, asking how many copies you want).

digitize — To convert sound, pictures, video, or any other kind of real-world sensory experience into the iMac's own numerical digestive tract.

DIMMs — The iMac's memory chips.

disk cache — A secret feature for making your iMac faster at the expense of memory. The iMac memorizes a few things that you do a lot and keeps them in a wad of memory called the *disk cache,* where they'll be immediately accessible. You set the size of the disk cache (the amount of memory reserved) in the Memory control panel.

disk drive — The machinery that actually reads what's on a disk (floppy, CD, SuperDisk, or other kind of disk).

document — A file that you create with a *program.* Examples: a memo (using a word-processing program), a logo (using a graphics program), or a spreadsheet (using a spreadsheet program).

documentation — A five-syllable way of saying *user's guide.*

DOS — Synonym for *IBM-style computers,* meaning the computers of the world that aren't lucky enough to be Macs. Stands for Disk Operating System.

dots per inch — A gauge of visual clarity, both on printouts and on the screen. The Mac's crystal-clear screen became famous for having a very high resolution — 72 dots per inch, or 72 *dpi.* A laser printer is much sharper, though, capable of printing at 300 or 600 dpi.

double-click — One of the most basic iMac skills: placing the on-screen pointer on an icon and, without moving the mouse, pressing the mouse button twice quickly. If you double-click an icon, it always opens into a window.

download — To transfer a file from one computer to another over phone lines.

dpi — Dots Per Inch a measurement of screen or printer quality.

drag — To position the cursor on something, hold down the mouse button, and move the mouse while the button is still down.

drawing program — A graphics program (such as the Drawing window in AppleWorks) that creates circles, squares, and lines. The iMac stores each object that you draw as an object unto itself, rather than storing the status of each screen dot. See also *painting program* and *bitmap.*

driver — A smallish file on your disk that tells the iMac how it's supposed to relate to a specific piece of equipment (such as a printer or a scanner) that it's never heard of before. A translator.

DVD — A new kind of CD, capable of storing an entire movie on a single disc. Some expensive Macs and PowerBooks have DVD drives instead of ordinary CD drives (although the DVD drives can *also* play the older CD discs).

e-mail — Electronic mail; messages that you read and write on the iMac screen without ever printing them. May also be short for *earth-mail,* because no paper (and no rain-forest acreage) is involved.

Ethernet — A system (wiring, connectors, software) of connecting Macs together in an office network, permitting quick transferring of files (see Chapter 10).

extension — Miniprogram that you install by dropping it in your System Folder (whereupon the iMac puts it in the Extensions folder). From that

moment on, the extension will run itself when you turn on the iMac and will be on all the time. Examples: virus protectors and screen savers.

fax modem — A modem (see *modem*), like the iMac's, that lets you send or receive faxes from your computer.

field — Computerese for *blank,* such as a blank in a form.

file — The generic word for one of the little icons in your iMac. There are two kinds of files: *programs,* which you purchase to get work done, and *documents,* which are created by programs. See also *program* and *document.*

File Sharing — A built-in iMac feature, wherein you can make any file, folder, or disk available for other people to go rooting through (as long as they're connected to your iMac by network wiring).

Finder — The "home-base" view when you're working on your iMac. It's the environment where you see the Trash, your icons, and how little space you've got left on your disk. Also known as the desktop or "that place with all the little pictures."

Fkey — Can refer to (1) the row of keys across the top of some keyboards: the *function* keys, labeled F1, F2, and so on. Or (2) a special built-in keyboard shortcut involving the ⌘ and Shift keys plus a number. The ⌘-Shift-3 function key, for example, takes a snapshot of the screen, and ⌘-Shift-1 ejects a floppy disk.

folder — In the iMac world, a little filing-folder icon into which you can drop other icons (such as your work) for organizational purposes.

font — (1) Apple's usage: a single typeface. (2) Everyone else's usage: a typeface *family* or package.

fragmentation — When something gets broken up into little pieces. Usually refers to the files on your hard disk (which, over time, get stored in little pieces all over the disk, making it slower) or to the memory in your computer (see *defragment*).

freeze — When your cursor becomes immovable on your screen, you can't type anything, your iMac locks up, and you get furious because you lose everything you've typed in the past ten minutes.

function key — See *Fkey.*

G3 — As of 1998, the fastest personal-computer processor chip available (and the one inside the iMac).

GB — Short for *gigabyte.*

GIF — A kind of graphics file, most often used on America Online and the Internet. Requires a special program, such as the America Online program, Internet Explorer, or GIF Watcher (shareware), to open and view it. (Stands for *graphic interchange format.*) Nobody quite knows whether to use a hard or a soft "G."

gig — The measurement unit for today's hard drives (short for *gigabyte,* which is 1,024 megabytes).

grayscale — An image in which all the colors are different shades of gray, like all the pictures in this book.

grow box — See *resize box.*

hang — Freeze (see *freeze*).

hard disk or **hard drive** — The spinning platters, usually inside your iMac but also available in an external form, that serve as a giant floppy disk where your computer files get stored.

hardware — The parts of your computer experience that you can feel, and touch, and pay for. Contrast with *software.*

header — Something that appears at the top of every page of a document, such as "Chapter 4: The Milkman's Plight" or "Final Disconnection Notice."

highlight — To select, usually by clicking or dragging with the mouse. In the iMac world, text and icons usually indicate that they're selected, or highlighted, by turning black or colored-in.

icon — A teensy picture used as a symbol for a file, a folder, or a disk.

iMac — The one-piece, high-speed, low-cost, see-through, blue-plastic, rounded-cased, G3-based Macintosh that debuted in late 1998 and became a smash hit. Beloved by many because of its simplicity — and grumbled about by a few because it has no built-in floppy drive.

initialize — To prepare a new disk for use on your computer. Entails erasing it completely.

inkjet — A kind of inexpensive, high-quality printer, such as an Epson Photo or DeskJet, that makes its images by spraying an incredibly precise plume of ink at the paper.

insertion point — In word processing, the short, blinking vertical line that's always somewhere in your text (see Chapter 4).

Internet — The worldwide network of computers joined by phone lines. Incorporates the World Wide Web, e-mail, and other features (see Chapter 11).

JPEG — Another graphics-file format found on America Online and the Internet (see *GIF*). This one has higher quality than GIF.

K — Short for *kilobyte,* a unit of size measurement for computer information. All the typing in this book fills about 2,500K. A full-screen color picture is around 1,000K of information.

label — A text tag or color tag used to identify icons by category. You apply a label to an icon using the Label command in the File menu.

landscape — Used to describe the sideways orientation of a piece of paper.

laser printer — An expensive printer that creates awesome-looking printouts.

launch — To open a program.

Launcher — The window containing jumbo, one-click icons that launch your favorite programs and documents (see Chapter 8).

leading — *(LEDding):* The vertical distance between lines of text in a document. Single-spaced and double-spaced are measurements of leading.

logic board — The main circuit board inside your iMac. Often at fault when your iMac refuses to turn on.

Mac OS — The System software (the behind-the-scenes operating software) that makes a computer act like a iMac. As distinguished from DOS or Windows. Continually improved: Most iMacs come with either Mac OS 8.1 or Mac OS 8.5 pre-installed.

Mac OS X — The late 1999 version of the Mac system software. Advertised to be faster, crash less, and do your dishes. Pronounced "Mac O. S. ten."

mail merge — Creating personalized form letters with a word-processing program.

MB — Short for *megabyte*.

megabyte — A unit of disk-storage space or memory measurement (see *K*). Used to measure hard disks, memory, and other large storage devices. There are 1,024K in a megabyte.

memory — The electronic holding area that exists only when the iMac is turned on; where your document lives while you're working on it (see Chapter 1 $^1/_2$).

menu — A list of commands that drops down from the top of the iMac screen when you click the menu's title.

menu bar — The white strip, containing menu titles, that's always at the top of the iMac screen. Not to be confused with *bar menu,* which is a wine list.

mezzanine slot — A mysterious expansion slot on the right side of the iMac. Mysterious, because the iMac is not advertised to be expandable.

modem — A phone attachment for a computer that lets you send files and messages to other computer users all over the world. Built into the iMac.

modifier keys — Keys that mess up what the letter keys do. Famous example: the Shift key. Other examples: ⌘ (Command), Option, Control, and Caps Lock.

monitor — The screen.

motherboard — See *logic board.*

mount — To bring a disk's icon onto the desktop so that its contents may be viewed or opened.

mouse — The rounded hand-held thing that rolls around on your desk, controlling the movement of the cursor.

mouse pad — A thin foam-rubber mat that protects the mouse and desk from each other and that gives the mouse good traction.

multimedia — Anything that gives you something to look at *and* listen to, such as a CD-ROM game.

network — What you create when you connect computers to each other.

NumLock — A goofy key, named by numskulls, on the keyboard. Pretty much does nothing except in Microsoft Word, where it switches the functions of the keys in the number pad. On the iMac, the same as the Clear key, which *does* do something (usually the same thing as the Delete key).

OCR — Short for *optical character recognition*. You run an article that you tore out of *Entertainment Weekly* through a scanner, and the iMac translates it into a word-processing document on your screen, so you can edit it and remove all references to Cher.

online — Hooked up to a dial-up network, such as the Internet.

painting program — A program with the word *Paint* or *Photo* in the title (or the Painting window in AppleWorks) that creates artwork by turning individual white dots black or colored on the screen.

paste — To place some text or graphics (that you previously copied or cut) in a document.

PC — Stands for *personal computer,* but usually means any non-Macintosh computer; an IBM clone.

peripheral — An add-on: a printer, scanner, iMac floppy drive, and so on.

PICT — The most common kind of Macintosh picture file.

pixel — One single dot out of the thousands that make up the screen image. Supposedly derived from *pic*ture *el*ement, which still doesn't explain how the *x* got there.

pop-up menu — Any menu that doesn't appear at the *top* of the screen. Usually marked by a down-pointing black triangle.

Paper: [US Letter ▼]
Layout: [1 Up ▼]

port — A jack or connection socket.

portrait — A right-side-up piece of paper; the opposite of *landscape* (see that entry).

PostScript — A technology, a printer, a trademark, a kind of font, a computer code language for displaying or printing text or graphics, a way of life. All of it means high-quality type and graphics.

Power Macintosh — The iMac's big brother: a line of expandable Mac models.

PowerBook — A Mac laptop.

PowerPC chip — The very fast main processor chip inside a Power Macintosh or iMac.

PRAM — *P*arameter *RAM:* the little piece of memory maintained by your iMac's battery. Helps explain how the iMac maintains its settings (mouse speed, printer choice, and so on) even when it's been turned off.

program — A piece of software, created by a programmer, that you buy to make your iMac do something specific: graphics, music, word processing, number crunching, or whatever.

QuickTime — The technology (and the little software extension) that permits you to make and view digital movies on your iMac screen.

QuickTime VR — A special kind of QuickTime movie that lets you change the camera angle by dragging your cursor around inside the picture.

quit — To exit or close a program, removing it from memory.

radio button — What you see in groups of two or more when the iMac is forcing you to choose among mutually exclusive options, such as these:

A System error has occurred. What result would you like?

○ Loud, static buzzing
◉ Quietly blink to black
○ A two-minute fireworks display

RAM — Term for memory (see *memory*) designed to intimidate non-computer users.

RAM disk — A way to trick the iMac into thinking that it has an extra high-speed hard drive. The RAM disk is actually a chunk of memory set aside to *resemble* a disk (complete with an icon on the screen). Explained in *MORE Macs For Dummies.*

reboot — Restart.

rebuilding the desktop — A troubleshooting technique (described in Chapter 16).

record (n.) — The computer word *record* refers to one "card" in a database, such as one person's address information. Contrast with *field,* which is one *blank* (such as a zip code) within a record.

relational database — A complex information list that you hire somebody to come in and set up for you, in which each list of information (such as a mailing list) is connected to another list (such as People Who Never Pay on Time).

resize box — The small square in the corner of a window that, when dragged, changes the size and shape of your window.

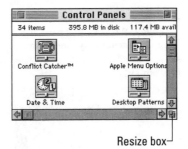

Resize box⌐

resolution — A number, measured in dots per inch, that indicates how crisply a printer or a monitor can display an image.

restart hole — A tiny pinhole (nestled among the jacks on the iMac's right side, behind the door), marked by a triangle. When a straightened paper clip is inserted into this hole, the iMac restarts.

ROM — A mediation mantra that you can use when contemplating the ROM chips, where the iMac's instructions to itself are permanently etched. (Actually, the iMac's ROM is mostly in a *file,* not a chip — it's in your System Folder and called Mac OS ROM.)

sans serif — A font, such as Helvetica or Geneva, with no little "hats" and "feet" at the tip of each letter. See Chapter 5.

scanner — A machine that takes a picture of a piece of paper (like a Xerox machine) and then displays the image on your iMac screen for editing.

Scrapbook — A desk accessory, found in your menu, used for permanent storage of graphics, text, and sounds. (Not the same as the Clipboard, which isn't permanent and holds only one thing at a time.) To get something into the Scrapbook, copy it from a document, open the Scrapbook, and paste it. To get something out of the Scrapbook, use the scroll bar until you see what you want, and then copy it (or cut it).

screen saver — A program (such as After Dark) that darkens your screen after you haven't worked for several minutes. Designed to protect an unchanging image from burning into the screen, but more often used just for fun.

scroll — To bring a different part of a document into view, necessitated by the fact that most computer monitors aren't large enough to display all 60 pages of your annual report at the same time.

scroll bar — The strips along the left and right sides of an iMac window. When a scroll bar's arrows, gray portion, or little white (or gray) square are clicked or dragged, a different part of the window's contents heaves into view *(scrolls)*.

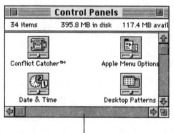

Scroll bar

SCSI — A high-speed, but complex and headache-inducing, connector on the back of every Macintosh model *before* the iMac. Used to connect scanners, hard drives, Zip drives, and so on; replaced by USB jacks on the iMac.

serif (n., adj.) — A term used to describe a font that has little ledges, like little "hats" and "feet," at the tip of each letter, such as Times or this font.

shareware — Programs that are distributed for free, via the Internet. The programmer requests that you send $10 or $20 to him or her, but only if you really like the program.

SimpleText — A basic word processor that comes free with every Macintosh.

sleep — Sort of like Off, except that the iMac remembers everything that you had running on the screen. When you want to use the computer again, you just touch a key; the whole computer wakes up, the screen lights up, and you're in business again. Used to conserve power.

software — The real reason you got a computer. Software is computer code, the stuff on disks: programs (that let you create documents) and documents themselves. Software tells the hardware what to do.

spreadsheet — A program that's like an electronic ledger book; you can type columns of numbers in a spreadsheet program and have them added automatically.

startup disk — *A* startup disk is one that contains a System Folder. *The* startup disk is the one that you've designated to be in control (in the event that you have more than one to choose among). The Startup Disk *control panel* is what you use to specify *the* startup disk.

stationery — Click a document icon, choose Get Info from the File menu, and select Stationery Pad. Thereafter, when you double-click that icon, it won't open; instead, an exact *copy* of it opens. This saves you the hassle of pasting the same logo into every memo that you write because you can paste it into your Stationery Pad document just once.

submenu — In some menus, you're forced to choose among an additional set of options, which are marked in the menu by a right-pointing triangle, like this:

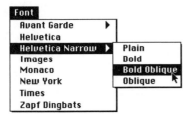

SuperDisk — A special kind of iMac disk drive (from Imation) that accepts both normal floppy disks *and* SuperDisks, which hold 80 times more.

System crash — When something goes so wrong inside your iMac that a bomb appears on the screen with the message "Sorry, a System error has occurred" — or not.

System file — The most important individual file inside a System Folder. Contains the iMac's instructions to itself, and stores your fonts, sounds, and other important customization information. A iMac without a System file is like a broke politician: it can't run.

System Folder — The all-important folder containing the software the iMac requires to run (see Chapter 8).

System Folder

telecommute — To work in T-shirt and slippers in a messy apartment, spending not one penny on transportation, and sending work to the office over the phone lines.

third party — (1) A company other than Apple, as in "You didn't get a mouse pad with your iMac? Well, of course not; you buy that from a third party." (You, by the way, are the second party.) (2) The New Year's Eve get-together at which you get the drunkest.

TIFF — Stands for *tagged image file format;* the kind of graphics-file format created by a scanner.

title bar — The strip at the top of a window where the window's name appears. Shows thin horizontal stripes if the window is *active* (in front of all the others).

toner — The powder that serves as the "ink" for a laser printer.

trackball — An alternative to the mouse. Looks like an 8-ball set in a pedestal; you roll it to move the pointer.

TrueType — A special font format that ensures high-quality type at any size, both on the screen and on any printer. Rival to PostScript but costs much less (nothing, in fact; it comes with the iMac).

upload — To send a file to another computer via modem.

USB — Describes rectangular metal jacks (USB *ports*), cables that plug into them (USB *cables*), and add-on appliances (USB *devices,* such as printers, modems, digital cameras, disk drives, and so on) that plug in there. On the iMac and some later Mac models, USB jacks, cables, and add-ons replace the keyboard, mouse, SCSI, and printer ports of previous models.

virtual memory — A chunk of hard-disk space that the iMac sets aside, if you want, to serve as emergency memory (see Chapter 16).

virus — Irritating, self-duplicating computer program designed (by the maladjusted jerk who programmed it) to gum up the works of your iMac (see Chapter 15).

volume — A disk of any kind: floppy, hard, cartridge, or anything represented on your desktop by its own icon.

VRAM — Stands for *video RAM.* Memory chips inside your iMac that are dedicated to storing the screen picture from moment to moment. The more VRAM you have, the more colorful your picture. The first iMac had 2MB of VRAM; in November 1998, iMacs started coming with 6MB instead, for better game-playing.

window — A square view of iMac information. In the Finder, a window is a table of contents for a folder or a disk. In a program, a window displays your document.

word wrap — A word-processing program's ability to place a word on the next line as soon as the current line becomes full.

WYSIWYG — Short for *what you see is what you get* — one supposed reason for the iMac's superiority over other computers. Means that your printout will precisely match what you see on the screen.

Zip disk — A slightly thickened floppy disk that holds 100MB (as much as a hard drive) and costs $15. To be used in Zip drives, sold by Iomega.

zoom box — The tiny square in the corner of a window (in the title bar) that, when clicked, makes the window jump to full size.

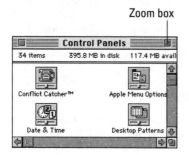

Zoom box

Appendix D

The Ultimate iMac Buyer's Guide

● ●

*W*hen the iMac first debuted, a great whine could be heard across the land. "It's got USB connectors?!" said the veteran Mac fans. "But what are we gonna plug *in* there? We need printers, scanners, cameras, mice, game joysticks, keyboards, modems, speakers, and stuff like that!"

They needn't have worried. This appendix lists dozens of gadgets and accessories that plug into the iMac's USB jack, many of which match the iMac's striking translucent teal-and-white looks. Get out your Visa card and go wild. (If this listing doesn't do it for you, visit Apple's iMac Product Web page at *www.apple.com/imac/usbindex.html*. It's kept current and has clickable links to the Web pages of every company listed here.)

As for the prices here — consider them rough guides. Not only do they rise and fall like John Travolta's career, but some companies list "street" prices (what you'll actually pay) and others list *list* prices, which nobody actually pays.

Printers & Printer Adapters

With the proper cables, you can plug your iMac into any of — get this — over 1,500 different printer models. For example:

Alps MD-1300 — Chapter 5 describes the most common kind of printers: inkjets and laser printers. There's a third kind, though: *dye sublimation,* which is less common because it's usually astronomically expensive. This photo-quality dye-sub printer, however, is only $400 — and unlike inkjets, the color printouts from *this* baby don't smear or fade. (It has a standard injket cartridge, too, for when you don't need the ultimate photo printouts. That's lucky, because the high-quality mode takes 15 minutes per page and requires special paper.)

Alps also makes an even higher-res photo printer, the $600 MD-5000 Desk Top Print Shop, shown here, which lays down a staggering number of dots per inch (2,400 dpi). A $99 USB adapter cable is required for both printers. Alps, *www.alps.com.*

Epson Stylus Color 740 — One of the most popular color inkjets for the iMac. The USB cable plugs straight into the iMac; prints five pages per minute up to 1,440 dots per inch. $280, Epson America, Inc., *www.epson.com/printer.*

Epson Almost Anything — If you're an Epson injket-printer kinda person, don't feel limited to the 740 model. Just buy Epson's $50 USB/Parallel Printer Adapter Kit, and then hook your iMac to almost any Epson Stylus color printer alive: models 440, 600, 640, EX, 700, 800, 850, 1520, or 3000, for example. Epson America, Inc., *www.epson.com/printer.*

HP DeskJet 670 and 690 — Hewlett-Packard has been making great printers for decades; with the addition of an HP Printer Cable Kit (about $70; includes cable and software), you can equip your iMac with either a DeskJet 670C (inexpensive black or color printing for about $160) or the $200 DeskJet 690 family (with six ink colors for better photo printing). Hewlett-Packard, *www.hp.com/peripherals2/supplies/imac-cable.html.*

iPrint — Farallon makes two $110 adapters that accommodate pre-USB Macintosh printers. One, the iPrint LT, is for *LocalTalk* printers (usually laser printers); you must also purchase a PhoneNet connector (see Chapter 5) for the printer, if you don't already have one. The other adapter, the iPrint SL, is for injket printers like Apple StyleWriters (models I, II, 1200, 1500, 2200, 2400, and 2500). Each iPrint plugs into your iMac's Ethernet jack. Farallon, *www.farallon.com.*

PowerPrint USB to Parallel — Talk about mind-blowing choices: This $100 adapter kit lets your iMac hook up to any of 1,500 different *IBM-compatible* printers — every conceivable kind, price, and model. Comes with software and a cable that hooks up to one of your USB jacks. Infowave, *www.infowave.com.*

iParallel USB Printer Adapter — Another adapter ($50) for connecting the iMac to IBM-type printers. Doesn't come with the necessary software for those printers, however. iMaccessories, *www.imaccessories.com.*

Serial, ADB, and SCSI Adapters

In case you were wondering, *serial, ADB,* and *SCSI* are three kinds of jacks not found on the iMac. (*Serial* means "modem or printer jack," *ADB* means "keyboard or mouse jack," and *SCSI* means "external hard drive, Zip drive, Jaz drive, or scanner jack.") But because all 150 previous Macintosh models had them, thousands of older, pre-iMac add-on gadgets are alive, well, and kicking around the offices of the world. Fortunately, they can connect to an iMac with one of these adapters.

Keyspan USB Serial Adapter ($80) or **Momentum uConnect** ($84) — Got an old Macintosh inkjet printer, PalmPilot, digital camera, or a digital drawing tablet — and nowhere to plug them into your iMac? Then get one of these adapters. Each plugs into an iMac USB port and provides one (uConnect) or two (Keyspan) old-Mac-style serial ports. Into these jacks, you can then plug such printers as StyleWriters, Epson Stylus printers (300 and 500), HP DeskWriters (600 and 800 models), the PalmPilot cradle, digital cameras  from Kodak, Olympus, Apple, Connectix, Agfa, Casio, Canon, Chinon, Epson, Ricoh, or Sony, and even Wacom drawing tablets. (This kind of adapter doesn't do MIDI, GeoPort, or LocalTalk, however, even if you know what those are. For those purposes, read on.) Keyspan, whose adapter is shown here, is *www.keyspan.com,* and Momentum is *www.momentuminc.net.*

iPort — This remarkable expansion card lets you plug a second *monitor* into your iMac. It also provides a *fully* functioning old-style Macintosh modem/printer port, into which you can plug not only pre-USB printers, digital cameras, modems, PalmPilots, and so on, but even MIDI interfaces and LocalTalk printers. iPort requires dealer installation or somebody smart to take your iMac apart. $70 from Griffin Technology, *www.griffintechnology.com.*

iMate — A little translucent adapter that lets you plug old-style (ADB) Macintosh keyboards and mice into the iMac's USB jack. $40 from Griffin Technology, *www.griffintechnology.com.*

Power Drive iMac — SCSI (pronounced "scuzzy") technology can be a royal headache, sometimes requiring much fiddling and experimenting. (SCSI is a type of connector and fat cabling found on all pre-iMac Macintosh models.) But if you've got some aging SCSI gadget (such as a Jaz drive, hard drive, or scanner) that you want to mate with your iMac, this $160 adapter board from iMaccessories is exactly what you want. A dealer (or some friendly techie) must install this card into your iMac. iMaccessories, *www.imaccessories.com.*

USB to SCSI Converter — Here's another solution to the SCSI-gadget problem: an $80 adapter from Microtech International. This one's just a cable, requiring no special installation; you can even safely connect or disconnect this cable while the iMac is turned on (unlike ordinary SCSI cables). Caution: This adapter can handle *only* storage gadgets like Zip, Jaz, or hard drives — not scanners. (Microtech plans to fix that limitation with a free software upgrade in early 1999.) Microtech International, *www.microtechint.com.*

Digital Cameras

As you can read in Chapter 18, as expensive gadgetry goes, these babies are pretty wonderful.

QuickCam VC — This $80 golf-ball-sized USB-jack camera can take still pictures (352 x 288 dots, which is pretty small) and even digital movies (at about 15 frames per second). It's got an adjustable focus lens and a six-foot cable. (The QuickCam itself is sold for Windows computers only. But the little secret is that, with the addition of the free software located at *www.logitech.com/Cameras/quickcamvcmac.html,* it'll work with your iMac, too.) Logitech, *www.logitech.com.*

Courtesy of Logitech

iSee Camera — This archrival to the QuickCam looks nearly identical: It's a two-inch gray sphere. But its picture-taking quality is better (640 x 480 resolution), and the price ($110) isn't bad. iSee plugs directly into your iMac's USB jack, and it can even make low-res digital movies. From Ariston, *www.ariston.com.*

DC 220 and 260 Cameras — These pro-quality digital cameras offer very high quality (1152 x 864 resolution on the DC 220 model, 1536 x 1024 on the DC 260), autofocus 3x zoom lens, time lapse and audio recording, and much more — and they plug directly into your iMac's USB jack. They cost $700 and $800, respectively; at this writing, the software requires Mac OS 8.5 (see Chapter 1). From Kodak, *www.kodak.com/US/en/nav/digital.shtml.*

ImageMate — Many digital cameras use, as "film," a removable memory card called a CompactFlash card. This $90 gadget is an external reader/writer of such cards, so that you can rapidly transfer pictures from thus-equipped digital cameras to your iMac. From SanDisk, *www.sandisk.com/cons/imagemate.htm.*

PC Card Reader or **CameraMate USB** — These machines accept *PC cards,* yet another form of "electronic film" used by today's digital cameras (including the abovementioned Kodak models). Fill up a PC card with pictures, slip it into a PC Card Reader, and it's transferred to your iMac. $150 for Ariston's card, *www.ariston.com,* or $90 for the Microtech CameraMate, *www.microtechint.com.*

Disk Drives

The iMac doesn't come with a built-in floppy drive. Although there are plenty of ways to back up your work without disks (see Chapter 4), most people prefer to be able to carry their stuff around on a disk. These gadgets plug into your USB jack.

Imation SuperDisk USB Drive — This fascinating, iMac-colored, translucent, two-in-one disk drive accepts *both* floppy disks (from Macs or Windows machines) *and* SuperDisks, which look like floppies but hold 83 times more (120 megs). The USB-cabled drive is about $140; disks are $65 for a five-pack. Imation, *www.imation.com*.

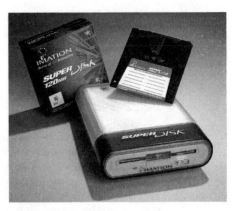

USB Zip Drive — This sleek, translucent blue USB device is a Zip drive, just like the millions found in Macs and PCs worldwide. It accepts Zip disks, which look like overweight floppies and hold 100 megs each. $150 for the drive, about $12 per disk. Iomega, *www.iomega.com*.

iDrive — Here it is, folks: the floppy-disk drive the iMac always wanted. $80; plugs into one of your USB jacks. From Newer Technologies, *www.newertech.com*.

SyQuest SparQ Drive — Each SparQ disk holds 10 times more than a Zip disk: 1 gigabyte per $50 disk, in fact. Get this one if you need to back up or transfer *big* files, like Photoshop or digital movie files. The drive itself ($250) is see-through red and very cool-looking. SyQuest, *www.syquest.com*.

High-Speed Modem (ISDN) Adapters

The iMac comes with a built-in modem, yes — but it's still a modem. If you're willing to fork over, say, $50 per month, you may be able to sign up for *ISDN* service. Using an *ISDN adapter* is a lot like using a modem (to connect to the Internet), but there's no actual dialing involved: You're online all the time, at three times the speed of the fastest modem. After contacting your phone company to see if this service is available, you then need an ISDN adapter, such as one of the following.

Sagem ISDN USB Adapter — Just plug this translucent thing into the open USB jack at the end of the iMac's keyboard, and you're ready to go (at 128 kilobits per second). Sagem, *www.satusa.com*.

WebShuttle — A $250, cool-looking ISDN adapter (due in the USA in early 1999) for your USB jack. From Hermstedt, *www.hermstedt.com*.

Joysticks and Game Pads

The iMac is a great gadget for games — especially if you bought one of the "version B" iMacs, those sold after November 1998 (with Mac OS 8.5 pre-installed). These "B" iMacs have juiced-up video circuitry for faster and more detailed screen display (translation: "better for games"). And if you do get into some of the great iMac games, you may enjoy flying your plane/spaceship/laser destroyer with one of these doodads instead of a mouse.

"Ares" Ultimate Warrior Joystick — According to Ariston (the maker), this $44 joystick is the most advanced analog joystick available today. *www.ariston.com*.

"Hermes" Gamepad — Another $44 game controller from Ariston. This one has a boomerang shape; eight specialized buttons, including throttle and rudder control; eight directional buttons; Turbo function; and an LED status light. *www.ariston.com*.

CH GameStick 3D, USB Version — A cool-looking black joystick from CH Products for $50. *www.chproducts.com*.

Kernel Joyport USB — This clever $50 adapter from Kernel Productions lets you equip your iMac with any of the hundreds of game controllers sold for Playstations, Nintendo 64, Genesis, Atari, and some PC-compatible computers. Talk about choices! *www.kernel.com*.

iGame USB Gameport Converter — Here's another converter ($25) that lets you adapt most analog joysticks, game pads, and pedals for your iMac. The four-position mode switch configures the adapter to work with various game controllers. iMaccessories, *www.imaccessories.com*.

ThrustMaster Top Gun — This $50 joystick is modeled after the grip found in the F-4 Phantom fighter jet. It has a patented, four-way hat switch, three beveled buttons, and a quick action trigger. ThrustMaster, *www.thrustmaster.com*.

The Fusion — This $20 ThrustMaster gamepad has 10 programmable buttons — and you can even use it as a mouse. *www.thrustmaster.com*.

Cyborg 3D Stick — According to the manufacturer, this $75, fully configurable joystick from Saitek has "precise 3D twist function; ratio digital technology; and up to 24 programmable actions." It's also really cool-looking. *www.saitek.com.*

iStick USB Flight Command Stick — A high-performance $50 joystick from iMaccessories with precision slide throttle, viewfinder hat switch, rapid-fire trigger, and three plastic and two realistic rubber function buttons. *www.imaccessories.com.*

iPad USB Reversible Controller — This $30 game pad is reversible, designed for both right- and left-handed game players. It's got eight function buttons for game setup; an eight-way directional pad; and an "X-traction knob" for precise movement when an ordinary knob just won't do. iMaccessories, *www.imaccessories.com.*

Keyboard and Mouse Replacements

What's great about the iMac's mouse and keyboard is that they're see-through and included in the price of the computer. What's not so great is that some people find the keyboard a little cheap and the mouse too round and too small. Thus is a market opportunity born . . .

Ariston Podiki Mouse — A *two*-button mouse, in iMac colors, right down to the transparent cord. (Each button does the same thing — click.) $25 from Ariston, *www.ariston.com.*

Cherry Keyboard — It's a keyboard! It's a USB hub! It's a keyboard *and* a USB hub! Get this clever keyboard, and you also get four empty USB jacks, suitable for plugging in all the other gadgetry in this chapter. (Read about USB hubs at the end of this chapter.) From Cherry Corporation, *www.cherrycorp.com.*

Evolution Mouse-Trak — This ergonomically designed, very large trackball has six big, programmable buttons around the ball, which you can set to (for example) click, double-click, or drag. $100 from Itac Systems, *www.mousetrak.com/evolutio.htm.*

iBall — A $30 trackball that's color- and design-coordinated with the iMac itself. From Macally, *www.macally.com.* It kills me that you can't see the cool blue color and see-through ball in this photo.

iMouse — A superbly sculpted, translucent blue, $20 USB mouse — shaped like a mouse, not like the iMac's yo-yo. (Pictured above at right.) From Macally, *www.macally.com.*

iBoard — A full-sized, nice-touch keyboard. Like the original iMac keyboard, it offers a spare USB jack where you can plug in another USB gadget. $80 from iMaccessories, *www.imaccessories.com.*

iKey — Here's a $70 translucent blue keyboard, full-sized, full keys. (Doesn't offer a spare USB jack, however, as on your original iMac keyboard.) From Macally, *www.macally.com.*

iPoint mouse — For $20, a great-shaped little iMac-colored, translucent USB mouse with a four-foot cord. From iMaccessories, *www.imaccessories.com.*

iPoint USB One Button Mouse — A comfortable, full-sized, ergonomic mouse, in matching iMac colors. $20 from iMaccessories, *www.imaccessories.com.*

iTrack ProBall — On this iMac-colored, translucent-blue plastic trackball, the central ball itself *lights up.* How cool is that? $40 from iMaccessories, *www.imaccessories.com.*

Scanners

As described in Chapter 18, a scanner is eyeballs for your iMac: It captures a flat image (usually a photo) and turns it into a graphics file (or even text file) on your computer.

Umax Astra 1220U — This USB scanner from Umax (pictured in Chapter 18) offers professional quality, 600 x 1200-dpi, 36-bit color output — for about $130. In my day, you'd have paid four times that. Even comes with photo-editing software and OCR (text-reading) software, so that scanned articles wind up as editable AppleWorks documents. *www.umax.com.*

Agfa SnapScan 1212u Scanner — Here's the Umax Astra's archrival: another high-quality, 36-bit, 1200 x 600 dpi color scanner, likewise equipped with OCR software. $120 from Agfa, *www.agfa.com.*

Security

Okay, so the iMac is an inexpensive computer. It's still no fun to find it missing. Therefore:

iMac Security Solution — This kit's interlocking steel plate attaches to the underside of your iMac, which adhesive holds down to your desk or table with 16,000 pounds of holding force. Unless you're robbed by marauding bands of bodybuilders, your iMac should be safe. $100 from FMJ/PAD.LOCK *www.fmjpadlock.com.*

iRack — Worried that a mere 16,000 pounds of adhesive strength won't keep your iMac safe? Then get an iRack: a 16-gauge steel shell that completely encloses your iMac (except the front, thank heaven, and the side panel). The shell covers up the iMac's cool shape and looks, but at least the steel is teal. $130 from Anchor Pad, *www.anchorpad.com.*

Cable Security — If you're not quite so paranoid as to require enclosing your iMac in solid steel, consider this $35 steel cable. It's vinyl-coated and three feet long; loop one end through the iMac's handle, and lock the far end to the desk with the included brass padlock. From Anchor Pad, *www.anchorpad.com.*

Speakers

Yeah, sure, the iMac has built-in stereo speakers already. But they're pretty small, and nowhere close to being able to shake the rafters. That's why you might consider plugging a pair of these into your USB jacks.

COZO Speakers — These high-quality speakers enhance both the SRS ("three-dimensional" sound, as heard when playing Nanosaur) stereo capabilities and the visual impact of your iMac. Available in translucent blue, amber, or red, COZO speakers add power to your iMac gaming, Web-radio, and audio playback. About $90 from Uchishiba Seisakusho, Inc., *www.uchishiba.co.jp.*

USB Hubs

Once you've read this chapter, you'll no doubt be salivating, shouting: "All — I want 'em *all!*"

Assuming your credit line can, in fact, handle such extravagance, only one more obstacle stands in your way: Once the keyboard and mouse are hooked up, your iMac has only two empty USB jacks. No matter — that's the beauty of ISB. Buy one of these *hubs,* and you've got yourself four or seven additional USB jacks, ready to accept a world of add-on gadgetry.

(By the way: There are close to 34 trillion different USB hubs for sale; even USB hubs *not* designed for the iMac work with the iMac. To keep this book below that consumer-sensitive 2,500-page break point, I've limited my listing to hubs designed specifically to match the iMac's translucent teal décor.)

iHub — Four USB jacks for $50. Macally, *www.macally.com*.

Entrega Hubs — Four jacks for $80, or seven for $130. From Entrega, *www.entrega.com*.

iHub — Seven jacks for $80 from Newer Technology, in a stackable case designed to complement the iMac. *www.newertech.com*.

USB iMac Hub — Four jacks for $50. The bottom is "iMac blue," and the top is clear. From Interex, *www.interex.com*.

iBus USB 4 Port Hub — Four jacks for $60, in a sculpted translucent case. From iMaccessories, *www.imaccessories.com*.

More to Come

As this book went to press, two companies announced complete lines of iMac add-ons, each clenching its teeth in determination to be the world's leading consumer of translucent teal plastic.

Belkin (*www.belkin.com*), for example, makes one of just about everything in this chapter: a mouse ($15), USB extension cables ($30), USB hubs ($90 for four extra jacks, $110 for seven), a serial-port adapter, a surge suppresser, and even translucent teal racks for your Zip disks and CDs.

Then there's NewMotion (*www.newmotion.com.tw*), whose lineup will include everything — iMac-coordinated mice, speakers, USB hubs, and adapters for older-Mac-style ADB, SCSI, and serial gadgets.

Mark my words: This time next year, we'll see a full line of translucent teal curtains, bedding, and all-terrain vehicles.

Index

YOUR ONLINE RESOURCE

WWW.DUMMIES.COM

Discover Dummies™ Online!

The *Dummies* Web Site is your fun and friendly online resource for the latest information about *...For Dummies®* books on all your favorite topics. From cars to computers, wine to Windows, and investing to the Internet, we've got a shelf full of *...For Dummies* books waiting for you!

Ten Fun and Useful Things You Can Do at www.dummies.com

1. Register this book and win!
2. Find and buy the *...For Dummies* books you want online.
3. Get ten great *Dummies Tips™* every week.
4. Chat with your favorite *...For Dummies* authors.
5. Subscribe free to *The Dummies Dispatch™* newsletter.
6. Enter our sweepstakes and win cool stuff.
7. Send a free cartoon postcard to a friend.
8. Download free software.
9. Sample a book before you buy.
10. Talk to us. Make comments, ask questions, and get answers!

Jump online to these ten
fun and useful things at
http://www.dummies.com/10useful

SURF THE NET

WWW.DUMMIES.COM

For other technology titles from IDG Books Worldwide, go to
www.idgbooks.com

Not online yet? It's easy to get started with *The Internet For Dummies®,* 5th Edition, or *Dummies 101®: The Internet For Windows®* 98, available at local retailers everywhere.

IDG
BOOKS
WORLDWIDE

Find other *...For Dummies* books on these topics:
Business • Careers • Databases • Food & Beverages • Games • Gardening • Graphics • Hardware
Health & Fitness • Internet and the World Wide Web • Networking • Office Suites
Operating Systems • Personal Finance • Pets • Programming • Recreation • Sports
Spreadsheets • Teacher Resources • Test Prep • Word Processing

IDG BOOKS WORLDWIDE
BOOK REGISTRATION

Register This Book and Win!

We want to hear from you!

Visit **http://my2cents.dummies.com** to register this book and tell us how you liked it!

✔ Get entered in our monthly prize giveaway.

✔ Give us feedback about this book — tell us what you like best, what you like least, or maybe what you'd like to ask the author and us to change!

✔ Let us know any other *...For Dummies®* topics that interest you.

Your feedback helps us determine what books to publish, tells us what coverage to add as we revise our books, and lets us know whether we're meeting your needs as a *...For Dummies* reader. You're our most valuable resource, and what you have to say is important to us!

Not on the Web yet? It's easy to get started with *Dummies 101®: The Internet For Windows® 98* or *The Internet For Dummies®,* 5th Edition, at local retailers everywhere.

Or let us know what you think by sending us a letter at the following address:

...For Dummies Book Registration
Dummies Press
7260 Shadeland Station, Suite 100
Indianapolis, IN 46256-3945
Fax 317-596-5498

BESTSELLING BOOK SERIES FROM IDG